CLIMB!

CLIMB!

Bob Godfrey and Dudley Chelton

Published for the AMERICAN ALPINE CLUB by

ALPINE HOUSE Publishing Boulder Colorado

Distributed by
WESTVIEW PRESS Boulder, Colorado

© Copyright 1977 by ROBERT GODFREY
Printed in the United States of America

Distributed throughout the world by
WESTVIEW PRESS, Inc.
1898 Flatiron Court
Boulder, Colorado, 80301
Frederick A. Praeger, Publisher.

ISBN 0-89158-318-1
Library of Congress Card Number 77-4436

Design and photographic prints by Bob Godfrey.

CONTENTS

Foreword, by Tom Frost ... vii

Preface ... viii

Acknowledgements ... ix

Introduction ... 2

PART I   THE EARLY DAYS

First Ventures 1820 - 1919 ... 6
Steep Faces and High Mountains 1920-1927 ... 24
Consolidation 1927-1949 ... 40

PART II   THE FIFTIES ... 53

New Techniques and Overhanging Rock 1949-1956 ... 54
Garden of the Gods ... 70
Transition 1956 ... 78

PART III   THE GOLDEN AGE ... 85

The Sixties ... 86
Big Walls in the Seventies ... 132

PART IV   THE FREE CLIMBING ERA ... 137

Free Climbing - The Sixties ... 138
Free Climbing - The Seventies ... 174

AN INTERVIEW WITH JIM ERICKSON AND STEVE WUNSCH ... 240

Index ... 274

Foreword

My first acquaintance with Colorado climbing came while a beginning climber in California in the late '50s. In those days, we were much more isolated and our techniques developed independently of other areas. We knew Colorado was a land of mountains, but disbelieved that they could compare in difficulty and size to Yosemite's sheer granite cliffs. We knew not what Colorado climbers were up to and therefore assumed they weren't up to much. In those days, occasional references to Hallett Peak and other climbs filtered through. The Diamond on Longs Peak was talked about, and we thought how silly it was for climbing to be restricted to such a "small" face.

My first tangible contact with Colorado and its mountain men came through association with Layton Kor during his visits to Yosemite in the early '60s. That was when I saw with my own eyes the superhuman qualities possessed by the Coloradans. I remember that Kor quickly climbed everything that we did, and that his endurance and speed surpassed ours. Upon finishing one Grade VI, he would search out a fresh climbing companion and immediately start up another big wall. The opportunity never developed for me to rope up with Kor. Subconsciously, I believe, I avoided it for fear of not measuring up.

Now the mystery is gone. Colorado's cliffs, located on the spine of the continent, have become the crossroads of American climbing. Climbers from east and west come here often. Test pieces, from the Naked Edge to the Yellow Wall on the Diamond, are fireside words from the Shawangunks to Yosemite. It is felt by many that Colorado is the subculture center of the climbing community; where climbing is a more serious way of life, and lived more fully by sizeable numbers of participants, than at any other place in the nation. From Colorado emanates the pulse of the sport, currently characterized across the land by an emphasis on short, hard, free rock climbing.

This definitive work by Godfrey and Chelton is a collection of rock climbing experiences which captures the essence, the challenge, and the spirit of the sport at its best. The inspiring text is supplemented by the finest collection of rock climbing photographs I have ever seen. One in particular, Bob Godfrey's classic photograph of birds and the Naked Edge, has long been one of my favorites. To me, this photograph represents Colorado climbing. In addition to photographs produced by the authors expressly for this book, there are a number of historical photos drawn from seventy years of technical climbing in Colorado.

Climbing has changed a lot since the Millards' ascent of the Third Flatiron in 1906. The refinement of climbing methods during the intervening years will be obvious as you read through this book, but the basic challenge is still the same: the perfecting of the individual toward the achievement of a goal.

Tom Frost 1977

PREFACE

The preparation of this book was an exercise in selectivity, and to some extent, an exercise in frustration. The main problem lay in deciding what to include, and what to leave out. From a handful of pioneers in the early days, rock climbing in Colorado has developed to a point in 1977 where many thousands of climbers are active. This number includes those who live permanently in Colorado, and the many who make pilgrimages from other parts of the country, for the mountains of Colorado have become a mecca for climbers throughout America. This book contains only a small sampling of this activity, from the turn of the century to the present day.

In choosing what to include, and what to leave out, a number of criteria were used. Generally, the climbs chosen for inclusion were first ascents, and those involved were pioneer rock climbers involved in redefining concepts of the impossible. Many of the climbs described have become established classics, in the sense that they have received wide recognition for their excellent qualities and have received many ascents. Others have not become classic in this sense, but have become firmly established in the mythology of Colorado climbing history based on the desperate adventures of those who first climbed them. Mention Kor on the Northwest Face of Chiefshead, Northcutt on the Diagonal, Stettner on the East Face of Monitor Peak, or Albert Ellingwood on Lizard's Head to knowledgeable Colorado climbers and watch the eyes imperceptibly widen, notice the slight intake of breath indicating recognition of wild adventures rarely repeated.

Other climbs included seemed particularly interesting at certain points in time because of the style in which they were done and the techniques that were employed. Occasionally climbs of advanced difficulty were accomplished because of the introduction of new equipment which made upward progress, or safety, possible in previously impossible situations. In other cases breakthrough climbs took place when a particular individual was able to shrug off psychological restraints and make advances through personal boldness and daring. We have tried to include climbs illustrative of these advances.

In some cases climbs and events have been included for their curiosity value. When climbers gather over late-night beers, or around glowing campfire embers, inevitably someone will say, "Do you remember the time when..." Stories are exchanged, laughter fills the air, suspense is generated, and the myths and legends of climbing folklore grow a little larger with each telling.

For many people, climbing is fun-in-the-sun, and they are not interested in challenging concepts of impossible verticality or in approaching rock climbing as a means of existential definition. At risk of being criticized for a one-sided approach, we have chosen to pay little attention to documenting this aspect of climbing and have chosen to pursue events which have taken place at the cutting-edge of the possible within each developmental period in Colorado's climbing history.

The factual information which we have included is as accurate as we have been able to make it by thorough research and considerable cross-checking of source materials. We have attempted to present accounts in as interesting and as lively a manner as possible, and with the exception of one or two obviously tongue-in-cheek renditions, they are neither exaggerated nor fictitious.

Many of the photographs were taken in prepared situations by jumaring fixed ropes alongside the climbers. However, none of the climbing was faked, and we have attempted to avoid tricks of camera-tilting to increase the sense of steepness. In a few of the photographs, as a result of awkward situations, the perspective is distorted. This is usually obvious, and generally the correct perspective can be gained by comparing the angle of the climbing rope, or a piece of equipment hanging down from the climber's body, to the vertical edge of the photograph.

We have been dependent upon climbing literature, in the form of published articles and guidebooks, supplemented by the memories and notes of many individuals who have played prominent roles in Colorado's climbing history. The Boulder region and Rocky Mountain National Park have seen the most intense activity over the years, and a good deal of description of these activities has been recorded. In contrast, the Garden of the Gods and the Pike's Peak Region near Colorado Springs have also seen considerable rock climbing activity, but few records exist, and events have taken place outside of the mainstream. No guidebooks exist to the Pike's Peak Region, and the most active climbers in Colorado Springs say simply that they prefer it this way. These feelings have been respected in the preparation of this book, and the small amount of information relating to traditions of climbing in the Garden of the Gods gives only the briefest notation of this richly varied area.

There are a large number of other lesser-known rock climbing areas in Colorado which, for reasons of time and space, have not been included. Within these limitations, the stories presented in the following pages describe the historical interplay between events and personalities in Colorado rock climbing, and show how the concept of the impossible has been progressively redefined.

ACKNOWLEDGEMENTS

This book could not have been written without the help of many people. Jim Erickson and Steve Wunsch were the most long-suffering in our attempts to portray events of the seventies. "Don't you find it difficult to write with both feet in your mouth?" Wunsch once tactfully enquired in a carefully composed margin comment. Erickson had the most expressive exclamation marks of all our critics, and three of them side-by-side (!!!) purged our prose of many inanities. These two patiently guided us and injected a thread of objective rationality.

Roger Briggs, a thinker and writer spanning two important eras, the Sixties and the Seventies, was a sage mentor. He labored physically, by helping us jumar and photograph scores of the most difficult climbs, and editorially, by debugging draft chapters.

Duncan Ferguson provided information on events of the seventies and was also stalwart where ropes and cameras were concerned.

Bob Culp was a constant source of information, inspiration, and good-humored tolerance of our attempts to make sense of the most complex period in Colorado's climbing history—the sixties. We visited his store many times, overused the telephone, and eventually the mess took shape.

David Rearick applied Occam's razor to our more gushy prose, and with mathematical precision identified redundancies and factual inaccuracies in Chapters I-IX.

Walter Fricke read draft versions of the early section of the book and made useful suggestions from the lessons he had learned in the production of his climber's guidebook to Rocky Mountain National Park.

George Hurley's background in English literature and Colorado rock climbing helped as he dissected split infinitives with the dexterity of a 5.10 face climber.

Larry Dalke was generous with anecdotes and provided a wide selection of original photographs of the sixties. Pat Ament, shared insights and photographs. Huntly Ingalls contributed pictures and wit.

Steve Komito laughed when we said we wanted to take his picture, and became bashful when the shutter clicked. Aware of his power as *Mountain* magazine's western correspondent, we dutifully presented the draft version of the sixties for comment. "Jolly good show," he chortled as his red pencil spidered across the pages.

Jack Turner flitted through Boulder, and beer and information flowed liberally. Tex Bossier visited briefly, entranced us with tales of the past and, "Did you hear the story about the black panties.......?" But we couldn't print it.

Stanley Sheperd wrote long letters from Belgrade about the "medieval period" of Colorado's rock climbing history.

Bill Forrest was generous with photographs and information on big wall climbing in Colorado.

Royal Robbins thought we were the C.I.A. when we called long distance and asked if we could tape record a telephone interview. He cooperated and also proof read and commented on the chapter on the Sixties.

Wayne Goss and Jim Logan filled in gaps in the text. Goss provided photographs of the first winter ascent of the Diamond, and other early gems.

Layton Kor provided a number of classic photographs of the sixties, and gave permission to reprint his account of the first winter ascent of the Diamond.

Cleve McCarty, knowledgeable from his guidebook research, had constructive comments to make on draft versions of the early chapters, through the sixties, and also provided photographs.

Ray Northcutt drank beer with us on a number of occasions and yarned about the years of the 1950's and early 1960's. He also provided photographs of that era.

Harvey Carter was kind enough to open his notes and his memory, and also provided early photographs of climbing in the Garden of the Gods.

Tom Hornbein provided a small gold mine of original color transparencies taken in Colorado during the 1950's, supplemented them with tape recorded information, and proof read Chapter IV. Dale Johnson provided information and photographs from the same period and read and commented on early drafts of the first five chapters of the book. Harold Walton, a neighbor in Boulder, provided information on the 1950's.

Carleton Long provided information on the early days of the San Juan Mountaineers. Melvin Griffiths did likewise and trusted us with over a hundred original negatives.

Joe Stettner spent many hours recounting his climbing adventures in the Colorado mountains over glasses of wine, and entrusted us with his original glass plate negatives from which to make prints.

Baker Armstrong provided information on the early days in the Boulder region, and unearthed the collection of original photographic negatives left behind by Ernest Greenman. Ralph Squires remembered many of the events portrayed and identified individuals.

Ken Wilson of *Mountain* magazine, and Nan Babb of *Mountain Gazette*, both provided constructive editorial comment.

Alistair McArthur of the Colorado Outward Bound School patiently read the final draft and made useful suggestions on the organization of the material.

Linda Morehead spent long hours editing and proof reading the final copy.

Grant Barnes arranged co-publication with the American Alpine Club.

To these, and to all those climbers who patiently endured clicking cameras, re-runs when the film came out underexposed, and "Hold it for a minute while we change lenses," our eternal gratitude.

Bob Godfrey and Dudley Chelton
1977.

Longs Peak from the eastern plains.

INTRODUCTION

In the European Alps of France and Switzerland, one sneaks up on the mountains through endless miles of narrow winding valleys. In Great Britain, the mountains of the Lake District, Wales, and Scotland are invariably introduced by preludes of rolling lower hills. In Colorado there is no such preamble. The Great Plains have been torn and rent by massive uplifting. A change of geomorphological tempo takes place that only a geologic Beethoven could have orchestrated, akin to inserting the fiery second movement of the Ninth Symphony into one of the most placid sections of the Pastoral. Forces of volcanic activity have split the earth, fragmented the fabric of the landscape, and thrust massive peaks up to fourteen thousand feet. To the west, as far as the eye can see, the Rocky Mountains of Colorado extend like a huge tidal wave frothed with sweep after sweep of towering mountain crests.

The region of interface between the Great Plains and the Rocky Mountains, commonly known as the Front Range, has been of major importance in Colorado's rock climbing history. Many dramas and significant developments have been played out on its steep cliffs. In some areas sedimentary rocks of sandstone, conglomerate, and mudstone are on the surface. In others, igneous granite has thrust through. Glacial activity and the erosional effect of fast-flowing water have cut steep-sided valleys that slice their way down to the plains. This mixture of sedimentary and igneous rock, coupled with differing erosional patterns, makes for a wide variety of types of rock climbing in a relatively small area.

The reasons for the concentration of rock climbing in the narrow Front Range Corridor of Colorado are many. Accessability has been important. In particular, the areas surrounding Boulder and Colorado Springs have seen the most development over the years. Both of these towns nestle close to the mountains and are surrounded by steep cliffs providing many fine climbs. Climate has also been important. The Front Range cliffs are at a lower elevation than many of the high mountain faces, and the relatively mild plains winter makes rock climbing possible year round. There are numerous mid-winter January and February days when it is possible to bask in shirtsleeves on sun-warmed rocks on the south facing cliffs of Boulder Canyon and the Garden of the Gods. The norm is blue skies, sun, low humidity, and predictably stable conditions for day after day.

The High Mountains

Scattered throughout the rest of Colorado are many high mountain faces which have seen exploration. Thirty miles from Boulder, to the northwest, lies Rocky Mountain National Park. Many of its summits are over 13,000 feet and present the technical climber with a variety of steep faces. Longs Peak (14,255 feet) is the dominant mountain in the Park, and its massive square top can be seen from miles in every direction. The East Face of Longs offers two thousand feet of vertical and overhanging rock, providing technical rock climbs of a wide range of difficulty in a setting of alpine grandeur as spectacular as one could hope for. In the center of the East Face is the Diamond: one of the most impressive pieces of rock architecture in Colorado. It is one of only a small number of faces in Colorado that deserve the decription *big wall*. The struggles that have taken place here are among the most dramatic in Colorado's rock climbing history.

Close to Longs Peak is Hallett Peak (12,713 feet). It has a steep face, a little less than a thousand feet high, which faces north. The face is not as steep as the Diamond and the climbs on the whole are considerably easier. Exploration of this face started in the mid-1950's, and its eventual ascent preceded the first ascent of the Diamond.

The East Face of Longs and Hallett's North Face have been the two classic Colorado high mountain faces over the years, in the sense that they have been focal points for climbers and have provided high concentrations of fine rock climbs.

Close to Rocky Mountain Park lies the thronged-with-tourists-in-the-summer-but-virtually-a-graveyard-in-the-winter township of Estes Park. Nearby, a series of granite faces up to eight hundred feet high, called Lumpy Ridge, has figured prominently in recent climbing developments. One hundred miles to the south, to the west of Colorado Springs, steep cliffs on the upper elevations of Pike's Peak have seen important recent activity, as have some of the little known rocks close to Aspen.

Elsewhere, the San Juan Mountains in the southern part of the state were explored by climbers prior to the 1920's and over the years have yielded a large number of climbs. The Crestones in the Sangre de Cristo Mountains contain a number of alpine peaks with many fine rock routes. Countless other cliffs exist in Colorado, some occasionally frequented, some still unexplored: enough rock to keep a climber busy for a lifetime.

Canyons and Boulders

There are two other facets of Colorado rock climbing that deserve mention in this introduction. Colorado possesses, in addition to its high mountains, a number of canyon systems. There are well-known canyons near Boulder and Colorado Springs, and the names Eldorado Canyon, Boulder Canyon, and North Cheyenne Canyon evoke familiar responses among climbers. Further west, buried deep in the mountains, are two canyons in particular which, though less well known and frequented, have figured in Colorado rock climbing history. Glenwood Canyon lies two hundred miles west of Denver, and its two thousand foot-high loose limestone walls have been the scene of numerous hair-raising adventures since the early 1960's. The Black Canyon of the Gunnison, to the south, is a canyon in a different sense from the aforementioned, in that one drives to its rim and descends its depths rather than starting at the bottom and working one's way upwards. Some three thousand feet deep and twenty miles long, it contains many steep rock faces, including the Painted Wall. The Painted Wall is two thousand three hundred feet of crumbling rock which repeatedly repulsed all attempts during the 1960's and early 1970's. It is considered the most serious major face in Colorado.

The second facet of importance takes one's attention away from massive canyon walls to another extreme, the macro-level of boulders. During the 1950's, a small number of Colorado climbers began working out on detached boulders as practice for longer, more demanding routes. Climbing on boulders was called "trick climbing" then. It was discovered that a climber could work out moves of maximum difficulty on boulders only a few feet from the ground in perfect safety. An hour's session of climbing on boulders enabled a climber to work on the finer points of technique and to push the standard of climbing to higher and higher limits. Individual moves could be worked on, and repeated time and time again, until perfected. During the later years of the 1950's, a small number of individuals developed bouldering to the point of an art form, an end in itself.

Rock Climbing and Mountaineering

Acknowledging the wide range of possible mountain experiences, and the rather narrow range considered in this book, a distinction needs to be made here between rock climbing and mountaineering, for in the minds of some climbers, the two are somewhat separate and possess rather different characteristics. Admittedly, there are many mountaineers who climb rocks, and most rock climbers occasionally ascend mountains, but there are also mountaineers who develop body tremors at the prospect of a piece of vertical rock, and rock climbers who break into a cold sweat at the thought of having to walk more than a hundred yards from the car.

Mountaineering, in the classic sense, involves climbing mountains by ridges and faces, where the attainment of the summit is the prime objective. Steep rock may be encountered en route, and rope may be used to overcome technical difficulties, but the emphasis is on the totality of the ascent, the hike in to the mountain, life at a high camp, and the aesthetics of the final summit push.

Rock climbing is more specialized than mountaineering, but rock climbers are inspired by no single motivational force. For many, a central part of the experience is simply strenuous physical exertion, stretching and exercising every part of the body. The beauty of high, airy places attracts others who remain content with easy climbs. The companionship and closeness that comes from being linked to a friend by a climbing rope is another important aspect. The spiritual core of rock climbing, the potential of the experience to connect the climber with normally untapped resources, in self and surrounding universe, has been progressively emphasized in recent years. On the material plane, it is possible to evolve a complete life-style around rock climbing, with periodic pilgrimages to the meccas of America, Europe, and further afield — and the expression "climbing bum" is not pejorative. For some, it is the aspect of competition which is most important; the measuring of one's ability and achievements against the best of one's contemporaries. However, overriding all these factors, the dominant force spurring Colorado climbers to work out progressively more and more difficult routes over the years has been the concept of adventure that can only come when the outcome of the climb is in question.

Prior to 1900, the guiding principle in Colorado climbing was to reach summits by the easiest, safest, and most reasonable way. Difficult and steep sections en route were negotiated with reluctance and distaste. After 1900, the tenets of "to get to the top" and "because it's there" (though not yet articulated by Mallory), were no longer sufficient for a small number of mountaineers. The concept of difficulty for difficulty's sake emerged, and the "adrenaline rush" of the modern 5.10 climber, spread-eagled on minute chalked-up holds, twenty feet above the last protection and about to take the sixth fall of the day, was not too far away.

As this development is traced in the following pages, it makes sense only if it is appreciated at the outset that rock climbing is, after all, a little bit absurd, and that all of the commonly offered reasons for rock climbing are characterized by an underlying irrationality. One can imagine a smile of condescending good humor coming to the face of Jean Paul Sartre, and other writers of his persuasion, if they were to read those eloquent texts of climbing literature which attempt to present climbing as completely rational. It is the very irrationality, the continuing fascination of brushing shoulders with something mysterious, intangible, indescribable, in the context of an uncertain outcome, that gives rock climbing its enduring allure, and ensures the continual redefinition of that most ubiquitous of rock climbing assertions......"Impossible!"

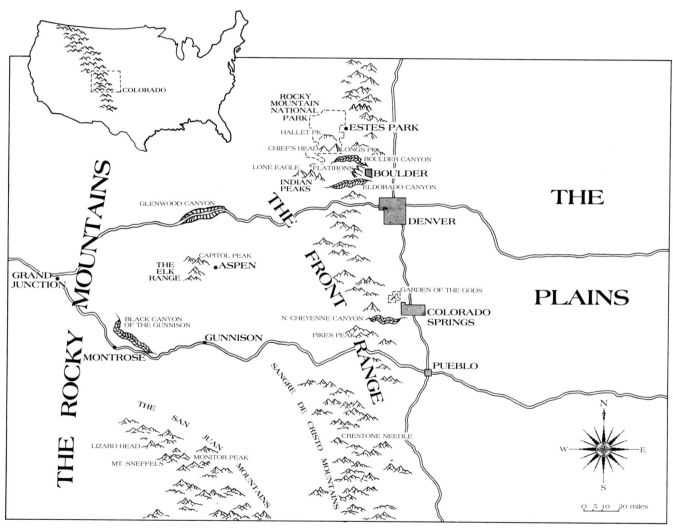

COLORADO

ROCKY
MOUNTAIN
NATIONAL
PARK

HALLET PK.

•ESTES PARK

CHIEF'S HEAD

LONGS PK.

BOULDER CANYON

LONE EAGLE

FLATIRONS

•BOULDER

INDIAN
PEAKS

ELDORADO CANYON

GLENWOOD CANYON

THE

DENVER

THE ROCKY MOUNTAINS

THE FRONT RANGE

THE
ELK
RANGE

CAPITOL PEAK

•ASPEN

GARDEN OF THE GODS

THE

PLAINS

GRAND
JUNCTION•

N. CHEYENNE CANYON

COLORADO
SPRINGS

BLACK CANYON
OF THE GUNNISON

PIKES PEAK

GUNNISON

MONTROSE

PUEBLO

SANGRE DE CRISTO MOUNTAINS

THE

SAN

CRESTONE NEEDLE

LIZARD HEAD

JUAN

MONITOR PEAK

MT. SNEFFELS

MOUNTAINS

N

W   E

S

0 5 10   20 miles

The major climbing areas of Colorado.

Part I

THE EARLY DAYS

The Rocky Mountain Climbers Club vehicle.
Circa 1910.

FIRST VENTURES
1820-1919

We used to scorn the use of a rope in rock scaling.
Ralph Squires describing climbing in 1919.

Recorded climbing in Colorado spans almost two centuries, and the Ute and Arapahoe Indians undoubtedly climbed mountains even earlier. Zebulon Pike was the first recorded individual to aspire to climb a Colorado peak in the sense of traditional mountaineering. He was a somewhat incompetent geographer who spent a great deal of his time wandering around watersheds in Colorado, not too sure of his bearings, engaged in government survey work. On November 15, 1806, he spotted Pike's Peak near Colorado Springs on one of his meanderings, estimated its height to be 18,581 feet (having guessed the plains to be 8,000 feet), and resolved to climb it. (The plains are actually a little over 5,000 feet, and the elevation of Pike's Peak is 14,110 feet). Seeing the mountain first from the site of the town of Los Animas, Pike described it as "a small blue cloud." [1] He decided to climb the mountain, but experienced the phenomenon of foreshortened distances which high mountains project, and after a number of days spent moving closer and closer, he found that the summit was still a long way away. From a point of view some fifteen or sixteen miles away from the summit, Pike recorded in his journal that it "would have taken a whole days march to have arrived at its base, when I believe no human being could have ascended its pinnacle." [2] It was left to members of Major Stephen Long's government exploration party to make the first ascent in the summer of 1820. Though the climb was a relatively straight forward hike, Long's party experienced it as a tremendous adventure, and their ascent became known as "the first successful ascent by white men of a major mountain in the American West." [3]

The major motivation in these early ascents was geographical, in the sense of wanting to reach vantage points "in order to be enabled from its pinical (sic), to lay down the various branches and positions of the country," as Zebulon Pike wrote in his journal. [4] However, the spark of excitement which gleams through Pike's writing indicates that the presence of the unclimbed summit of the mountain was motivation in and of itself.

There is nothing in the literature available to indicate that Pike and Long, and the other early pioneers involved in the exploration of the Colorado mountains, had any knowledge of the developments that were taking place in the European Alps at this time. Mont Blanc had been climbed by Balmat and Paccard in 1786, some thirty years prior to the ascent of Pike's Peak by Long's expedition. Longs Peak, forty miles northwest of Boulder, was first climbed in 1868 by a party including Major John Wesley Powell, famous for his explorations of the Colorado River, and William Byers, the founder and editor of the *Rocky Mountain News*. The ascent took place only three years after the first ascent of the Matterhorn in Switzerland in 1865. The first ascent of the Matterhorn was conducted by Edward Whymper and a party of experienced climbers for whom mountaineering was a firmly established sporting activity for gentlemen. They accomplished the Matterhorn climb with the use of ropes, ice-axes and rudimentary rock climbing techniques. In contrast, the ascent of Longs was by a group of explorers interested mainly in treading new ground, and who possessed no real concept of mountain climbing as a sport.

The East Face of Longs Peak

In 1890 Frederick Chapin, a climber from the east coast, published a small book entitled *Mountaineering in Colorado: the Peaks about Estes Park*. (A must for connoisseurs of early climbing history.) He made an early ascent of Longs Peak, and two things stand out in his writings. First, he climbed for the sport of it, and secondly, he was aware of mountaineering developments in Europe. Writing of Longs Peak, he stated, "It has been rather fancifully named the 'American Matterhorn'; but when we consider that one side is actually inaccessible, perhaps it is worth the comparison —for the Matterhorn has been ascended by aretes on all sides..." [5] Chapin pointed out that "about one hundred people have been on the mountain (Longs) annually for several years past," [6] indicating that mountain climbing had become somewhat established as a leisure-time activity in Colorado by 1890. He also commented on mountaineering developments in the

Enos Mills.

Alps and the Caucasus, indicating that some international exchange of information was taking place in 1890.

Chapin makes comparisons between the East Face of Longs Peak and the East Face of the Matterhorn, pointing out that whereas the Matterhorn's East Face is "scarcely more that 40°...the tower on Longs Peak exposes an unbroken front of 1,200 feet, as smooth as the side of Bunker Hill Monument."[7] The most interesting statement in his description occurs when he examines the East Face of Longs and pronounces it "actually inaccessible." To have come to this conclusion he must have examined the face for a potential route. It is somewhere around this point in time, during the period 1870-1890, that one finds the seeds of technical rock climbing on vertical faces. Perhaps Frederick Chapin was not the first to entertain the germ of the idea of climbing the East Face of Longs Peak, but it is certainly the first recorded hint that exists in the literature.

The chronology of this period is somewhat murky. Chapin published his book in 1890. It is likely that his climbing activities took place in the 1880's, or possibly even the 1870's. At approximately the same time, a feat of mountain daring took place on Longs Peak which was in dramatic contrast to the accepted way of behaving in the mountains in those days. The Reverend Elkanah J. Lamb had reached the summit of Longs via the regular hiking route through the Keyhole, and via the Homestretch, on an August day in 1871. After perusing the view from the summit for a while, he decided to instill a little variety into his day's outing by descending the east side of the mountain. Considering the reputation of the East Face at the time, as expressed in Chapin's writing, this had to be one of the most audacious adventures ever to be undertaken in the Colorado mountains. Alone, without mountaineering equipment, and with only the vaguest notion of where he was heading, Lamb embarked over the edge and started down. He later described his adventures in his journal:

> After one hour's feasting of my mental and spiritual and somewhat poetic nature (on the summit), I concluded to go down the eastern face of the mountain, where man had never gone before...After getting down more than a thousand feet from the summit I began to realize the rashness of the undertaking....I concluded to go back if possible, and go down the old way; but, I soon realized the fact that I had already passed dangerous points and sloping icy places that were almost impossible to round or ascend. [8]

Lamb apparently descended via the Notch Couloir to Broadway, which he traversed to a steep snowfield at the south side of the face which was later appropriately named "Lamb's Slide." At one spot on the edge of the snowfield he encountered his worst trouble:

> With finger holds in meager niches of the wall and my feet pressing the edge of the ice, I started across this dangerous section. Quicker than I can tell it, my hands failed to hold, my feet slipped, and down I went with

The East Face of Longs Peak showing the approximate line of descent followed by Elkanah Lamb in 1871 and Enos Mills in 1906.

almost an arrow's rapidity. An eternity of thought, of life, death, wife, and home, concentrated in my mind in those two seconds—. Fortunately for me, I threw my right arm around a projecting bowlder (sic), which stood above the icy plain some two or three feet. Getting my knife out of my pocket, I opened it with my teeth, then reached half-way to the rocks of safety and began digging a niche in the ice for a toe hold, when my knife broke in two. So, putting the tip of my left foot in the shallow niche I had cut, (knowing that if my foot slipped I was a lost lamb), then working my arm to the top of the rock, I gave a huge lunge, just managing to reach the foot of the mountain. I immediately fell upon my knees and thanked God for deliverance. [9]

A later pioneer, Enos Mills, who had spent a number of years living in a cabin at the base of Longs and guiding parties up the peak, decided to emulate Lamb's descent some thirty years later in 1906. Mills followed approximately the same descent route as Lamb had taken, as far as one can tell, and had a similar gripping adventure. The descent was described by a friend of Mills, Earl Harding, in a periodical of the time called *Outing*. "Once the descent began," writes Harding, "peril was lost sight of in the ethereal excitement that comes from facing death, whether it be in the battle charge or in scaling the forbidden heights." [10] Lower down the face, Mills became entangled in an avalanche in Lamb's Slide. Harding describes Enos Mills's adventure in epic terms:

Cracking of ice warned him that another avalanche was starting...springing twenty feet from the cliff, (he)

was whirled away—to death or safety? Here's peril and sensation new, even to the man whose only stimulant is danger, mad racing down a mountainside, riding on the very wings of death.

Needless to say, (the gods look after those who dare?) Mills lived through his adventure. For many years he was a guide and naturalist on Longs Peak, and took it upon himself to travel the country, generating support for the establishment of a National Park for Longs Peak and the surrounding area.

These two isolated events, hairy solo descents of the East Face of Longs Peak, characterized the beginning of an aspect of mountaineering that was quite different from the commonly held guiding principles of the late 1800's. An English lady, Isabella Bird, making a very early ascent of Longs Peak in September 1873 (five years after its first ascent) summed up quite succinctly the attitude to difficult rock climbing which generally prevailed in Colorado up to 1900. This attitude had stood Indians, miners, surveyors, trappers, explorers (and even mountaineers!) in good stead for the century preceding the audacious ventures of Lamb and Mills. She wrote:

At the 'Notch' (i.e., the Keyhole) the real business of the ascent began...to me it was a time of extreme terror...my feet were paralyzed and slipped on bare rock...while crawling on hands and knees, all the while tortured with thirst and gasping and struggling for breath, this was the climb. [11]

8

The Third Flatiron (right) with Boulder spread out below.

The Boulder Region

At the turn of the century, Boulder was a small university town, a social and cultural melting pot, with vertical acres of fine steep rocks only minutes away. The Flatirons at the edge of town were the most notable local landmarks—a series of sedimentary rock slabs that leaned at a fifty degree angle. The Third Flatiron presented a single, unbroken sweep of rock almost thirteen hundred feet high.

Boulder had become a favorite vacation place for well-to-do Texans, some of whom enjoyed mountain hiking. In 1896, a group formed the Rocky Mountain Climbers Club. The main activity of this group was mountain hikes in the vicinity of Boulder, the Indian Peaks around Brainard Lake, and the Arapahoe Glacier. Some members of the group started to take an interest in the rock faces close to Boulder. Chautauqua Park was a favorite meeting place, and the Flatirons provided a backdrop to steak frys and hikes on the trails of Green Mountain. Inevitably, the attention of some of the group turned towards trying to climb the Flatirons. In 1906, Floyd and Earl Millard made the first ascent of the thirteen hundred-foot east face of the Third Flatiron, giving the earliest recorded rock climb of its kind in the state. For many years it remained the only one. The experts of the Rocky Mountain Climbers Club had it as their exclusive domain, and it was looked upon as being the ultimate in difficulty and danger.

Rudolph Johnson, a Swede who practiced law in Boulder during those years, was a particularly active member of the Rocky Mountain Climbers Club. He was one of the group's ''crack'' rock climbers and specialized in ascents of the Third Flatiron. Johnson differed from his companions because he took a particular delight in leaving the beaten track in the mountains and searching for thrills and excitement on steep rock faces. His description, ''Scaling the Flatirons,'' published in *Trail and Timberline* in 1923, leaves no doubt as to the fearful perils of these rocks:

> Scaling the face or east side of either the first or third Flatirons, those jutting rocks of Fountain sandstone a mile to the southwest of Chautauqua Park, Boulder, will be found to be a most difficult climb, to be attempted

In Green Canyon. *Ernest Greenman.*

First Ventures

only by the most experienced and intrepid rock climbers. These are the most dangerous climbs I have ever attempted but the thrill and pleasure have tempted me to perform the feat a number of times, as it has tempted other thrill seekers in Boulder. Either of these two flatirons can be climbed from the south side, by working along from one shelf to another, and even in this way the ascent is difficult and dangerous enough, with uniform steepness, smooth places where one can hardly find a hand or foot hold, and chimneys in which to climb straight up. But in case of fall one would not roll all the way down. In going up the face, however, a slip would mean a fall all the way to the bottom, 700 feet more or less. And on the face there are long distances of terrifically steep inclines, more nearly perpendicular than one cares to contemplate, in some places worn smooth from running water and without hand holds or foot holds or even finger holds big enough to be seen. In places one must lie flat and worm his way, sticking to the rock by aid of the palms of the hands and friction of the clothes. In such places the descent is even worse for the nerves than going up. But the rocks are solid and do not give away or tear loose. There are occasional shelves or wind holes where one may rest. And the climb is exhilarating and thrilling above any I know.

In climbing either Flatiron with a party I have always used a rope, and it has been a life saver several times, but the first man up or the last man down gets no advantage of the rope. As to footwear, I prefer wearing hob nailed boots, but have found rubber soled shoes, or even stockinged feet to be satisfactory, except in wet weather, when rubber is exceedingly dangerous, while hob nails will stick anywhere on any sort of rock in any sort of weather.

I am not recommending the Flatiron climb for any except the most foolhardy rock climbers, but to mountaineers who want real thrills no better climb can be found. To such kindred spirits I would recommend that rock climbing and the scaling of precipices be more generally entered into, and I would advocate scheduled trips of the more venturesome members of the Club up the Flatirons or similar climbs. [12]

R.M.C.C. members. *Ernest Greenman.*

What a delicious adventure climbing must have been in those days, with so little known of technique, and equipment virtually non-existent.

It is of interest to note Johnson's remarks in 1923 about the use of a rope. During the period 1910 to 1920, it was generally felt that the use of a rope in climbing the Third was somehow "cheating." Ralph Squires, who was the president of the Rocky Mountain Climbers Club in those days, was alive and active in Boulder in 1977 when this book was written. He says that most rock climbers of the day "scorned" the use of a rope in "rock scaling," though occasionally one was carried to protect other members of the party after the first one had climbed up. Squires recollects that "often the first man up would have the rope tied around his waist. He would just sit down on a handy ledge and other members of the party would use it for a hand-hold, suspended from his waist, as they climbed up." [13]

Prominent in the Rocky Mountain Climbers Club in those days were Ernest and "Ma" Greenman. Ernest arrived in Boulder in 1896 and worked for a number of years as a surveyor on the local narrow-gauge railway. He was one of the climbers in charge of the club's "graduated program." This program was designed for

R.M.C.C. transportation. *Ernest Greenman.*

Snowballs in the Arapahoes. *Ernest Greenman.*

Arapahoe Glacier hikers. *Ernest Greenman.*

A hardy Rocky Mountain Climbers Club group braves the rain. *Ernest Greenman.*

The Ladies on a Flatirons hike. *Ernest Greenman.*

Pa Greenman.

people who came from the east coast and the prairie states and who wanted to climb a high mountain. Greenman used to talk humorously of "those fat old schoolmarms" who came out wanting to climb Longs Peak. They would pay a dollar and sign up for the club's program. The first event was usually a hike up to the base of the First Flatiron, followed by a moonlight steakfry. Up to one hundred and fifty people would crowd around the glowing fire, and Ernest Greenman and Rudolph Johnson would lead the group in raucous song until the late hours. The program would continue with a hike up Flagstaff Mountain, and eventually progress to an ascent of a high peak in the vicinity of Brainard Lake.

Greenman developed a strong personal interest in the Third Flatiron. During succeeding years, he climbed it over one hundred times. He was a tall, somewhat gaunt man, but of friendly appearance, and was noted for his consideration toward beginners in the mountains. On most of his hikes and climbs he carried a bulky old Kodak folding camera. His photographs preserved from this period are the earliest records of technical rock climbing in Colorado. He kept his negatives filed in envelopes, with names, places, and dates meticulously inscribed on the outside in spidery copperplate handwriting. His photograph of a roped party on the final pitch of the Third Flatiron, taken in 1919, is the earliest record of technical rock climbing in the Boulder region. Ralph Squires clearly remembered the day the picture was taken and chuckled to himself, saying that they weren't going to use the rope but that Greenman shouted across to them to throw it down so as to make a better picture.

In these early days, the favorite footwear was a tight-fitting pair of baseball shoes, with soft rubber soles. The modern rock climber also wears a tight-fitting climbing shoe with a smooth rubber sole which gives extremely good frictional qualities on smooth rock. The

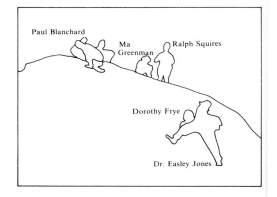

Paul Blanchard
Ma Greenman
Ralph Squires
Dorothy Frye
Dr. Easley Jones

Ma Greenman.

The summit of the Third Flatiron. Ralph Squires standing on the left. *Ernest Greenman.*

Baker Armstrong

baseball shoes used in 1919 had some of these same properties. Ernest Greenman's photographs show some rather remarkable similarities to modern smooth-soled rock climbing footwear.

The official photographer of the Rocky Mountain Climbers Club was Ed Tangen, who worked with the cumbersome view camera and tripod of those days, recording the activities of the group from underneath his black cloth. One day in 1911, Tangen was strolling in Chautauqua Park when the piercing screams of a young lady heralded danger. Dashing gallantly to the rescue, Tangen followed the lady, a nurse, to a large rock, atop of which a small boy of five was firmly stuck and squealing at the top of his lungs. Tangen assisted the child down and made his first acquaintance with Baker Armstrong. Baker's solo ascent of this rock at the age of five was the first ascent of a lifetime of climbing in the Boulder region. Tangen, almost twenty five years older, adopted him in a sense, and they became climbing companions for many years to come.

Baker Armstrong hiked and climbed in the Boulder region from the day of his rescue by Tangen in 1911 until the late 1960's. His slow Texan drawl, indefatigable patience, and interest in the welfare of beginning climbers made him a welcome companion over the years. After his first solo rock climb at the age of five, Baker accompanied Tangen and members of the

Rocky Mountain Climbers Club on many of their mountain hikes; but mountain hikes were not sufficient. He possessed a sense of adventure, and the steep rocks of the Flatirons drew him like a magnet. He had a long-standing ambition to climb the face of the Third Flatiron and related this humorous story of his first experience:

> The Third Flatiron was supposed to be one of the worst climbs in the country. My dad was awful good to me and I tried never to displease him. He told me to keep away from it. Anyway I wanted worst in the world to climb that thing. There was a fellow named Paul Blanchard who did a lot of climbing. He used to climb at night with a flashlight in his mouth. But finally when I got to be twenty I just had to do it. I got Mr. Greenman. He was about 48. My father had more confidence in him than in Paul and said it was all right. Mr. Greenman carried a window sash cord. Maybe 30 feet long. He said, "I don't think we will need this." We went up in 18 minutes. He said the best way to get down was to get all five points in contact with the rock. You put your hands flat. Feet flat. We wore basketball shoes. We came down in 22 minutes. [14]

Dale Johnson climbing the Third Flatiron in the 1950's - in roller skates! *Dale Johnson.*

R.M.C.C. outing group. *Ernest Greenman.*

Sometime after his ascent of the Third Flatiron with Greenman, Baker Armstrong came across a book containing a picture of a climber who was descending a steep rock face by wrapping a climbing rope around his body and using the friction gained to slide down the cliff. The new method was called "rappelling." Borrowing a hemp rope from a friend, Baker took the book and climbed solo to the top of the Third Flatiron. Arriving there, he decided he was going to use the method of descent illustrated to lower himself over the steep west side. A spike of rock provided a secure attachment for the rope. Spreading the pages of the book out beside him, he attempted by trial and error to figure the correct way of wrapping the rope in order to make the rappel. His first effort almost ended in disaster. Somehow he arranged the ropes incorrectly and promptly turned upside down as soon as he put his weight on it. Panting and somewhat dishevelled, he

managed to right himself, and his next attempt proved successful.

Since these early adventures, the Third Flatiron has been climbed regularly. It has had speed ascents recorded faster than ten minutes. It was climbed in the 1950's by Dale Johnson wearing roller skates, and was streaked by Gary Neptune when streaking was fashionable in the early 1970's.

Even though the Third is an easy climb for the experienced, it is also one of the state's most dangerous pieces of rock. Only ten minutes' easy hike from a nearby parking lot, its relatively easy angle has lured many unsuspecting beginners. Two youths spent the night on the face in 1973 after being overcome by darkness. It snowed that night and they were both dead from exposure the following morning. Discounting occasional incidents of this nature, the Flatirons have become a favorite place for climbers. The climbs are

Colo. Sight Seeing Company. *Ernest Greenman.*

R.M.C.C. outing group. *Ernest Greenman.*

long, face east into the morning sun, and meander up gently sloping slabs, with the vastness of the Great Plains stretching out below to the horizon.

In 1912, James Grafton Rogers of Denver started the Colorado Mountain Club. It was more broadly based than the Rocky Mountain Climbers Club, both geographically and in terms of its activities. Very little rock climbing took place in the club's early days, and this group, too, was involved mainly in hiking and in the ascents of easy peaks. It is interesting to note that one of the goals of the club in those days was to spread propaganda on Colorado and to attract people from the midwest and east coast. This undoubtedly stemmed from the fact that many early members were businessmen and members of the local chamber of commerce.

The Pike's Peak Region

One hundred miles south of Boulder lies Colorado Springs, noted as the soft rock climbing center of Colorado. Close to the edge of the town is a crenellated series of rock spires and pinnacles up to three hundred feet high. The rock is an atrociously soft sandstone—so soft that new holds appear, and old ones disappear, at a fast rate under the hands and feet of climbers. Exploratory rock climbing started here in 1914, and the nature of the rock contributed to the development of a local school of climbing with some rather significant differences in style, technique, and rock climbing philosophy, when compared to climbing in the Boulder area.

During later years, a friendly, and sometimes not-quite-so-friendly, rivalry developed between the Boulder contingent and climbers from the Springs. Debate took place on such matters as the relative difficulty of the hardest routes, on styles of climbing, and on the relative merits of differing techniques.

To the hills . . . . *Ernest Greenman.*

Garden of the Gods. *Chris Wood.*

During the period 1914-1919, the influence of European mountaineering was felt more strongly in Colorado Springs than in Boulder. This was due to the activities of a single climber, Albert Ellingwood. Ellingwood attended Colorado College in Colorado Springs as an undergraduate. In 1910, he was awarded the Rhodes Scholarship for Colorado and attended Merton College of Oxford University in England from 1910 to 1913. The Oxford Mountaineering Club was very active at the time, and it is reported that Ellingwood climbed in Wales, the Lake District, and the Alps in the summer. Inquiries with the Oxford University Mountaineering Club were unproductive, and no details of his climbs are recorded. One can only speculate on what he did. In the English Lake District,

Wasdale Head was a popular climbing center, and classic routes such as Napes Needle (Haskett-Smith, 1886), Scafell Pinnacle (Haskett-Smith, 1884), Moss Ghyll (J.N. Collie, 1892), and Botterill's Slab (Fred Botterill, 1903) had already been done. In the 1925 journal of the Colorado Mountain Club, Ellingwood writes of Wasdale Head as "the most famous climbing rendezvous in England,"[15] indicating that he had climbed there during his stay and had likely learned technique on the climbs of Haskett-Smith, Collie, and Botterill. The well-known English climbers Herford and Sansom were also active throughout the Lake District from 1910 to 1914. Ellingwood's note indicates that he climbed at Wasdale, and perhaps even knew these climbers, but we do not know for sure.

Based on his rock climbing experiences in England, Ellingwood returned to Colorado Springs in 1914 and embarked on a series of climbs, the likes of which Colorado had not seen before. He possessed a relatively sophisticated rope technique, knew how to belay a rope (though only by anchoring it statically to the rock or a piton), and had brought back a few soft iron pitons from Europe. Crude as these techniques were, they gave him the tools to go where climbers had not dared previously. Ellingwood possessed the pioneering instinct and gazed at the Colorado mountains with "the questioning look of those who wish to ascend by hitherto untrodden ways." This combination was explosive. While the rock climbers of Boulder meandered up and down the face of the Third Flatiron, Ellingwood pulled off a series of technical rock climbs of impressive quality and difficulty. In keeping with the style that was traditional in Europe at that time, he was active on both the lower rocks close to Colorado Springs and in the high mountains.

Hardly any climbing had taken place in the Garden of the Gods in Colorado Springs at this time. It was known that Indians had climbed some of the easier pinnacles, and people had scrambled on the rocks, but technical rock climbs were unknown. Ellingwood, equipped with hemp rope, a soft iron piton or two, nailed boots, and a taste for adventure, embarked on a steep series of ramps and chimneys on the west side of Greyrock in the Garden of the Gods. A steep bulge blocked the ascent part way up. Ellingwood placed a piton for protection and made two or three traversing moves around the bulge which today are graded 5.6. The climb, later to be known as the Ellingwood Ledge, was the most technically advanced of the day, and, along with ascents of the Third Flatiron, marked the start of modern rock climbing in Colorado.

Ellingwood worked out a number of other short technical climbs in the vicinity of Colorado Springs in 1914 and 1915, including Ellingwood's Route on Keyhole Rock, and the route which became known as The Old Climbers Route on Greyrock. The difficulty of these climbs was approximately 5.6 by modern standards, and they generally followed large chimneys and ledge systems.

Ellingwood was responsible for initiating technical climbing of a high standard, characterized by bold and unprotected leads, in the Colorado Springs area. More importantly, he began a line of development in Colorado Springs which stemmed from a tradition of rock climbing in Great Britain. Its main characteristic was a specified minimum use of pitons, either for direct aid or for protection on free climbs. There was little communication between Boulder climbers and Colorado Springs climbers up until the 1940's, and it is interesting to note that rock climbers in Boulder were unaware of this tradition. Pitons were used more extensively in Boulder, and, as a result, climbing developed somewhat differently than in Colorado Springs.

The activities of Boulder climbers on the Flatirons, and of Ellingwood in the Garden of the Gods up to 1920, were of crucial importance in the development of rock climbing in Colorado. Techniques were practiced. The crude use of climbing ropes was mastered. Rock climbers began to develop the necessary confidence and psychology to venture onto steep rock walls. The eyes and thoughts of the leading climbers of the day began to turn toward the big faces of the high mountains. The East Face of Longs Peak, the steep faces of the Sangre de Cristos, and the crags of the San Juan Mountains were to be the main arenas of development after 1920.

REFERENCES

1. Donald Jackson, *The Journals of Zebulon Montgomery Pike*. Vol. 1 (Norman: University of Oklahoma Press, 1966), p. 345.
2. *Ibid.,* p. 351
3. William M. Bueler, *Roof of the Rockies* (Colorado: Pruett Publishing Co., 1974), p. 24
4. Jackson, *op. cit.,* p. 349.
5. Frederick A. Chapin, *Mountaineering in Colorado* (Boston: W.B. Clarke and Company, 1890), p. 34.
6. *Ibid.*
7. *Ibid.*
8. John L. Hart, *Fourteen Thousand Feet: A History of the Naming and Early Ascents of the High Colorado Peaks* (Denver, Colorado Mountain Club, 1925), pp. 34-35.
9. *Ibid.*
10. Earle Harding, *Outing,* 1904, in Enos A. Mills, *The Rocky Mountain National Park* (New York: Doubleday, Page and Company, 1924), p. 56.
11. Isabella Bird, *A Lady's Life in the Rocky Mountains* (New York: G.P. Putnam and Sons, 1880).
12. Rudolph Johnson, "Scaling the Flatirons," *Trail and Timberline,* March, 1923, p. 4.
13. Ralph Squires, *interview,* 1976.
14. Baker Armstrong, *tape-recorded interview,* 1975.
15. Albert R. Ellingwood, "The Eastern Arete of the Crestone Needle," *Trail and Timberline,* June, 1925, p. 6.

Albert Ellingwood (second
from right) on an outing in
the Wind Rivers. *Eleanor
Ehrman.*

STEEP FACES AND HIGH MOUNTAINS
1920-1927

We can worry about that when we get there.
Paul Stettner (1927)

The year 1920 saw the start of the development of difficult technical rock climbing in the high mountains. Prior to 1920, the ascent of Capitol Peak in the Elk Range near Aspen, and some of the Needles in the San Juan Mountains of southern Colorado, had required moderate rock scrambling. No ascents demanding difficult technical rock climbing had been made.

Lizard Head: Nailed Boots, Hemp Rope, and Rotten Rock.

In 1920 Albert Ellingwood turned his attention to the high peaks of the San Juans and made a climb which has become noted for its boldness. Lizard Head (13,113 feet), even today, is considered to be the most difficult summit to reach in Colorado. The top of the mountain is a four hundred-foot tower of rotten, crumbling rock. Ellingwood's ascent in 1920 with Barton Hoag was a landmark in Colorado climbing history. Today the crux section is graded 5.7+, and modern climbers still talk with bated breath of the looseness of the rock. Ellingwood and Hoag's climb in 1920 with hemp rope, nailed boots, and only three soft iron pitons for protection has become legendary.

The two reached Lizard Head in the early morning, and it was immediately apparent that nasty work lay before them. The surface of the rock was rotten, and "pebbles rained from its sides as readily as needles from an aging Christmas tree." Ellingwood commented in his account of the climb that "one could with one hand pull down hundreds of pounds of fragments, and occasionally we could hear the crashing of small avalanches that fell without human prompting."[1] They dismissed the east and north faces as being out of the question, and eventually found a promising crack on the west face. Ellingwood started up the crack at noon, sending down rattling showers of stones in the direction of Hoag, who sought shelter behind a protruding corner of rock. About eighty feet up, Ellingwood arrived at a good ledge and brought Hoag up to join him.

Twenty feet above the ledge he was faced by a fifteen-foot vertical wall of loose rock split by fractured cracks. Larry Dalke, a noted rock climber from

Lizard Head. The Ellingwood route lies just out of sight around the right side. *Mel Griffiths.*

24

eft. Robert Ormes belaying Jim Munroe on an nsuccessful attempt on Lizard Head in 1932. _A_unroe is just below the crux 5.7+ section led y Albert Ellingwood in nailed boots in 1920. _1el Griffiths._

Larry Dalke on the crux of Lizard Head in 1967. He is a little higher than Munroe in the picture to the left, and the photo is taken from the belay ledge. _Courtesy Larry Dalke._

Boulder, climbed the same route in the 1960's and reported that this section of the climb was "at least 5.7 and perhaps harder."[2] Ellingwood hammered in a piton, and, wearing his nailed boots, made the touchy moves over the difficult section. After further struggles, including a fight with a loose and overhanging chimney, Ellingwood and Hoag reached the summit of Lizard Head at 4:25 p.m.

They were still faced with the difficulties of descending. After climbing down part way, the steepest section of the climb lay before them. Ellingwood anchored the doubled rope around a spike of rock, and they both descended by rappelling. Ellingwood gave a tug on one end of the rope to pull it down, but the rope would not come. As he shook it in an attempt to loosen it, a stone as large as a fist was dislodged and landed squarely on his head, breaking the skin and nearly knocking him from the ledge. Feeling faint, Ellingwood

clung to the rock for support. Struggling back up the rope again, he was unable to get it into a position so they would be able to retrieve it after the rappel. Bemoaning their bad luck, he pulled up the rope and tied it off singly to the spike, hoping that the increased length would enable them to reach the bottom of the face. By this time it was dark. Using the rope as a handhold, Hoag made his way down. The rope ended some twenty feet from the ground. As he searched around for the small holds they had used in their ascent, Hoag slipped and plunged fifteen feet downwards, "leaving a section of his pants behind."[3] Fortunately he was not hurt, and Ellingwood followed more cautiously, saying goodbye to a rope that had served him well for five seasons. The 1920 ascent of Lizard Head by Ellingwood and Hoag was a climb ahead of its time in terms of technical difficulty and the psychological problems of dealing with rotten rock.

26

Professor J. W. Alexander below the Chimney
on the second ascent with Jack Moomaw. *Jack Moomaw.*

Jack Moomaw - "The Old Chromogen." (1933).
*Courtesy Times-Call Publishing Company,
Longmont, Colorado.*

The East Face of Longs - First Ascent

In Boulder, up to the early 1920's, the attention of climbers had focused on repeating ascents of the Third Flatiron, and on making relatively easy ascents of high mountain peaks. Longs Peak was the most popular alpine climb. Other than the epic descents of the East Face by Elkanah Lamb and Enos Mills, ascents of Longs were confined to the hikers' route via the Keyhole and the Homestretch. Rock scrambling was involved, but no real rock climbing. No one had ascended the great East Face.

In 1922, a group of climbers from Denver made plans for the first ascent of the East Face of Longs Peak. The face was examined from the vicinity of Mt. Lady Washington and Chasm View, and possible routes were discussed. The party was led by Carl Blaurock of Denver and Dudley Smith, and included a climber of German origins named Herman Buhl (not the famous Austrian climber). Dudley Smith had been studying the face and plotting the route for two years. Buhl had climbed frequently in the European Alps and was a member of the Swiss Alpine Club prior to his emigration to the U.S. after World War I. He was familiar with the use of modern climbing equipment, including pitons, crampons, carabiners and ice axes, as well as with the technique of rappelling and the use of rope for protection against a fall. The group planned their ascent of the East Face for Labor Day, 1922. They were astonished and disappointed to read in the *Rocky Mountain News* only three days before their planned ascent that the face had just been climbed solo by Professor J.W. Alexander of Princeton University. "For the first time in...history," the newspaper account read, "the sheer precipice which rises 2,200 feet on the east side of Longs Peak from the waters of Chasm Lake has been scaled."[4] The *Rocky Mountain News* had the following to say about the ascent:

Alexander climbing Alexander's Chimney during the second ascent. (Note that he is unroped). *Jack Moomaw.*

Professor Alexander left the Hewes-Kirkwood Inn at 8:30 a.m. on the start of his perilous journey and returned to the hotel at 6 p.m. The actual climbing time on the face is given as three hours and twenty minutes.

In crossing the Glacier at the foot of the precipice Professor Alexander was required to cut seventy-six steps in the ice and from then on completed his climb by clinging to the small projections of the rock in constant peril...Climbing the face of the precipice is a task which has always been the subject of much discussion among mountaineers in the park, many old-timers and guides claiming that the feat was impossible.[5]

Professor Alexander repeated the climb a day or two later with Park Ranger Jack Moomaw. Moomaw described their ascent in his book, *Recollections of a Rocky Mountain Ranger - The East Face Climb:*

Professor Alexander, a post-graduate math. teacher from Princeton, and I made the first recorded climbs of the east face of Longs Peak in 1922. In some ways I have regretted it, because for quite a time thereafter many climbers were killed attempting the feat. It also caused me a lot of hard work because afterward, every time there was an accident up there, they naturally assigned the job to me.

We had earlier scanned that side of the Peak with binoculars for several days from the top of Mount Lady Washington, and picked out a feasible route and set a day for trying the climb. But on that day, my wife's riding horse was missing in the morning, and the Professor went up alone and succeeded. Two days later we went up together and I took pictures of the climb. Some of these pictures were used in newspaper and magazine articles, but I do not believe I was given credit for them.

To Alexander goes the honor of naming the traverse ledge, about half way up, called Broadway. The crack or chimney on the lower part of the climb also was later named after the Professor. He did not use this chimney on his first climb, but we did on our climb. We took ropes and crampons along, but did not use them.

Alexander later confessed to me that since early boyhood he had always had a terrible fear of high places; and

Jack Moomaw on the second ascent of Alexander's Chimney. *J. W. Alexander.*

The third ascent party below Alexander's Chimney in 1922. Herman Buhl standing in the middle of the group. Carl Blaurock on the right pointing. *Courtesy Carl Blaurock.*

Carl Blaurock leading on the third ascent of Alexander's Chimney. *Courtesy Carl Blaurock.*

that the first time he climbed Longs Peak, by the regular trail, he almost "gave up" at the Key Hole. Here is something for the psychologists to mull over.

While climbing out of the Notch Chimney, the professor kept losing his hand-holds. I was just behind him on good footing, and braced myself but I did not try to boost him because I felt that it might hurt his pride. He finally made it, and as he sat puffing on the rim, he said, "Thank you." So I guess I was right. My kodak got in the way and I darned near did not make it out of the couloir, and when he reached down and gave me a hand it did not hurt my pride a bit. And I said, "Thank you."

On reaching the summit after his first East Face climb, Alexander did not record it in the register on top. But I inserted it later because I thought it should be there.

We did not descend by any regular trail or route but crossed over to Mt. Meeker and went down the long scree slopes. By making a running-jump into this scree one could slide forty or fifty feet; another jump, another fifty feet.

Alexander was wearing tennis shoes and we had gotten our feet wet in the snow banks. This scree-jumping bruised the bottoms of his feet and his soles peeled off later. He was 'laid up' for the rest of that vacation and spent most of his time playing cards with the women at Hewes-Kirkwood Inn, one of whom he referred to as "Timid, the cold-footed vamp."

The professor had married a Russian woman. And in these days, I suppose, would be referred to as a pink. However, being pink was somewhat fashionable in those days, among the intelligentsia.

Many times I have been asked if I was not afraid on these climbs. Without boasting, I can honestly say that I was not, and that I never felt any particular thrills. This does not mean that I was not always very, very careful.

Blaurock, Smith, and Buhl continued as planned and repeated the ascent on September 10. The party totaled seven, including Buhl's wife, and two men whom Blaurock described as having "never been on a mountain before". They reached the top of the mountain at six p.m. and descended in the dark. A rescue party was mounted and headed up the mountain, only to meet the

tired climbers descending. Carl Blaurock remembers that the rescue party carried window sash cords twenty-five feet in length as their only rescue equipment!

The ascent of Alexander's Chimney in 1922 opened up the great East Face of Longs Peak to Colorado climbers. For a number of years to follow it remained the most difficult climb on the face. Walter Kiener climbed the face in 1924 via the snow chute of Lamb's Slide, and after traversing part way across Broadway, diagonaled across the upper face to the summit (the route of descent followed earlier by Elkanah Lamb and Enos Mills). The North Chimney was climbed in 1925 and, undoubtedly, other exploratory scrambles took place on the face, but these climbs were all easier than Alexander's Chimney.

The East Face of Longs - Alexander's Chimney

The Ellingwood Arete

During the early 1920's, Albert Ellingwood continued his activities in other parts of the state. In 1916, he and companions had explored the peaks of the Sangre de Cristo Mountains and had climbed Crestone Peak and Kit Carson Peak. Ellingwood called the Sangre de Cristos the "romantic range of the state par excellence." He wrote that "they have that rare combination of strangeness and beauty...necessary to give the romantic character."[6] In 1924, Ellingwood climbed the northeast arete of the Crestone Needle. This route, which became classic as a high mountain rock climb, became known as the Ellingwood Arete.

The east face of the Crestone Needle is a rock wall which averages well over one thousand feet in height for its entire breadth of about a mile. Immediately below the summit of the Crestone Needle the wall reaches its maximum height of almost two thousand feet. A steep buttress flanked by an arete extends for most of this distance and was the line of ascent chosen by Ellingwood in 1924.

Ellingwood had examined the route in 1916. The lower section lay back at an angle of 55° and appeared to present no particular problem. He was pessimistic about the last five hundred feet, where the precipice seemed to attain verticality, and wrote that "near the top...a huge boss of well-polished rock was certain to force us into an enormous overhang from which we could discern no avenue of escape."[7]

Ellingwood's companions consisted of Eleanor Davies, Marion Warner, and Stephen Hart. They set their hopes on a line which followed the arete itself. Three hours of climbing up grassy ledges and easy crack systems took them to the top of the first fifteen hundred-foot section. They lunched on a small ledge and debated whether to continue or retreat. Clouds descended, a strong wind arose, and before long it began to hail. Ellingwood noticed a long thin crack running up to the right of the arete and decided to continue. The rock was wet and slippery and each handhold had to be swept clear of hail. At intervals, the crack opened to the width of a chimney, though rarely enough to permit the consoling security of a full body wedge. In his account of the climb, Ellingwood described this section as "a diddle-diddle-dumpling sort of climb—one foot in and one foot out, and hands usually clawing at such minute molecules of rock as have survived the process of erosion."[8]

They finally reached the base of the high, unbroken final rock wall. The situation looked grim, and at first Ellingwood could see no way past it. A ledge led off to the left. Ellingwood's account continues:

> Five or six feet above our heads, a small ledge, no larger than a dinner plate, marked the beginning of a crack that led up somewhere at least, and might lead out. Unfortunately, a bulge in the wall prevented an honest approach to this vantage point on foot. From a short chimney in the corner of our porch I could just reach the ledge with the right foot, but my center of equilibrium was well out in mid-air, and there were no handholds available to defeat the law of gravity. Below the crack, the wall sloped inward and a three-man-stand would have been decidedly precarious. Again I tried the chimney, this time facing in, and from a high crossbrace leaned far back and got my fingers in a small crack just above the ledge; thus spread out spider fashion, like a skin stretched out to dry, I found I could back up and hold myself close in against the wall, and by a twisting motion wriggled to a sitting position on the ledge. The crack itself proved readily negotiable, although straight up for fifteen or twenty feet. Again we were on the arete, and again it led us presently into what looked like a cul-de-sac. This was an enormous crack almost wide enough to drive a wagon through; deep, too, and high but closed in at the top by an impetetrable roof. Again our sally-port was found to consist of a high crack on the right-hand wall, reached from an all but impossible crossbrace well up in the chimney, and the shorter members of the party found the rope a very present help in time of trouble. Twenty-five feet of squirming brought us to gentler slopes, where hands were no longer necessary for locomotion and an easy scramble soon landed us upon the summit ridge, scarcely a hundred feet south of the cairn.[9]

The ascent of this route in 1924 was to be the last of Ellingwood's new and technically difficult climbs. Today it is graded 5.6-5.7, depending on the exact route taken. Ellingwood climbed regularly in subsequent years prior to his untimely death from illness in 1934, but none of his ascents after 1924 possessed that unique combination of technical difficulty and psychological daring which characterized Lizard Head and his route on the Crestone Needle.

For the next two years, no new ascents of significance took place. Lizard Head, Alexander's Chimney, and the Ellingwood Arete were the major difficult climbs in the high mountains. By comparison, Alexander's route on the East Face of Longs was far easier than Ellingwood's climbs on Lizard Head and Crestone Needle. Climbers like Walter Kiener and Alexander continued to explore the East Face of Longs, but did not have the skill or confidence to venture onto the steeper rocks of the main face. The East Face waited, broodingly, its major rock walls virgin.

The Crestone Needle showing the route followed by Ellingwood
and party in 1924 - The Ellingwood Arete. *Chris Wood.*

Joe and Paul Stettner fuel up in Chicago on their departure for the Rockies in 1927. *Courtesy Joe Stettner.*

Stettners Ledges

In 1927, Colorado's climbers were aced out of the next major route to be developed on the East Face of Longs by two Bavarian brothers who drove out to Colorado from Chicago on motorcycles. The two brothers were Paul and Joe Stettner. Born in Munich, Joe Stettner trained as a coppersmith and Paul Stettner served his apprenticeship as a photoengraver. Between 1919 and 1925, the two brothers climbed in Germany and in the Austrian Alps. America was the promised land of economic opportunity, and Joe emigrated in 1925 to obtain work as a coppersmith in Chicago. The following year Paul joined him. Obtaining two Indian Chief "72 cubic inch" motorcycles, the pair toured Illinois and Wisconsin searching out low-lying rocks on which to climb, but they pined for the high peaks. On Saturday, September 3rd, 1927, they assembled their climbing equipment, loaded the motorcycles, and left Chicago heading west for the mountains of Colorado. Their journey took five days and was to be almost as much of an adventure as the climbing they were to accomplish.

Most of the journey was over rugged dirt and gravel roads, and the stiff suspension of their motorcycles made every bump noticeable. Near Freemont, Nebraska, it began to rain. Their coveralls, supposedly waterproof, possessed the water-repellent quality of sponges. Noticing a haystack close to a coffee shop, the two brothers pitched their small pup tent and retreated into the coffee shop's warmth to dry out. Returning to the tent later, dry and warm, and looking forward to a comfortable night's rest, they found the tent a flattened wreck and saw a pack of dogs disappearing into the distance. Most of their food and belongings were still intact, fortunately, and they were able to re-erect the tent and spend a comfortable night. The following day they resumed their journey, and five days after leaving Chicago they reached the Colorado mountains.

The Stettners had a small number of pitons and carabiners with them which they had brought from Europe (probably the first time carabiners had been used in Colorado). They had not been able to find a rope in Chicago, however, and hoped to purchase one in Colorado. After spending one day warming up in the Garden of the Gods, during which they climbed the Kissing Camels, they headed up towards Longs Peak, intent on investigating the possibility of a new route on

First view of the Rockies. *Joe Stettner.*

Joe Stettner on the Kissing Camels in the Garden of the Gods, warming up prior to Longs Peak. *Paul Stettner.*

Left. Joe and Paul Stettner at the old Timberline Cabin. Longs Peak in the background.
Courtesy Joe Stettner.

the East Face. At the Longs Peak Inn they found a rope, but its owner refused to sell or lend it, warning that it was too late in the year for such a hazardous climb. Eventually, after some searching, they found one hundred and twenty feet of thick hemp rope at the general store in Estes Park.

Joe Stettner reports that they knew of Alexander's Chimney, as well as Kiener's route via Lamb's Slide and the Notch Couloir, but the two brothers were looking for new adventures. Their experiences in the Alps had taught them that climbs were feasible even on apparently impossible faces, if there were sufficient holds, and cracks for pitons. They spent the night in the old timberline cabin below the East Face of Longs and the next morning examined the face through binoculars. About two hundred feet to the right of Alexander's Chimney, up a section of steep and intimidating rock, they noticed a system of cracks and ledges leading to Broadway, the ledge system running across the face at mid-height. Joe wrote in his account that the cracks "looked challenging enough for us," and they headed up towards the face. He was apparently a little bit pessimistic, suspecting that some of the cracks might be icy, but Paul's response was, "We can worry about that when we get there." [10]

They were wearing nailed boots for the hike in and changed into felt-soled climbing shoes on reaching the foot of the face. "Paul was eager to go on," wrote Joe, and started climbing without bothering to tie in to the climbing rope. Joe followed, also climbing solo, carrying the heavy pack. The pack made the climbing difficult, and on catching up with Paul, he said, "All right, you lead, but take the rope and put it on, and keep it on for the rest of the way." [11] Paul led the remainder of the climb, with Joe climbing second, carrying the pack. Part way up the climb they arrived in a flat-floored alcove. The rear wall of the alcove proved vertical, but Paul was able to free-climb it, using an occasional piton for protection. In subsequent years this section has sprouted so many pitons that it has become known as the "piton ladder." It was probably at this place that Joe, who was getting tired from carrying the pack, shouted up to warn Paul that he was about to peel at any moment. He did lose contact with the rock, but Paul was well belayed and was able to lower him ten feet to a good foothold. Joe writes that he remembers "several places where we thought it was impossible to get over, but with the use of pitons for protection Paul was able to negotiate them." [12] It began to snow as they reached Broadway, but they reached the summit of Longs rapidly via the Notch Couloir. The climb had taken the two brothers six-and-a-half hours.

Left. Joe Stettner (left) and Paul Stettner (right)
inside the Timberline Cabin. *Joe Stettner.*

Paul Stettner approaching the East Face of Longs. *Joe Stettner.*

Stettners Ledges on the East Face of Longs Peak.

Stettner's Ledges became, and has remained, a classic
ascent. In 1927 it was the most difficult Colorado high
mountain rock climb and probably the most difficult in
the United States. It was graded 5.7 in Walter Fricke's
1971 *Climbers' Guide to the Rocky Mountain National
Park,* which advises that a confident climber should
carry three pitons, eight slings, one nut, and ten
carabiners to supplement the many pitons already in
place. Fricke adds:

> While the Piton Ladder is often done on aid, one
> should know that the first ascent was done free. This
> route was for more than 20 years by far the hardest climb
> around. Time and modern technique have hardly made it
> any easier. [13]

Ellingwood's ascent of Lizard Head some seven years
prior to the Stettner's climb was comparable in technical
difficulty, and Ellingwood and Hoag had rotten rock to
contend with. These two climbs were the most advanced
technical rock routes in Colorado in the 1920's. No
other climbs were to occur in Colorado until the
mid-1940's surpassing them in daring and technical
difficulty.

Equipment used by the Stettner brothers. *Joe
Stettner.*

REFERENCES

1.   Albert R. Ellingwood, *Outing Magazine,* November, 1921, p.
     54.
2.   Larry Dalke, *tape recorded interview,* 1975.
3.   Albert R. Ellingwood, *Outing Magazine,* November, 1921, p.
     92.
4.   *The Rocky Mountain News,* Sept. 8, 1922, p. 1.
5.   *Ibid.*
6.   Albert R. Ellingwood, "The Eastern Arete of the Crestone
     Needle," *Trail and Timberline,* June, 1925, p. 1.
7.   *Ibid.,* p. 8.
8.   *Ibid.,* p. 9.
9.   *Ibid.*
10. Joseph Stettner, in William M. Bueler, *Roof of the Rockies*
     (Pruett Publishing Co., 1974), p. 91.
11. *Ibid.*
12. *Ibid.*
13. Walter W. Fricke, Jr., *A Climber's Guide to the Rocky
     Mountain Park* (Colorado: Paddock Publishing Co, 1971), p.
     44.

The North Face of Lone Eagle Peak, showing route followed by Joe and Paul Stettner in 1933.
Courtesy Rocky Mountain National Park.

CONSOLIDATION 1927-1949

The period 1927-1949, subsequent to the ascent of the East Face of Longs by the Stettners, was a period of consolidation for technical rock climbing. Climbers continued their explorations of major faces in the high mountains, and were also active in the vicinities of Boulder and Colorado Springs.

In 1929, Carl Blaurock, Bill Ervin, and Stephen Hart made the much-publicized first ascent of Lone Eagle (11,920 feet) in the Indian Peaks close to Boulder. This rocky mountain was a spectacular granite spire when viewed from the north, but the ascent via its south ridge proved to be no more than a stiff scramble.

The Stettner brothers paid one of their lightning visits to Lone Eagle in 1933 and produced a fine rock climb on its north face, which local climbers had not even attempted. The Stettners climbed the face from Crater Lake to the summit in the remarkable time of two hours. With their usual modesty, they did not publicize the climb, and a Colorado Mountain Club party including Roy Murchison and Bob Ormes climbed it in 1940, assuming they were making the first ascent. Of the 1940 climb, Ormes wrote:

> There are several reasons for ranking this climb among the very best in the state: the rock is not surpassed anywhere for firmness and dependability; the ascent has considerable technical variety; it has quantity of climbing; its climax, like that of the Ellingwood Arete on Crestone Needle, is at the top where it should be; and while it is not at all a dangerous climb for people of the right experience, it is undeniably a thriller of the first rank. [1]

The climb was certainly of excellent quality, but it lacked the technical problems of the Stettners' route on Longs and had none of the combination of difficulty and bad rock which characterized Lizard Head.

The San Juan Mountaineers

A small group of energetic climbers emerged in southwestern Colorado during the late 1920's. They called themselves the San Juan Mountaineers (S.J.M.). The driving force behind the group was Dwight G. Lavender. Lavender was an active climber as well as an industrious writer on climbing subjects. Largely as a result of his initiative, the group produced in typewritten form *The San Juan Mountaineers Guide to Southwestern Colorado.* [2] Lavender wrote over half the book himself. The section on the Needles-Grenadiers

Top. Paul Stettner leading on Lone Eagle. *Joe Stettner.*

Bottom. Joe Stettner signing in on the summit of Lone Eagle. *Paul Stettner.*

group was contributed by Carleton Long, while Melvin Griffiths contributed an appendix on the Black Canyon of the Gunnison. Other members of the group were Henry L. McClintock, Gordon Williams, Lewis Giesecke, and Everett Long.[3]

Dwight Lavender was Colorado's authority on rock climbing equipment during the 1930's, to the extent of manufacturing his own pitons (pronounced pi-tones in those days). He described them in an article in *Trail and Timberline* in 1933. His homemade pitons were four inches in length and were made from malleable wrought iron. They were designed with an open eye, rather than with the closed eye which has since become accepted practice. At this time Lavender was apparently unaware of European soft-iron pitons, or did not have carabiners to use in closed eyes. His reason for leaving the eye open was that the climbing rope could be run directly through it to protect the leader in case of a fall. One shudders today to think of taking a serious fall on a steep rock face, with the climbing rope running through the open eye of one of these pitons as the only protection.

Lavender describes one of his first attempts at constructing a piton in 1933. He writes, "Unwise in the ways of mountains we erred on the side of safety. It was made of one-inch steel, was about eight inches long, had a ring as large as a turkey egg, and required nothing less than a sledge hammer to drive it into a very large crack."[4] Baker Armstrong of Boulder acquired his first piton in 1934, and he reports that it was one of the open-eyed variety made for him by Dwight Lavender. Carl Blaurock had similar pitons manufactured at this time and used them in his rock climbing activities in the vicinity of the Flatirons and in the high mountains.

In the 1930's climbing ropes were made of hemp and manila, with 7/16-inch linen yacht rope being the preferred favorite. The strength of these ropes was a little over two thousand pounds when new. A hundred foot length of linen yacht rope cost $7.25 in 1933. Lavender felt that this was the best rope available; it was relatively soft, was easy to tie and handle, and was much less apt to be cut on sharp rocks than either manila or Italian hemp.[5]

One can imagine modern rock climbers salivating at the thought of a hundred feet of the best climbing rope of the day for $7.25. Though, even with the handling advantages mentioned by Lavender, the linen ropes suffered from the same disadvantage as hemp and manila; namely, that although their tensile strength was reasonably high, they possessed virtually no elasticity, and the shock load of a fall made rope failure a real possibility.

During this period in the 1930's nothing was known of dynamic belaying methods. In the eventuality of a fall, the rope was simply held as tightly as possible, and in some cases wrapped around a spike of rock. The result was that a fall would produce a tremendous shock

Carl Blaurock with his rope clipped into an open-eyed piton. Circa 1940. *Courtesy Carl Blaurock.*

Climbing equipment used by the San Juan Mountaineers: nailed boots, linen yacht rope, and hand-made pitons.

Bob Thallon on top of Wolf's Tooth, a pinnacle on the west side of Mt. Sneffels. *Dwight Lavender, courtesy Mel Griffiths.*

Robert Ormes leading on a practice outcrop in the 1930's wearing the same kind of basketball shoes as those used by the Greenmans in Boulder in 1919. *Mel Griffiths.*

load on the belayer, compounded by the fact that the ropes of the day had no stretch to help absorb the tremendous forces generated. Despite these inherent dangers in rope work and piton construction, there exist no reports in the literature of the period of serious accidents, or death, from leader falls in technical rock climbing. One can only assume that the small numbers of climbers active in those days adhered firmly to the Geoffrey Winthrop Young maxim that the leader shall not fall.

A short article appeared in the 1932 *American Alpine Journal,* giving a description of the relative merits of soft steel pitons and "safety snaps" (carabiners) available from European manufacturers. An accompanying photograph showed both the open-eye pitons, of the type manufactured by Dwight Lavender, and also closed-eye and ring pitons. The article stated that the open-eye pitons were "very secure...if driven in at least two-thirds of the shaft," but points out that the closed-eye varieties were "by far the best rock pitons, and an assortment such as the one illustrated would meet the requirements of any grimpeur." The article contained a strong statement which anticipated future developments: "Not withstanding feeble protests by a few climbers, mostly of the past generation, hammers, pitons and safety snaps have definitely entered into modern climbing technique."[6]

Writing in *Trail and Timberline* in 1932, Dwight Lavender commented on some of the distinctions he saw in those days between mountaineering and rock climbing. "It is surprising that only a few of our mountaineers know the fundamentals of rock climbing," he wrote.

> What we must learn is to handle a rope; and that a piton is superior to a spike...A rope is fairly cheap life insurance, and it is much more fun to practice using the rope on a nearby cliff in the foothills than it is to plod up a talus slope for hours on end just to say you have qualified by climbing a fourteen thousand footer.[7]

With these words as something of a motto, the San Juan Mountaineers were active on Mt. Sneffels and its outlying rock pinnacles; in the Needles and Grenadiers, and in the Black Canyon of the Gunnison. They produced many fine high alpine ascents involving various degrees of technical rock climbing, but none of the members of the group possessed that rare combination of exploratory instinct and psychological readiness for risk-taking to really tread new frontiers. Beuler says in his book *Roof of the Rockies* that the group was "the first to search out new and difficult routes."[8] New routes they sought out for sure, and of some difficulty, but none of their climbs compare to those of Ellingwood and the Stettners in the 1920's as far as technically difficult rock climbing is concerned.

Mt. Sneffels (14,150 feet) in southern Colorado possesses a large number of outlying rock pinnacles on its ridges. The San Juan Mountaineers group spent a

Ernest Ranzio practice climbing in the Shavano Valley. *Mel Griffiths.*

Charles Kane accepts a helping shoulder from Mel Griffiths. *Courtesy Mel Griffiths.*

good deal of time making ascents of these pinnacles in the early 1930's. Gordon Williams, climbing with Melvin Griffiths and Dwight Lavender, gives an account of the first ascent of one of these pinnacles, called "The Hand":

> For our first climb we chose the second highest of the needles. To begin with, we christened our victim "The Hand," because it slightly resembles the palm of a hand, with the thumb to the south, and the tips of the fingers overhanging a little to the east.
>
> After a brief reconnaissance, Mel decided he could make the almost vertical northern extremity, i.e., the little finger. This turned out to be shingled with very loose rock, and the general structure decreased in stability higher up. Mel saw fit to retreat, after gaining about fifty feet, and descended on the doubled rope to the col at the north end.
>
> Our next attempt was on a ledge on the west side of the arete. This route proved successful, but the climbing was again slow because of the loose hand and foot-holds and perched boulders. I did considerable grumbling about the non-technical climbing and the dangers of rotten rock. From the ledge the crest of the arete was gained and followed about two hundred feet to a small gendarme. Beyond this we could see no feasible route to the summit. Mel led over the gendarme and shouted back that the needle would go, but that there would be an exposed traverse. Dwight and I agreed, with the proper invectives, as we came in sight of the difficulty.
>
> The only possible route lay across the balls of the fingers, so to speak, just above the overhang and a sheer drop of about three hundred feet. The last fifteen or twenty feet were up a rotten little chimney which was practically as exposed as the traverse itself. We examined the traverse closely and noted that there were a few projections dotting the face of the smooth and now solid rock. All agreed that the traverse would be possible, but that the psychology born of the sheer drop below would present a handicap.
>
> We estimated sixty feet to the "crow's nest" which is practically the summit of the peak. I then untied so that Mel would have sufficient rope to pass the traverse, ascend the chimney, and reach the "crow's nest." I belayed the rope over a projection of rock, and Mel cautiously stepped out over the abyss. It seemed an age before he reached a ledge which would accommodate both of his feet at once. This ledge was half way along the traverse and the belay seemed puny enough at that distance. From his position the leader drove a piton into a crack at arm's length above his head. To the piton he hung a karabiner (sic), and in that the rope was snapped. With such additional assurance, the first part of the traverse was duplicated, except that the chimney was, if anything, a little more difficult than the face.
>
> Securely belayed from the summit above, I next and then Dwight reached the top...For Dwight and me, at least, the descent was not as bad as we had anticipated. Belayed as we were from above, we backed down from memory; the theory was good but our memories were bad, and as Dwight avowed, when we looked down between our legs for verification it took us five minutes to see the bottom. Mel came down by two stages, en rappel from a rope ring at the nest to the piton, and from the piton by semi-climbing and rappelling to our notch.[9]

Williams' account shows that the members of the San Juan Mountaineers were making use of pitons and

Direct aid - 1930's style. *Mel Griffiths.*

Consolidation

Mel Griffiths climbing on Courthouse Peak in the San Juan Mountains. *Courtesy Mel Griffiths.*

carabiners at the time of this ascent (1932), and that rappelling as a technique of descent was commonly used. Mel Griffiths' photographs show that nailed boots were still preferred for moving around in the high mountains, and that the same kind of tight-fitting baseball shoes used by Greenman on the Third Flatiron in 1920 were carried for more difficult rock sections.

Mel Griffiths wrote a two article sequence in *Trail and Timberline* in 1932 entitled "Rock Climbing," which summarized the known techniques of the day. His article illustrates the state of the art at that time, and gives first mention of techniques which were to become part of the basis of modern rock climbing:

> For mountaineering purposes a chimney may be defined as a fissure which is large enough to admit a climber's entire body, while a crack is smaller. The choice of two methods of ascending a chimney should be determined by the nature of the rock within it. If it is well broken up the best method is to climb directly up, using the holds and keeping the body away from the sides, but if its walls are comparatively smooth, friction must be resorted to. By placing the back against one wall and the feet or knees against the other and pushing almost horizontally from side to side, a firm position is obtained. Ascending is accomplished by alternately raising the back and the legs. The process is easier when the chimney is narrow if one of the feet is dropped across onto the wall supporting the back and the body raised by rocking back and forth on the feet and hands. The rucksack should be taken off at the foot of a difficult chimney and hauled up on a line after the first man has reached the top.
>
> The key to many a ticklish climb has been found in some impossible looking crack. The ascent of any crack calls for friction climbing pure and simple. If the crack is large enough it can be utilized by jamming the arm and leg into it. From this predicament the ascent is via a series of convulsions. Sometimes the climber can make headway by also clawing at the corner of the crack with the outside foot. When the fissure is too small to admit the arm and leg, the fingers and toes still remain to carry on. Any of these methods calls for the superlative in gymnastic ability. [10]

Modern climbers will smile at the instructions to proceed via a "series of convulsions" and to "make headway by clawing at the corner of the crack with the outside foot," and will note that in 1932 Griffiths talks of "jamming" and describes the embryonic beginnings of modern crack climbing technique.

The Black Canyon of the Gunnison - First Explorations

The San Juan Mountaineers made the first rock climbing explorations of a unique area which was to figure prominently in Colorado rock climbing during the 1960's and 1970's, called the Black Canyon of the

Robert Ormes gives a shoulder belay.
Mel Griffiths.

Gunnison. It is a steep, narrow defile, eroded by the Gunnison River to depths of three thousand feet. Members of the San Juan Mountaineers made a number of climbs in the Black Canyon in the early 1930's. Their climbs tended to follow pronounced ribs of rock reaching up from the river to the canyon rim. Melvin Griffiths described his reactions to the canyon in an appendix to the *San Juan Mountaineers Guide to Southwestern Colorado* in 1932:

> ...the climbs on the ribs are more inviting than the descents into the canyon. Perhaps this is due to the psychology born of the surroundings. On such a descent, one leaves a bright, sunny world behind and climbs down into a rocky, forbidding hole eighteen hundred feet below the warm, inviting soil above, a hole which is filled with the terrifying boom of the river and the gloomy, grotesque aspects of water-worn rock. One comes away with an overwhelming realization of the titanic forces of nature. Since the normal procedure is reversed, the ascent following the descent, one will do well to watch his time, remembering that it will take him longer to get back out than it took him to descend. [11]

Griffiths' brief note describing the uninviting nature of descents into the Black Canyon gives no hint of the horrors which lurk in the steep gullies leading down from the rim to the river, ready to trap the unwary. Many of them are steep, loose, and plain nasty. Talus with the consistency of polished ball bearings lies on top of slabby rock, ready to catapult the careless rock climber into the depths of the canyon. Vegetation in the gullies and on much of the canyon bottom has justly earned the canyon its reputation among climbers as the poison ivy center of Colorado. These hazards have never deterred rock climbers. The canyon walls are precipitous and vast, and many major climbs have been developed in recent years. In 1932 the canyon was unknown and the explorations of the San Juan Mountaineers, though they did not tackle the major steep walls, were noteworthy for that day and age. On July 11, 1932, William Macomber, Charles Kane, Gordon Williams and Melvin Griffiths descended a gully running down from Echo Point on the west rim. After descending for several hundred feet, they were able to attain a ridge which rose towards a detached island of rock well out from the main rim. Three massive gendarmes guarded its beginning. After avoiding the first two by a traverse around the north side, they were able to surmount a steep buttress of rock some thirty feet high by a steep crack at the northwest end. This maneuver enabled them to traverse the face of the third gendarme by means of a narrow ledge and to reach the crest of the ridge. The ridge led easily along to the summit of the fourth gendarme. After dropping down to the south side of the ridge, they found a series

Gordon Williams leading the tricky hand traverse on the Echo Point climb in the Black Canyon. Running belays were unknown in the 1930's and the main climbing rope runs behind a flake of rock to give protection in case of a fall. *Mel Griffiths.*

of narrow ledges which gave promise of a route. Progressing part-way around the gendarme via this ledge system, they were faced with an exposed rock wall. After some discussion and exploration of possible alternatives, Gordon Williams led out across the wall. A line of holds provided the promise of a hand traverse to another ledge system. Running belays were unknown in those days, and Williams slipped the main climbing rope behind a detached flake of rock to give some measure of security in case of a fall. Another member of the party belayed the rope out through the dubious security of the flake, and, with its protection, Williams was able to complete the traverse and to reach the continuation of the ledge system. Mel Griffiths was nicely positioned behind the belayer to record the adventure on film. At the end of the hand traverse they were able to follow ledges on the south side of the ridge, bypassing a mass of smaller gendarmes, and to reach the foot of a two hundred-foot-high chimney which led upwards. The chimney contained some of the most difficult climbing on the route, particularly at the top where it widened, and they lost the security of being able to progress by back and knee methods. In his account of the route, Mel Griffiths pointed out that it was of a high order of difficulty for that time. He also added, "the surface has not been scratched as yet. This short treatment of a few climbs only hints at the exploration which remains to be made." [12] His words were prophetic, and the Black Canyon was to become an important area in Colorado rock climbing in future years.

Longs Peak

Thanks mainly to the efforts of Enos Mills, Congress passed a bill in 1915 designating Longs Peak and its surroundings as the Rocky Mountain National Park. By 1930, the Park was firmly established and was administered by government rangers. The early park rangers were mountain men, and one of them, Jack Moomaw, had made the second ascent of Alexander's Chimney in 1922 with Alexander. By the early 1930's Longs Peak had seen the establishment of a simple cabin at the boulder field (12,000 feet), and mountain guides were in residence to escort tourists up and down the peak.

The Longs Peak guides were primarily interested in guiding their clients up and down the regular route on Longs. Everett Long, who was a Longs Peak guide at this time, and a companion, attempted to expand the

Routes on the East Face of Longs Peak in 1936. *Warren Gorrell.*

R — Regular route up Gully & along Broadway; W. Kiener, Agnes Vaille & C. Blaurock, 1924.

A — Alexanders Chimney: E. W. Alexander, solo, 1922, the first ascent of the East Face. He went up the Chimneys off Broadway, which is the usual line today.

S — Stettner Ledges: — Joe and Paul Stettner, 1927.

K — The Second, or Kieners Chimney: — E. K. Field and W. Gorrell, Jr., 1936.

N — The North Chimney: — E. H. Bruns and W. F. Ervin, 1924.

NC — Notch Couloir: — D. Smith, C. Blaurock, H. Wirtman, J. L. J. Hart, Mr. & Mrs. H. Buhl & F. Shirmer, 1922, three days after Alexander's first ascent of the cliff.

RS — Staircase; RB — Slabs; LN — Little Notch: — regular lines to the summit.

RX — The Corner: the sheer drop from this point is a third of a mile.

T — The Thumb, yet unscaled.

E — The Eighth: — Paul Hauk, E. K. Field & W. Gorrell, Jr.

J — Joes Solo: Joe Stettner, 1936. This, E & TR reach summit via Meeker Traverse.

BC — Broadway Cutoff; W. Gorrell, Jr. and E. K. Field, 1936.

M — The Meadows, wide grassy ledges; Broadway extends from here all the way to L, where E. J. Lamb left the Face on his solo descent of the cliff in 1871.

C — The Cable, put up in 1925; E. Mills was first up this North Face, about 1912.

business by inserting a series of large iron belay spikes in the face of the Third Flatiron in 1931. Their hope was that the Third Flatiron might become popular with tourists, and that they might be able to do business as guides in the vicinity of Boulder, as well as on Longs Peak. Apparently this scheme did not work out too well and little business was forthcoming. The eye bolts are still there today and provide convenient anchor points for climbers.

It seems that the Longs Peak guides were unaware of the Stettners' route on the East Face, until the climb was "rediscovered" by Warren Gorrell and Charles Hardin in 1935. While attempting to make the second ascent in 1935, Warren Gorrell took a bad fall and broke his foot. A rescue was mounted and he had to be carried out from the face. Undeterred, he returned the

The Boulderfield Shelter Cabin on Longs Peak. 1925-1937. *Ev. Long.*

Longs Peak guides Hull Cook (left) and Clerin Zumwalt (right) buildering on the walls of the Boulderfield Cabin in 1932. The "ice axe" brandished by Zumwalt was brought up by a tourist for the ascent of Longs! No one knows where the hats came from. *Ev. Long.*

following year with Charles Hardin, Ernie Field, and Eddie Watson, and made the second successful ascent of the Stettners Ledges in 1936. Even after Gorrell's second ascent in 1936, Stettners Ledges still remained shrouded in mystery to Colorado climbers. Warren Gorrell's fall, and subsequent rescue, in 1935 had given the climb an aura of great difficulty, and those climbers active during the 1930's were hesitant to attempt it. In August 1938, Fritz Wiessner and Chappel Cranmer made an attempt on the route. Jack Fralick (co-founder of the Chicago Mountaineering Club) spoke with Wiessner after his attempt. "In 1941," Fralick writes, "I asked Fritz Wiessner about this attempt (on Stettners Ledges), and he told me he could not find the route! Coming from one of the outstanding mountaineers of the world, this was indeed a resounding testimony." [13] After Wiessner's attempt in 1938, a decade was to pass before another ascent of the route was made by climbers other than the Stettners. The climb's aura of great difficulty, and the problems of finding the correct route, kept the climb in obscurity for twenty-one years. The Stettner's first ascent in 1927, Gorrell's second ascent in 1936, and an ascent by Joe Stettner and Bob Ormes in 1942, were the only successes between 1927 and 1948.

In 1936, Joe Stettner paid a solo visit to the East Face of Longs Peak. Reaching Broadway, he climbed alone to the summit ridge of Longs via a line of ascent just left of the Notch Couloir. This ascent has been much discussed during subsequent years. Warren Gorrell had a photograph of the East Face showing the line of Joe's solo ascent. Stettner examined the photograph in later years and felt that the line was correct. Modern climbers who have explored this region of the East Face have returned impressed with its steepness and difficulty. Walter Fricke, in his climbers guidebook writes, "Close inspection from several angles suggests the unlikelihood...of an unbelayed solo route continuing in this line." [14] Joe Stettner remains convinced that the line shown in Gorrell's photograph is correct and that he cut left only about a hundred feet from the top. In his words, he found the upper part "very hard and felt that I took chances on it." [15] In retrospect, it is impossible to ascertain with complete certainty the exact nature and line of Joe Stettner's solo climb. It is possible that he

Left to right - Ernie Field, Warren Gorrell, Baker Armstrong, and an unknown companion, after an ascent of Zumies Chimney in 1937. *Courtesy Baker Armstrong.*

The East Face of Monitor Peak. Stettner-Fralick-Speck route marked. *Courtesy Joe Stettner.*

overhang at about two-thirds of the height of the gully.''[16] They climbed up steep rocks on the left side of the gully, with Stettner leading, and eventually found themselves some way below the major overhang which they had seen from below. Fralick's account continues:

> When the chimney finally intersected the big gully, we found ourselves still below the ominous overhang and separated from it by a steep zone of smooth slabs forming the left wall of the gully. In this series of slabs we placed a number of pitons for security. Much loose rock had been encountered thus far, and it caused a near accident in this section. Tiny fingerholds gave way under John's hands, and he swung and fell at the same time from a point below and to the right of me. I was unable to hold him and keep my feet in doing so. Checking his rope instinctively, and perhaps too rapidly, I stopped the running of the rope, but was pulled off and down to the next ledge about 5 feet below. Our combined fall came heavily on Joe, but he held us on the piton and karabiner (sic) through which he was anchoring me. John and I were able to quickly take our weight off the rope, and the incident was soon forgotten. However, only Joe's caution in anchoring me, while I belayed John, had saved the day.[17]

From this point, slabs of rock led upwards to a small ledge directly beneath the overhang. It occupied the left wall of the gully and barred further progress up that side. Inspection of the right wall of the gully revealed a steep lie-back crack which appeared difficult but possible. Stettner climbed delicately across the gully to reach the lie-back and:

> ...made two unsuccessful attempts to start the crack. These spoke eloquently of its great difficulty, but Joe's only comment was his request for a shoulder stand. John dropped down to the floor of the gully, crossed the slab nicely, anchored himself to a piton, and wedged into the bottom of the crack as securely as possible. Using the rope sling and John's shoulder as footholds, Joe managed to get started in the crack. With his hands gripping the right edge, Joe Stettner did a lie-back up the 30 foot crack and climbed into the steep rocks above it before he could pause for even the briefest respite from his exhausting efforts. It was the hardest work to that point, and it forced Joe to the limit of his exceptional strength and ability.[18]

The crack led the party onto steep rock to the right of the gully. Fralick writes that they ''had entertained no thought of finishing the climb by means of the great central face.'' The lie-back crack led them into a position where they now found themselves committed to this course. The climbing on the central face was

was mistaken on examining Gorrell's photograph, and that his actual line of ascent was further left on more broken and easier ground. However, there is no doubt that he was climbing at a high technical standard during the 1930's. It is quite possible that, in the excitement of finding himself alone on that great face, all of his energies, spurred on by the unthinkable consequences of an unroped fall, motivated him to follow the difficult line indicated on Gorrell's photographs.

The East Face of Monitor Peak

In 1947 Joe Stettner, rather than remaining in contented obscurity in Chicago, paid another vacation visit to Colorado. Twenty years had passed since his ascent of Stettners Ledges with his brother Paul. In 1947 Joe Stettner was 46 years of age. He arrived in Colorado in the company of John Speck and Jack Fralick. Their objective was the previously unclimbed 1,200 foot East Face of Monitor Peak in the Needles of the San Juan Mountains.

In an article written for *Trail and Timberline* in December 1947, Jack Fralick wrote that ''a very steep gully marking the left hand margin of this great central face appeared to be climbable, providing that a way could be found over or around an ominous black

The bivouac high on the East Face of Monitor Peak. *Joe Stettner.*

Jack Fralick (right), Joe Stettner (center), and John Speck (left), in 1947 at the time of the ascent of the East Face of Monitor Peak. *Courtesy Joe Stettner.*

difficult and sustained, but they found the rock firmer than below. At this point they found themselves nine hundred feet up the wall, with darkness coming quickly. Finding a convenient ledge, the three decided to bivouac for the night. The remaining three hundred feet the next day presented sustained difficulties involving a one hundred and forty-foot pitch with two very delicate traverses. In his summary of the climb, Fralick wrote:

> Joe Stettner......considers that (the East Face of Monitor Peak) is the most difficult climb he has ever accomplished—even more severe than the North Wall of the Grand Teton and the Stettner Ledges route on the East Face of Longs Peak. The difficulties increase as height is gained—building up to two passages of the utmost severity, the lie-back crack and the "140 ft. lead."[19]

The pattern of events subsequent to Stettner's ascent of the East Face of Monitor Peak with Speck and Fralick paralleled closely the events which followed Stettners Ledges in 1927. A period of twenty-one years elapsed before the face received a second ascent! The second ascent was made in 1968 by Larry Dalke and Paul Stettner Jr., Joe's nephew. They started up a different line of ascent, to the right of the 1947 route, but joined the original route about three hundred feet from the top. When interviewed about the East Face of Monitor in 1975, Dalke remained very impressed by his recollections of the technical difficulties of the face, and by the rotten nature of much of the rock. During the interview he remarked, "It's one of the few climbs I'd never want to repeat."[20]

The ascent of Stettners Ledges in 1927, the North Face of Lone Eagle in 1933, Joe's solo ascent of the East Face of Longs in 1936 and the East Face of Monitor in 1947, firmly established the Stettner brothers as the most daring and technically advanced rock climbers active in Colorado during the 1930's. Their climbs are all the more impressive when one remembers that their home was in Chicago and that their climbs were made on brief vacation visits to Colorado. Who knows what they might have accomplished had they lived closer to the high mountains?

REFERENCES

1. Robert Ormes, "Lone Eagle—North Face," *Trail and Timberline,* September, 1940, p. 137.
2. Dwight G. Lavender and Carleton Long, "*The San Juan Mountaineers' Guide to Southwestern Colorado,*" Colorado Mountain Club Library, 1932. (Typewritten.)
3. Bueler, *op. cit.,* p. 142.
4. Dwight G. Lavender and T. Melvin Griffiths, "Notes on Equipment," *Trail and Timberline,* November, 1933, p. 16.
5. Dwight G. Lavender, "Climbing Ropes," *Trail and Timberline,* May, 1933, p. 67.
6. Notes, *The American Alpine Journal,* Vol. 1, No. 4, 1932, pp. 526-527.
7. Dwight G. Lavender, "Correspondence," *Trail and Timberline,* May, 1932, p. 73.
8. Bueler, *op. cit.,* p. 142.
9. Gordon Williams, in Dwight G. Lavender and T. Melvin Griffiths, "Climbing in the Mount Sneffels Region, Colorado," *The American Alpine Journal,* Vol. II, No. 2, 1934, pp. 97-98. 97-98.
10. T. Melvin Griffiths, "Rock Climbing," *Trail and Timberline,* September, 1932, p. 131.
11. Dwight G. Lavender and Carleton Long, "The San Juan Mountaineer's Guide to Southwestern Colorado," Colorado Mountain Club Library, 1932. (Typewritten.) p. 195.
12. *Ibid.,* p. 202.
13. Jack Fralick, *personal communication,* 1976.
14. Fricke, *op. cit.,* p. 60.
15. Joe Stettner, *personal communication,* 1976.
16. Jack Fralick, *Trail and Timberline,* December, 1947, in Bueler, *Roof of the Rockies* (Pruett Publishing Co., 1974), p. 170.
17. *Ibid.,* p. 170
18. *Ibid.,* p. 171
19. *Ibid.,* p. 171
20. Larry Dalke, *interview transcript,* 1976.

Part II

THE FIFTIES

Bob Riley (left), Tom Hornbein (center), and Dick Sherman (right) on top of the Third Flatiron after their first ascent of the Northwest Passage. *Courtesy Tom Hornbein.*

NEW TECHNIQUES AND OVERHANGING ROCK
1949-1956

I'd ...had nightmares about this climb. It was...the only thing I had ever climbed that I would never care to repeat. Tom Hornbein describing the Hornbein Crack (1953)

Between 1949 and 1956, developments took place in Colorado rock climbing which radically changed its nature. New equipment and the introduction of more advanced techniques made possible a new psychological approach.

In 1947 Arnold Wexler published his paper "Belaying the Leader."[1] Wexler's central concept was a system of rope handling which gave some degree of protection to a rock climbing leader in the eventuality of a fall. He pointed out that, "if a leader falls clean from over eight to ten feet, sustaining a sheer drop of sixteen to twenty feet or more, the rope (*any* rope practical for climbing purposes) thus rigidly fixed, will most certainly snap."[2] The English climber Geoffrey Winthrop Young had recognized this fact many years before. Young had only a relatively ineffective method for dealing with a leader fall and suggested belaying the rope around a rock with "corrective action...practically confined to doing all we can to spring the rope, with arm, hand or body, so as to lessen the chance of its snapping."[3]

Young understood well the dangers of the static belay and had concluded that it was virtually impossible for the second climber to hold a leader fall of more than a few feet. This led him to generate his classic maxim that it was entirely unjustifiable for the leader to risk a fall. Based on this reasoning, Young, and others of that period, concluded that if the leader fell, he had knowingly violated his obligations to the rest of the party and "must therefore ruthlessly be sacrificed."[4] This sacrifice was to be accomplished very effectively; they frankly recommended that the second man use a static rock belay which would almost certainly result in the breaking of the rope if the leader fell.

Wexler concluded that the frequently used shoulder belay "was found to be the weakest of all," and that "the soundest of the body belays was the hip belay."[5] However, even with a seated hip belay, Wexler found that a fall of about seven feet was the maximum that could be held using static methods. Falls of more than seven feet presented danger to back and kidneys and tended to jerk the belayer out of his stance. After some experiments with weights and various systems of pitons, Wexler concluded: "Surprising as it

may seem, a ten-foot fall can easily be held by only one hand if proper technique is used."[6] The technique which Wexler recommended was called the dynamic belay. In the eventuality of a leader fall, the second man was to allow the rope to slide some distance and gradually bring the falling leader to a halt. Wexler found that, in practice sessions, a fall of eighteen feet could be easily held if correct dynamic belaying methods were employed. Falls of more than eighteen feet were not tried in practice, but Wexler felt that his system would hold much longer falls, without ripping the belayer from his stance.

During this same period, the army carried out comparative studies of all available climbing ropes, and subsequently ordered two million feet of nylon rope for the Mountain Troops on the basis of the results. The use of nylon climbing ropes and dynamic belaying methods were to have a significant effect on the course of technical rock climbing during the following decade.

In the *American Alpine Journal* of 1948, Fred Beckey presented a short description of "contraction bolts." The bolts he described were 5/8 of an inch in diameter and three inches long. The use of these bolts necessitated the climber drilling a hole in the rock. Beckey stated in his article that it took thirteen minutes on the average to drill the necessary three-inch deep hole. The appearance of these bolts in rock climbing introduced a new dimension. Previously, rock climbers had been confined to cracks in the rock to provide placements for pitons. With drilled holes and bolts, the climber could patiently engineer his way up blank sections of rock. Beckey stated in 1948 that he did not believe in "blacksmithing a route," but did recommend their use if a blank section were to be encountered on a longer climb. He finished his article by asking a question which has not been answered fully even today, "how far shall we go in using artificial aids?"[7]

At approximately the same time that Beckey described contraction bolts, John Salathé and Ax Nelson made their legendary five-day ascent of Lost Arrow Spire in Yosemite Valley (1947). Allen Steck called this ascent "the greatest achievement of its kind in the history of tension climbing."[8] In 1949, John

Salathé and Alan Steck succeeded in climbing the North Face of Sentinel Rock in Yosemite, using "seventy-six pitons plus nine bolts" for the final eleven leads.

Colorado rock climbers in 1948 were unaware of these events in California, and the terms "aid climbing" and "tension climbing" were virtually unknown. Word had not yet filtered through about Salathé's climbs in Yosemite, and knowledge of equipment and technique was limited. Wexler's work on dynamic belay methods was also unknown. Colorado climbers were still at the stage of making things up as they went along, and developing new techniques "in situ".

The First Ascent of the Northwest Passage

In 1949, a young geology student at the University of Colorado named Tom Hornbein (later to climb Everest on the successful 1963 American expedition), was active in the Boulder vicinity. After repeating a number of routes on the Flatirons and the Maiden, he began to turn his attention to some of the unclimbed lines. His first new climb in 1948 was a relatively easy route up the east face of a pinnacle called the Willy B. During one of these climbs, the steep and overhanging west face of the Third Flatiron caught his eye. In 1949 the face was virgin and had been dismissed as impossible by climbers of earlier generations, who occasionally had rappelled down it as a descent route after climbing the east face.

Hornbein and two other young rock climbers, Bob Riley and Dick Sherman, began exploring possible lines up the face. Hornbein remembers "cutting mineralogy laboratory" and arriving mid-afternoon at the face for these early exploratory efforts. They chose a line which trended leftwards across the main face, following a natural line of rock strata which eventually led out onto the east ridge at a prominent notch. Just below the notch was a large overhang split by a crack. They expected this overhang to be the most difficult section of the climb.

After an initial easy crack, Bob Riley found himself in a rocky corner containing large quantities of avian deposits. After appropriate excavations had been made the corner was christened the "birds nest" and became the position of the first belay point. Hornbein remembers that they "pounded all kinds of pitons up in that corner to try to keep the belayer in place,"[9] but

Top. The pendulum across Skid Row.

Center. Bob Riley moving round the overhang on direct aid.

Bottom. Stretch in the rope drops Riley down below the overhang, out of reach of the next piton placement. *Photos Tom Hornbein.*

that the anchors were somewhat unsatisfactory. The pitons they had at this time were of soft steel, and all of them were of the ex-army variety, consisting of the standard army angle (approximately six inches long and three-quarters of an inch wide) and horizontal, vertical, and "wafer" pitons. They all owned, and were rather proud of, reversible Army surplus parkas, white on the outside and with fur around the collar. Hornbein recollects that Riley and he "were enamoured of little Alpine felt hats" and that they wore them for all of their climbs. Their boots in those days were also army surplus and had Goodyear rubber lugged soles.

The first major difficulty consisted of a steep slab, subsequently to be called "Skid Row." Bob Riley led the slab and made a descending traverse to a belay ledge on the left. Hornbein and Sherman followed the slab by penduluming across, with the rope running through Riley's high protection piton.

Between the belay stance and the crack leading up to the overhang was a short steep wall. After a number of attempts they found themselves unable to climb it, and there were no suitable cracks for pitons. They fiddled around for a number of afternoons attempting to drill holes for expansion bolts which they had purchased in the local hardware store. These bolts were half-inch in diameter, and Hornbein says that they didn't really know how to use them. To the best of his knowledge, no one had used them before in the Boulder area. After spending a long time drilling a hole above the belay stance, in an attempt to facilitate an upward ascent into the crack beside the overhang, Riley reached the moment of truth. He attempted to pound the bolt in and succeeded only in stripping the threads. This was a little discouraging after all the time they had spent drilling. They then adopted an alternative technique which was to attempt to lasso a point of rock up in the crack which seemed to be reasonably solid. This technique involved standing on a tiny ledge facing outward and then, without too much "body English," flipping the rope with a loop on it repeatedly until finally, by sheer luck, the little promontory was snagged. They then prusiked up the eight or ten feet into the crack. Hornbein reports that during these maneuvers they "were all duly awed and impressed" by the tangles they could easily create…"with piles of rope hanging here and there."

The lasso and prusik had brought them to a point directly beneath the final overhang. After experimenting with a number of alternative ways of engineering it,

Riley climbed up and hammered in a piton. He let himself out from this and hammered in another piton further out in the crack. From this he suspended the main rope with a foot loop tied in the end. The intention was that the belayer would pull on the rope and Riley would slowly rise over the overhang. These levitational aspirations did not work too well in practice. When Riley put his weight on the loop, the stretch in the rope between him and the belayer was so much that he ended up dangling in space below the overhang, far out of reach of the next piton placement. He was hauled back into the belay ledge and, after some reassessment of the situation, the three decided to make a short foot loop from a separate length of rope to hang directly from the piton. (It is of interest to note that Hornbein, Riley and Sherman were unaware of stirrups (etriers) in 1949, despite the fact that they had been in use in Europe, and in California, for some time.) The short loop proved to be the key to the climb. Riley was able to stand in it and reach around the corner and place a piton above the overhang. A second piton was placed a little higher, and after some grunting and heaving Riley disappeared from view to make the successful first ascent. The party called the climb the Northwest Passage. It was the first climb in Colorado to tackle a major overhang using artificial aids, and to attempt to overcome a blank section of rock with expansion bolts.

The Maiden Rappel

There were very few climbers in the Boulder area searching for new and more technically difficult climbs in 1948. Hornbein, Riley and Sherman climbed together on a regular basis, and their ascent of the Northwest Passage was a landmark climb. In 1948 two other climbers appeared who were to be very active in exploratory rock climbing during the early 1950's. The two were Brad Van Diver and Bill Eubanks. Their first recorded new climb, of no great difficulty, was up the East Ridge of the Matron, a sister pinnacle to the Maiden. The climb is now an easy classic graded 5.5. Hornbein and Van Diver occasionally climbed together, and one day in 1950 found themselves on top of the Maiden's spectacular summit, making what was then the fourth or fifth ascent.

Since its first ascent in 1944 by Roy Peak and Mark Taggart, the spire of the Maiden has become famous throughout the United States, and many tales are told of it. Some climbers have even camped overnight on its summit. Cleve McCarty and Margaret Powers once climbed to the summit equipped with nets and bottles on an errand for the biology department of the University of Colorado. The trip was a success. In a small water-filled basin at the summit they found fresh water shrimp!

Hornbein and Van Diver knew that on earlier ascents the climbers had descended via the regular ascent route on the north face. It is unclear who actually came up with the suggestion, but during the course of conversation an idea emerged of rappelling from the summit, over the massive overhanging west face. In their rock climber's guide book, *High Over Boulder*, Ament and McCarty give the following description of this rappel. "During high winds, the rappel becomes a ballistics problem, with the bombardier calculating himself as a human bomb while being blown through the air like a pendulum. The target seems no larger than a doormat and is only a point on a ridge. This point is called the Crow's Nest and is 115 feet from the top. Vertical walls drop for 120 feet either side of the narrow ridge."[10]

Appropriate discussions of the situation took place. Bill Braddock, who was along, would climb horrendous routes, but firmly announced that he had no intention of lowering into mid-air over the overhang, particularly with such a narrow exposed landing point. Brad Van Diver was elected to be the first hero. The start of the rappel was awkward. One plan was to start somewhat to the right of the anchor point and "sort of pendulum in decreasing arcs until things got under control."[11] This didn't appeal too much to Van Diver, who slid gently over the edge directly below the anchors. Hornbein reports that they belayed him down with a safety rope and that "it was a spectacular thing to watch as he spun gently down onto the narrow ledge." It has been said of the Maiden rappel, "fall off that one and you'd fall for the rest of your life."[12]

The Northwest Overhang of the Maiden

In 1950 a young blond-haired Boulder climber named Dale Johnson made the second ascent of the Northwest Passage on the Third Flatiron and became intrigued with the new possibilities which pitons and expansion bolts opened up. Johnson had an inventive side to his nature, and after his ascent of the Northwest Passage set about trying to improve upon the rather crude direct aid techniques which were then being used. Somewhere he had come across a picture in a magazine of the French climber, Gaston Rebuffatt, climbing the underside of an horizontal overhang in the Alps by hammering in upside-down pitons. After studying the photograph for a while, he thought to himself, "His technique is terrible, we can do better than that." Co-opting Phil Robertson and Bob Sutton, they selected a large overhang on Castle Rock in Boulder Canyon as a good place to work out the new ideas. Rebuffat's technique was to suspend a short ladder from pitons hammered into the overhang. He would then sit with a leg through the rungs of the ladder, and reach out to hammer in the next piton. Johnson examined this technique and tried to figure out a way of being able to lay out horizontally underneath the overhang, to extend his reach, and thereby reduce the number of pitons needed. To assist in this process he developed a "diaper seat" made from nylon webbing which enabled him to suspend himself close up to the piton and to reach out two or three feet to the next piton placement.

This technique depended on double-rope tension climbing. At first this system required two belayers. Johnson would clip in one rope, clip in a stirrup, and haul himself as tight into the piton as he could. One belayer would then hold him in place while he hammered in the next one. Once it was hammered in, the second rope would be clipped in and a stirrup attached. Dale would swing across to it, and the second belayer would hold him in tight. It was a strenuous technique and left the leader puffing and panting from exertion. They eventually did engineer their way across the underside of a twenty foot overhang on Castle Rock, claiming a first for this kind of climbing in the Boulder region.

The overhang which the three climbed became known as the "practice roof." It is only about thirty feet up from the ground and has given many climbers their first practice in direct aid technique over the years. Boulder Creek runs by only a few feet away, and numerous fishermen have rubbed their eyes in amazement at seeing a suspended spidery figure, encased in a cocoon of tangled ropes, inching across the underside of the roof. Sometime during the early 1950's the story is told of James Peterson using a rather unconventional technique for belaying the roof. He anchored the climbing ropes from the lead climber to the bumper of his car and carried out his belaying responsibilities from the driver's seat, moving the car back and forward to give the climber the appropriate amounts of slack and tension.

In addition to their experiments on Castle Rock,

Johnson and his companions would try out new methods on the inside of the University field house. They would read of some new technique in a climbing magazine and then head down to the field house with ropes and carabiners to try it out. The tall windows of the field house had chain-link fences covering them to protect them from flying balls. Dale recounts the consternation experienced by the other users of the field house when they noticed strange figures, swathed in climbing equipment, inching their way via various tangled rope maneuvers up the chain-link fences toward the field house rafters.

Feeling confident after his experiments on the practice roof and on the chain links of the field house, Johnson began to search around for an unclimbed rock on which to employ the new methods. His ascent of the Northwest Passage enabled him to consider climbing a new major overhanging face, and he had also made the second ascent of Shiprock in New Mexico.

Soft iron pitons were still being imported from Europe, and there was a good deal of army surplus hardware available, but local climbers did not have a high regard for much of it. Roy Holubar employed a local Colorado blacksmith to manufacture steel pitons, which were stronger than either European imports or army surplus. One of the real problems in engineering overhanging rock was the quantity, and weight, of the equipment which had to be carried. It was not unusual

Dale Johnson loaded down with direct aid equipment about to embark on the first ascent of the Northwest Overhang of the Maiden. *Courtesy Dale Johnson.*

for Dale Johnson to carry thirty heavy pitons, as many steel carabiners, as well as a hammer, expansion bolts, and other odds and ends. It was a real boon during this period when Raffi Bedayn of California produced the first aluminum carabiners. They were strong, yet light, and significantly reduced the amount of weight the climber had to carry on long overhanging faces requiring extensive direct aid.

Johnson acquired some of these new carabiners and felt well prepared to attempt a major new route of his own. The route he selected was up the steep and intimidating Northwest Overhang of the Maiden—the route of the dizzy rappel pioneered by Brad Van Diver a year or two previously. This was an audacious choice on Johnson's part. It involved starting the climb from the Crow's Nest, the small platform on the narrow ridge at the foot of the Northwest face, which meant that he had a sheer drop of over a hundred feet to contend with before even placing his first piton. Few climbers had considered the face as a possible route of ascent. Those few who did venture to the summit of the Maiden in those days, via the regular north face route, felt well satisfied to gingerly lower themselves over the top of the Northwest Overhang, close their eyes, and pray silently during the slowly spinning descent to the Crow's Nest.

Johnson assembled Dave Robertson and Cary Huston at this exposed spot on an October day in 1953. They had a large number of pitons of different sizes and shapes, eight expansion bolts, three drills, three 120-foot climbing ropes, one 120-foot length of 1/8-inch parachute cord for hauling equipment up and down, carabiners, hammers, and a camera.

Dave and Cary confessed that they had no interest in going first and promptly handed all of the equipment over to Dale. Staggering under its weight, he selected a line which led more or less straight up to the summit. The first ten feet were steep friction—no mean feat carrying forty pounds of iron—and led to thirty feet of direct aid up a series of excellent cracks. Some twenty feet higher the wall overhung steeply, and the difficult climbing started in ernest.

It took Johnson twenty-five minutes to drill his first expansion bolt hole. The bolts used were acquired at the local hardware store, and were of three different types: a "lead shield" version, 3/8-inch diameter with a separate hanger; a "Phillips Redhead," which was a self-driving bolt with its own teeth; and a "split rivet" type, which was 1 1/2-inches long and expanded when hammered into its hole. All three types required drilled holes.

Johnson and other climbers of the day were connoisseurs of equipment, including the finer points of expansion bolts. During the 1970's, climbers have

become more sensitive to the deleterious side-effects of the indiscriminate use of hardware. In 1950 there were very few active climbers and acres of virgin rock. The new toys were very seductive in their appeal; they opened up so many new possibilities. Johnson says that he never thought about damaging the rock, that it just wasn't a concern among the few individuals then climbing. In fact, he and his companions would head up to the cliffs occasionally, select a blank rock wall, and patiently drill a row of expansion bolts in a vertical line upwards, "just for practice."

After placing his first bolt, Johnson reports that the next three placements took two and one-half hours of drilling. Suspended from his diaper seat, he was continually faced with the excruciating prospect of leaning backwards at a twenty-five degree angle and pounding on his drill bit at arm's length above his head.

He was disturbed in his labors at one point by a call of "Hey, Johnson, lean out a little more into the sun." One of his belayers had gone truant from the Crow's Nest and was trying to frame Johnson and the overhang into a nice composition through the viewfinder of the camera!

Two or three piton placements brought him to a point underneath a large overhang. He was able to place a piton halfway into a poor crack. Warning Dave and Cary to be ready for a fall, he cautiously shifted his weight onto it and felt immensely relieved when it held his weight. An even smaller crack was now within reach and accepted the tip of a piton driven in only about a quarter of an inch. Johnson inspected this dubious placement and somehow deluded himself into believing that it had some chance of holding his weight. This was an early example of that inspired combination of wishful thinking and blind faith which has been a characteristic of technical rock climbing up to the present day. Whispering a silent prayer to himself, and shouting down "red alert" to his anxious belayers, Johnson clipped in a foot sling and gingerly transferred his weight. The next instant, the piton went flying past his head and he followed it downwards. He fell clear of the rock for some six feet, expecting his last half-driven piton to be pulled out by the impact of the fall. By some miracle it held. Dave Robertson grasped the belay ropes tightly and brought him to a stop after a free fall of some twelve feet through mid-air.

In his account of the climb, Johnson writes that moving up on the tip of the shallow driven piton was a "calculated risk." He felt that if the piton failed, and if the half-driven one immediately below also failed, the expansion bolts would for sure hold the fall. In actuality, he moved onto the piton soberly considering the prospect of a twenty foot fall through mid-air, some one hundred and fifty feet above the ground. This kind of "calculated risk taking" was to become the keynote of the more difficult rock climbs.

Wexler's belaying techniques, the development of nylon climbing ropes, improved carabiners and better pitons, were all intended to provide a greater margin of safety in the rather unlikely eventuality of the leader falling. The maxim was still that the leader must not fall. Paradoxically, the greater safety margin actually served to increase the incidence of leader falls. Johnson took his "calculated risk" reasonably confident that he would live through it, should the piton give way. During the later 1950's, and through to the present day, the art of calculated risk-taking has developed to the point where controlled falling, rather than something to be avoided at all costs, is now a technique in its own right, and is accepted by many climbers as being on par with good ropework, agility, and crack jamming expertise. In Johnson's time, calculated risk-taking in such exposed positions was new, and rare. Fortunately, his fall had no serious consequences and he was able to climb back up again and complete the route.

In 1953, calculated risks were taken only after careful consideration. In general, climbers stayed well within their limits and avoided falling like the plague. When asked during an interview if this was conscious, deliberate style, Dale Johnson crisply replied, "It was probably pure cowardice."

Johnson's description of his fall on the Maiden overhang in 1953 is the first recorded event of its kind in Colorado climbing literature. In the Colorado Springs region at this time, the notions which Albert Ellingwood had brought back from England were prevalent, and climbers just didn't fall.

The East Face of Longs Peak - The Window

In 1950 the eyes of Hornbein and his companions, and Eubanks and Van Diver, began to turn away from the Flatirons towards the vast East Face of Longs Peak. The Face had seen no real exploratory activity since the ascent of Stettners Ledges in 1927. In 1948, with the ascent of the Northwest Passage completed, with a rudimentary knowledge of tension climbing techniques, with pitons for direct aid on overhanging rock and expansion bolts for blank crackless sections, the scene was set for exciting events. On the great East Face of Longs, attention focused on the major precipitous cliffs and towards the Diamond.

Bill Eubanks (top) and Brad Van Diver (bottom) on the first ascent of Chasm Cut Off (5.7). *Tom Hornbein.*

The progression of this group, from activities on the lower cliffs to searching out difficult climbs on the high mountain faces, has had many replications in Colorado's climbing history. Ellingwood had learned technique and psychology on the lower cliffs of the Garden of the Gods before making his classic ascents of Lizard Head and the Crestone Needle. This pattern was often repeated in later years. In Hornbein's case, his experiences on the Northwest Passage were to give him the confidence to begin exploration of the Diamond.

During the 1930's, Warren Gorrell happened to be sitting up at Chasm View and noticed the sun shining through a hole in the buttress of rock which bounds the south side of the Diamond. Eubanks and Van Diver were aware of this mysterious hole. They figured that the hole through the rock, which came to be known as the Window, indicated the presence of a crack and chimney system, and the promise of a route.

On August 21, 1950, Dave Hornsby and Harold Walton headed up the East Face. They had both climbed a good deal in the vicinity of Boulder. Walton had made the first ascent of the Cussing Crack on Castle Rock in Boulder Canyon earlier that summer, and they felt optimistic that they had the ability to work out a route through the Window. On arrival at the Longs Peak Campground, they bumped into Eubanks and Van Diver and were disappointed to learn that they had just made the first ascent of the Window. After chatting with the pair about the first ascent, Hornsby and Walton headed for Chasm Lake to try the route themselves. They spent the night at the lake and were on Broadway by eight the next morning. The climb starts in the Broadway Cutoff, the first gully north of the Notch Couloir, and follows an upward traversing line to the right, to reach a long shelf angling across to the Window. Harold Walton gave an account of the climb in the February 1951 issue of *Trail and Timberline*. He writes:

> The first hundred feet of this shelf is just a scramble over broken rock, not all of it sound. This section gets steeper near the top and ends in a short chimney. The leader anchors himself on a piton just below the chimney. Above the chimney you stay right in the corner between the shelf and the vertical right-hand wall, which is the Diamond itself. This pitch is really a 60-foot lieback, for there are very few footholds, but the angle is easy and the groove in the corner is undercut on both sides. At the top is a ledge on the left, narrow but adequate for a stance. [13]

The ledge at the top of the sixty-foot corner brought Hornsby and Walton to the foot of the Window proper. Walton's account continues:

Rappelling down the Hornbein Crack prior to the successful ascent. Harvey Carter's direct aid finish goes up the thin crack to the right of the rappel. *Tom Hornbein.*

From here to the Window is probably the hardest fifty feet of the climb. It is delicate slab climbing of the most refined sort, at an angle decidedly steeper than our Boulder Flatirons. The exposure is terrific, but does not seem so as the slab. . . .slopes in toward the face of the Diamond. The hardest move is probably the first, a short traverse to the right, but this is secured by a piton. Then you keep as far to the right as you can. We used more pitons and one or two "holds" which Brad had kicked in the edge of the snow. [14]

The two hundred-foot slab leading up to the Window is often covered with hard snow, or ice. Early in the season it is sometimes possible to cut steps, or crampon, for its full length, using ice-screws for protection. Fricke, in his 1971 guide book, states that some climbers have rated the moves on the upper part of the slab as high as 5.8 when free of ice and snow. The Window itself makes an interesting belay perch. It is only a few inches wide, about six inches deep, and eighteen feet high. By leaning out slightly, one can look down on Broadway and Mills Glacier hundreds of feet below. Fricke gives the Window route a 5.7 grading by modern standards and says that "the Window route done consecutively with Stettners Ledges is a sort of classic grand tour, being the only Grade IV that is entirely free, and ascending 1300 feet in some thirteen leads and some traverses." [15] After the second ascent in 1950, Walton felt that "the average standard (of the Window) is higher than that of (Stettners) Ledges, but that there was no pitch on the Window route quite as hard as the hardest pitch on the Ledges."

The East Face of Longs: Further Explorations

The combination of the Window route in 1950 with Stettners Ledges provided a long climb of a high standard of technical difficulty on the East Face of Longs. The Diamond remained sternly inviolate. Hornbein probably had the strongest aspirations of anyone in 1950 to climb it, but even his experiences on the Northwest Passage had not fully prepared him for such a major challenge. He climbed the Window route during this period, and continued to search for new lines on the East Face.

High up on the south edge of the East Face is a spectacular aiguille of rock named Zumies Thumb, after Clerin Zumwalt, a Longs Peak guide during the 1930's.

Tom Hornbein completing the Hornbein Crack with an overhead belay on his second attempt to lead it. *Courtesy Tom Hornbein.*

Hornbein, along with Dexter Brinker and Harry Waldrop, made the first ascent of the thumb in 1951 during one of their exploratory ventures. They were able to rappel down into the notch behind the thumb after scrambling down ledges from the saddle between Meeker and Longs. A friend accompanied them and was able to photograph the ascent from a vantage point on the ridge. The crux pitch involved some combined tactics of dubious security. Hornbein recalls that he overcame the crux moves by "standing on top of Harry Waldrop's head who was standing on a tiny ledge attached to a small army wafer piton." The maneuver, shaky as it was, proved successful and enabled Hornbein to reach a series of holds leading to a shelf at the foot of the summit block.

During the period 1950 to 1953, Hornbein made a number of attempts to climb from Broadway directly up to Chasm View, resulting in a lead which was one of the most difficult free climbing pitches in Colorado rock climbing at that time, and which was to remain so for a number of years after 1950.

At the northern end of Broadway is a massive square cut chimney-couloir which leads directly up to Chasm View. It is of relatively low angle in its lower reaches, but steepens and overhangs slightly at the top. Hornbein, accompanied by Eubanks and Van Diver, made a first attempt in 1950. They were unable to reach Chasm View directly and followed a diagonalling line across a steep face to the right. The climbing was generally easy, consisting of scrambling along traversing ledges, with one or two difficult moves in between. The ledge system led to the ridge between Chasm View and Mount Lady Washington, and they called the climb the Chasm Cut-Off. Hornbein returned with Dexter Brinker in 1951 to again attempt to reach Chasm View directly, and gives the following account:

> Brinker and I headed up peeling off huge wads of unconsolidated rock in the lower part of the chimney. At one place a whole mass came out from beneath my feet and left me hanging by one hand as it began its descent onto the climbing rope, and Brinker, who ducked behind a rock. Fortunately no one was hurt. We got up to the ledge at the foot of the final crack that day in a fairly steady drizzle and were rescued by Otto Von Alman, who was bringing a guided party down the cables and hauled us out.[16]

The first ascent of Zumies Thumb. Tom Hornbein standing on Harry Waldrop's shoulders. *Courtesy Tom Hornbein.*

Alman threw a rope down to the pair, and Hornbein was able to climb the final crack with the security of an overhead belay. Despite its steepness and difficulty, he felt that there was a strong possibility that he could lead it.

Hornbein's second attempt on the crack was made the following year, in 1952, with Bob Riley, one of his companions from the Northwest Passage. His account of this attempt reveals an unexpected occurrence and a second rescue:

> The second attempt was made with Bob Riley and we made very good time up to the last ledge. We encountered pitons left by Bob Ormes or somebody who had made the first attempt on the thing many years before and had gotten up within a couple of fairly short leads of the final ledge. We were sitting on the final ledge contemplating the last lieback, nibbling our lunch and sort of cursorily watching a couple who had climbed Alexanders or Stettners getting ready to descend from Broadway. As one of them stepped on the snow of the glacier he slipped, took off like a bullet and kept going faster and faster, obviously completely out of control, spinning head over heels. At times he left the snow as he gained momentum. He cleared rocks, narrowly missed the eastern corner and disappeared down into the rocks below the outrun. We were certain he'd been killed but we found out later he had hit at a place miraculously where there weren't large boulders. He was terribly bruised and beaten but was able to walk out under his own power. The episode took away what little ambition I had to lead the last 40 feet. Fortunately Bob Frausen, who was a Longs Peak ranger, was up above at the time with the intent of protecting us from any rocks that might be dropped by curious visitors up the cable route. He flipped us a rope and belayed me out. [17]

These two unsuccessful attempts only served to encourage Hornbein. He returned in the following year, the summer of 1953, with Cary Huston:

> We headed up from the campground early one morning. I was in a big hurry and Cary wasn't going very well and as we crossed the flats above timberline I kept getting further and further ahead and he kept getting more and more put off by the whole deal. We got up to the base of North Chimney and in my compulsiveness I persuaded Cary not to rope-up in order to save time. I promptly succeeded in heading up a wrong draw and getting myself hung up so that Cary had to climb around above me and drop me a rope. We finally got untangled and were rope climbing North Chimney when a little while later he slipped and fell with a belay from above. We decided that it wasn't really our day for climbing the thing.
>
> A week later we returned, camped at Chasm Lake and had a couple of friends in support who were going to

Hornbein and Waldrop on top of Zumies Thumb, belaying Dexter Brinker to the summit. *Courtesy Tom Hornbein.*

...he East Face of Longs Peak. TL - Table Ledge. ZT — Zumies ...humb. W - The Window. HC - Hornbein Crack. CC - Chasm Cut ...ff.

go up a ledge system called 42nd Street and protect us from rocks from Chasm View. We started out at about six in the morning, and scrambled up the North Chimney with a rope on this time and were at the base of the last pitch by 9 o'clock. The other party was still wandering around on 42nd Street and we could not see them but we were able to bounce our voices off the east face and communicate with them perfectly easily. It was quite obvious that they were going to be another hour before getting to Chasm View and it was obvious to me that if I waited another hour I would probably have no inclination to climb the thing. Harvey Carter had climbed a crack to the south about 10 feet a couple of weeks earlier using aid, much to my distress, because I was convinced the climb could be finished free and therefore shouldn't be sullied by mechanical approaches. I suppose this must be one of the earliest examples of these conflicts of philosophies and freedoms. We put an angle piton in down on the ledge and then I took off like a scared rabbit which I distinctly was. By the time I reached the chockstone 10 feet below the top I was scrambling with no pretense of technique at all, completely out of breath from either the effort or the fear or both. I stuffed myself into the crack and panted for about five minutes before climbing the last section to the top. It was with a great feeling of triumph for I'd on occasions had nightmares about this climb. It was also with conviction that this was the only thing I had ever climbed that I would never care to repeat. At the present time there are a lot of other things that I neither would care to or could, but that was the only thing I ever attempted that at the time I did it I knew it was the one and only. I brought Cary up after me. He did it as a lieback, pausing a couple of times to hang on the rope while he rested his arms. [18]

Cary Huston climbing Alexander's Chimney, circa 1952. *Tom Hornbein.*

Left. A member of Tom Hornbein's party traversing out along Table Ledge, two thirds of the way up the Diamond, inspecting for a possible route in 1952. *Tom Hornbein.*

New Techniques and Overhanging Rock

Hornbein's lead was certainly the hardest free climbing pitch in the Colorado high mountains at the time. Even though he had top-roped it twice before, his unprotected ascent was a magnificently bold achievement for 1953.

Hornbein's remarks about Carter's use of pitons for direct aid as an alternative to free climbing the final pitch up to Chasm View give first hints of the debate on this issue which has grown in intensity to the present day.

The Diamond

In 1952 Tom Hornbein made a serious exploration of the Diamond, prospecting for a feasible route. He climbed over the summit of Longs and attempted to traverse out towards a crack system in the middle of the face via a wide ledge system. This ledge, called Table Ledge, became progressively thinner and thinner. Eventually it petered out completely and the party had to retreat, leaving a number of old army ring angle pitons in place that were to puzzle climbers of later generations. This was Hornbein's last attempt to find a possible route on the Diamond, and he later concluded, "I don't think our techniques had evolved nearly enough to the point where we could have managed it at that time."

After his successful ascent of the Northwest Overhang of the Maiden in 1953, Dale Johnson began discussing the possibility of climbing the Diamond with Bob Sutton. From their observations, they were not sure "if there were decent crack systems or not," so they practiced putting in lots of bolts. It was during this period that Johnson spent a number of afternoons patiently drilling vertical lines of expansion bolts up blank rock walls in the Boulder vicinity. Later climbers have scratched their heads in wonderment, for some of the bolt rows stop in the middle of nowhere.

In 1954, after three months of intensive preparation, they felt ready to make an attempt on the Diamond. Anticipating prolonged direct aid stretches suspended in stirrups, Bob Sutton's wife had made him a special pair of pants with a zipper in the seat! They had also manufactured a large number of continental-style wide wooden wedges for direct aid in wide cracks.

Dale Johnson recollects that, "rather than marching up there to the Diamond and just trying it, we went over and told the rangers at Park Headquarters what we had in mind. The Park Service immediately forbade it." The climbers had a long and heated discussion with the rangers, during which tempers became frayed, but to no avail. There was no stated policy against climbing the Diamond, but knowing that the climbers planned to use expansion bolts, the rangers made it clear that they would take action against the climbers for defacing the rock. Johnson feels that this was an excuse and states that, "they were determined to keep us off the mountain, or to punish us if we tried." During the years following 1954, Johnson made a number of other attempts to obtain permission for a Diamond ascent, and each time was refused.

The community of serious technical rock climbers in Colorado at this time still amounted to a small handful. Around Boulder there were a dozen or so difficult technical rock climbs, and only a small number in the vicinity of Colorado Springs. In the high mountains, Lizard Head, Lone Eagle, Monitor, the East Face of Longs Peak, and the Sangre de Cristo Mountains contained a small number of difficult rock climbs. In a sense, 1954 was the twilight of an older and more traditionally based period of rock climbing. The activities of Hornbein and Johnson heralded the approach of the modern era.

REFERENCES

1. Richard M. Leonard and Arnold Wexler, *Belaying the Leader* (San Francisco: The Sierra Club, 1947).
2. *Ibid.,* p. 2.
3. Geoffrey Winthrop Young, *Mountain Craft* (London), p. 221, in Leonard and Wexler, *op. cit.,* p. 5.
4. Young, *op. cit.,* pp. 260-263.
5. Leonard and Wexler, *op. cit.,* p. 5.
6. *Ibid.,* p. 6.
7. Fred Beckey, "Contraction Bolts," *American Alpine Journal,* 1948, p. 230.
8. Allen Steck, "Ordeal by Piton," *The Sierra Club Bulletin,* 1951, in Galen A. Rowell, *The Vertical World of Yosemite* (California: Wilderness Press, 1974), p. 211.
9. Tom Hornbein, *tape recorded communication.* 1976.
10. Ament and McCarty, *op. cit.,* p. 187.
11. Hornbein, *op. cit.*
12. Dale Johnson, *personal communication,* 1975.
13. Harold Walton, "Through the Window," *Trail and Timberline,* February, 1951.
14. *Ibid.*
15. Fricke, *op. cit.,* p. 64.
16. Hornbein, *op. cit.*
17. *Ibid.*
18. *Ibid.*

Harvey T. Carter. *Michael Kennedy.*

GARDEN OF THE GODS

Harvey would fix routes with his gold painted army angle pitons and we'd sneak by later and remove them, just for the fun of it...it used to make him madder than hell.
Gary Ziegler (1976)

In 1914 Albert Ellingwood had returned from his three year visit to England and had brought with him to Colorado Springs the seeds of a traditional English approach which had as its central concept an emphasis on free climbing with a minimum use of pitons and mechanized methods. During the late 1920's and the 1930's, Robert Ormes climbed with Ellingwood and learned from him this traditional approach. Both men were intellectuals and both became professors at Colorado College. The self-imposed discipline of rock climbing with a minimum of reliance on mechanized methods for either protection or direct aid appealed to their sense of aesthetics. Had Ellingwood and Ormes chosen to use pitons more extensively, there is no doubt that they would have been able to ascend steeper and more imposing rock faces than they actually did, but to

them the price was well worth it. They were also aware that the soft sandstones of the Garden of the Gods were delicate and would not withstand the effects of hammered pitons. At a later date, during the 1940's, these same ideas were embraced by Stanley Boucher. The line of development espoused by these three, Ellingwood, Ormes and Boucher, was to form the basis of a tradition which guided Colorado Springs climbers during the late 1940's and early 1950's.

The rocks of the Garden of the Gods are composed of soft sandstones and conglomerates of late Paleozoic age. It has been pointed out that "they have limited fracture crack patterns, and the soft scaly nature of the rocks...has led to a tradition of balance/friction climbing." [1] The softness of the rock has to be experienced to be believed. New holds can be created

Garden of the Gods. *Chris Wood.*

Herby Hendrix party on the first ascent of Inferno on North Gateway Rock. *Harvey Carter.*

Right. A free ascent of the traverse on Pete and Bob's whi▍ was originally climbed usi▍ expansion bolts for direct a▍ (5.10).

easily with a few scrapes or chips with a piton hammer. Small existing holds can easily be enlarged or broken off. Some face climbs depend on minute flakes of soft sandstone which will easily become detached by an outward pull. Climbers in the Garden learn to use these flakes with extreme delicacy, keeping their weight above and downwards, and wherever possible distributing their weight evenly between feet and hands to reduce the chance of a flake breaking off. For climbers unused to sandstone, it is an eerie and unnerving experience to meet these conditions for the first time. Garden climbers delight in telling stories of 5.10 expert rock climbers from other areas who have come down pale-faced and shaking at the knees after a first experience with a 5.6 soft sandstone classic. It takes a special control to remain calm while perched on minute holds which threaten to disintegrate at the smallest jerkiness or hint of rough usage.

In Colorado Springs during the late 1940's and early 1950's, the emphasis among the leading climbers was on developing free climbing, with direct aid being used only as a last resort to overcome short, difficult sections on longer, predominantly free climbs. In 1945 Stanley Boucher and Vernon Twombly, later to found the Colorado College Mountain Club, began to climb together. They used double-gated saddle cinches as carabiners and climbed in army combat boots with leather soles. Together they pioneered a number of climbs in the Garden of the Gods. These included the North End Chimney on the Practice Slab on North Gateway Rock. On top of North Gateway was a formation known as the Kissing Camels. Unaware that the Stettner brothers had climbed over them in 1927, Boucher and Twombly believed they had made the first ascent. The climb was fairly easy but exposed, and the camels were three hundred feet from the ground, providing a spectacular finish.

Another prominent climber who appeared on the scene at this time was Harvey T. Carter. Carter was introduced to mountain hiking by his father, a professor at Colorado College, in 1945 and began technical rock climbing in 1950. He climbed with Stanley Boucher and later became a climbing instructor with the mountain troops at Fort Carson, serving there from 1950 to 1954. Carter became a well known figure in North American climbing. After his beginnings in the military in 1950, he climbed in almost every major climbing area in the United States from Yosemite, to the Shawangunks, to Shiprock, to the sandstone spires of the desert. His climbing adventures span a quarter of a century.

Still climbing hard in 1977, Carter has long been recognized as a controversial character on the American

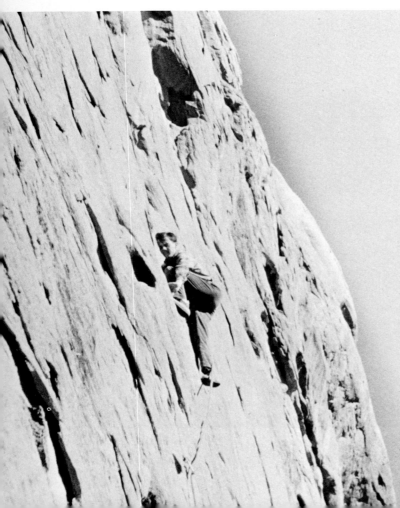

Pete Croff on the first ascent of Pete and Bob's. *Courtesy Pete Croff.*

Right. The first lead up to the Finger on Trick's (5.8/5.9).

Art Howells leading Crackup on the east face of Red Twin Spire. *Harvey Carter.*

climbing scene, noted for his stubborn nature and a certain verbal pugnacity in his dealings with the world.

In the mid-1950's, Carter was instrumental in forming a group called the American Mountaineering Association. One of his central ideas in forming this group was to attempt to develop a more uniform system of rating the relative difficulty of rock climbs in different parts of the country. He felt that the decimal grading system, which assessed a rock climb by identifying the single most difficult move, did not give a fair representation of the overall nature of the climb. He proposed a system which he called "the Universal Standard," developed from his military experiences in Colorado Springs. In Carter's system, such factors as the amount and quality of protection, the nature of the rock, and the degree of exposure and danger present, were all coupled with the actual technical difficulty of the hardest moves, to provide an overall rating of each pitch. The total difficulty of a particular climb was then calculated numerically by averaging the individual pitch gradings. Carter was unsuccessful in his efforts to encourage a greater degree of uniformity between rock climbing gradings in different parts of the country, and his grading system was poorly received by contemporary rock climbers. Heated discussion still goes on about the relative difficulties of climbs in Colorado, Yosemite, the Shawangunks, and other areas.

When Carter climbed with Stanley Boucher in 1950, he became aware of the traditions which had been established by Albert Ellingwood, and he adopted similar principles in his own climbing in the Garden of the Gods. During subsequent years he was to establish many new climbs in Colorado Springs and the Pike's Peak region. Due to a lack of information, the majority of these climbs have fallen into obscurity. They are known to a small number of local Colorado Springs climbers and by word of mouth to the rare visitor from other areas.

The year 1950 saw the beginning of the modern era of rock climbing in Colorado Springs. Ellingwood, Ormes and Boucher had followed classical precepts in their climbs, and their ascents invariably followed obvious lines of natural weakness—chimneys, ramps, ledges, and corners. They occasionally tackled a short, steep wall, but in the context of a longer climb.

In the early 1950's, Harvey Carter and his companions were faced with a problem to solve. In keeping with trends in rock climbing at that time, their eyes and aspirations were turning away from the chimneys, ramps and ledges of the established classic routes, towards the steep, blank major faces of the Garden of the Gods. Close inspection of these faces

Layton Kor leading the overhanging crack of Anaconda on the first ascent. John Auld belaying. *Wayne Goss.*

revealed small flakes, and occasional pockets and holes in the rock, giving the promise of exciting new climbs. None of the existing methods of protection provided them with sufficient safety to venture onto the faces. A small number of climbs were done on which protection was obtained from pitons driven part way in and then tied-off near the rock with a nylon sling to reduce leverage. Carter was aware that tied-off pitons provided mainly "psychological protection", and that there was little chance of them holding a fall. The expansion bolts available at the time were small, and though they were solid enough to hold a climber's weight, they were inadequate in the case of a leader fall due to the soft nature of the rock. After some experimentation, Carter devised a system for providing secure protection on the blank walls. He would drill a hole as though for an expansion bolt. Into the hole he would drive a sawn-off army angle piton. The drilled hole was smaller than the piton and the piton's "V" shape would compress as it was driven in. Fixed protection on popular climbs eliminated the problem of damage to cracks which accompanied repeated insertion and removal of pitons, as was the style in Boulder and California at this time. Carter felt that a drilled-in angle piton, well placed, was bombproof. With this secure method of protection, he and his contemporaries embarked on a series of new climbs up the intimidating, steep walls of the Garden of the Gods.

As he developed new routes in the Garden of the Gods during the 1950's, Carter remained strongly influenced by Stanley Boucher and the tradition which had come down from Albert Ellingwood. He designed new climbs to follow what he felt were logical lines, and he used the drilled-in piton with discretion. It would have been easy to use this new technique to establish major direct aid routes on the walls. Carter insists that the emphasis of himself and his climbing companions in the 1950's was to keep the use of pitons and bolts to an absolute minimum. They were used to provide essential protection for the leader on free climbs, and were occasionally used for direct aid to overcome short sections of blank rock in the context of a longer free climb. Carter felt strongly at this time that he wanted to preserve free climbing traditions in the Garden of the Gods. To this end climbs were designed and graded according to a prescribed amount of protection. He was careful to use drilled-in pitons sparingly and to position them either below, or to the side of, crux moves. In this manner they could not be used for direct aid on a crux, but were sufficiently close to provide adequate safety in case of a leader fall.

Carter felt that this method of leaving fixed protection on classic free climbs had much to

Kor (top) and Auld (seconding) on the first ascent of Anaconda on the Tower of Babel. *Wayne Goss.*

recommend it. Even on harder rock, problems are created by the repeated insertion and removal of pitons. On popular climbs which are unsuited to nut placements, a system of occasional fixed pitons, specified in the guidebook route description, has considerable merit.

During the 1950's in Colorado Springs, Harvey Carter was successul in maintaining a simple and tradition-based approach to rock climbing in the Garden of the Gods. There were only a small number of climbers active at the time, and he was successful in convincing the local climbing community of the values of fixed protection.

In contrast to his free climbing emphasis in the Garden of the Gods, Carter was later to gain a reputation as a specialist in direct aid. On visits to the Boulder region, Rocky Mountain National Park, other parts of Colorado, and the sandstone spires of the southwestern deserts, he put up many routes which involved direct aid.

During the 1950's Carter organized an event which has become regarded as a curiosity in Colorado's rock climbing history...the first National Championship Meet for competitive rock climbing. Traditionally, overt competition has been disdained by rock climbers. Undeterred, Carter organized a points system for competition on demanding boulder problems. Paint demarked allowable holds, and climbers endeavoured to outdo each other on progressively more difficult problems. The championships were held on Carter's home turf, and, considering his experience on the routes, it was not surprising that he won the event and became the first officially recognized "Master of Rock Climbing." Carter's championship approach never caught on and served more as a source of amusement than as a serious endeavor among other Colorado climbers.

During the 1960's younger climbers appeared who were less convinced than Carter of the value of demarcating routes with fixed protection. Gary Ziegler, who was an active climber in the Garden of the Gods during the 1960's says, "Harvey would fix routes with his gold painted army angle pitons and we'd sneak by later and remove them, just for the fun of it...it used to make him madder than hell."

During the late 1950's other notable climbers began to make their names in the Garden of the Gods. Steve Cheyney, a Colorado Springs schoolboy, was something of a child prodigy and began leading difficult climbs at the tender age of twelve. He climbed consistently in the Colorado Springs region during following years, founded a small boot repairing business, and his little shop, "the Cobbler," is still the best place in Colorado Springs for visitors to obtain reliable information on local climbing. Cheyney climbed regularly with Pete Croff and Bob Stauch, both of whom were responsible for advancing climbing standards in the Garden. Croff in particular was noted as an outstanding free climber. Their "Pete and Bob's" was an elegant line on the 300 foot west face of North Gateway Rock, and "Psychic Grandma" on the same rock was a six pitch climb rated 5.9, giving long run outs of poorly protected face climbing.

A California climber named Rick Tidrick climbed regularly in the Garden of the Gods around 1960 and one of his routes, later named "Tidrick's," established him as a master of delicate face climbing on small holds and was the most difficult free climb in the region. At approximately the same time, Mike Borghoff, the "Mad Bolter," nailed a route on North Gateway which became known as Borghoff's Blunder, which later became a challenging free climb.[2]

Gary Ziegler, a climber from Colorado College, and John Auld made a number of important ascents in the Garden of the Gods during the early sixties, including a long, predominantly free climb with a small amount of aid for the crux section, called the Pipe Route, on the west face of South Gateway Rock. Other very active climbers during this period were Art Howells, Herby Hendricks, Andy Spielman, John F. Able, Paul Radigan and Don Doucette.

During the 1960's, possibly as an outgrowth of the drilled piton technique, some climbers began to force bolt ladders up large blank faces. These aid climbs did not follow natural lines and once the bolts were in place they required little skill to repeat. By the mid-sixties the Garden of the Gods contained over two hundred climbs ranging from twenty foot extended boulder problems to complicated 300 foot mixed free and aid climbs on the larger spires. With the addition of the unfortunate bolt ladders, virtually all of the obvious lines and faces had been climbed, and the attention of climbers turned towards other cliffs in the Pike's Peak region.

REFERENCES

1. Harvey Carter, *unpublished notes, 1976.*
2. Jim McChristal, "A Rock Climber's Guide to the Garden of the Gods," *Colorado College Mountain Club,* 1975, pp. 12-15.

Ray Northcutt "trick climbing" on Flagstaff Mountain.

TRANSITION 1956

*Suddenly a terrifying sensation
pierced every fiber in my body. My
right edge had given way, leaving
me hanging by the fingertips of my
right hand.*

Ray Northcutt (1956)

Technical rock climbing, though still the esoteric pastime of a handful of devotees, was firmly established in Colorado by the mid-1950's. Hornbein's ascent of the Northwest Passage, Johnson's ascent of the Northwest Overhang of the Maiden, and exploratory efforts on the East Face of Longs Peak had set the stage for spectacular developments. 1956 was an unusually important year.

Eight miles to the south of Boulder lies Eldorado Springs Canyon. Of all the rocks in Colorado, the steep walls of Eldorado have been pre-eminently important in the overall development of rock climbing. Driving into the canyon, one is immediately impressed by the size and steepness of its walls. One drives in through the remains of the old Spa (so fashionable in the thirties that President Eisenhower spent his honeymoon here), pays the toll entry fee to the current owners of the access rights, crosses the narrow bridge over the creek, and immediately develops a crick in the neck from attempting to see the top of precipitous cliffs. A steep rock wall rises abruptly on the left-hand side of the road, so close that one can step directly onto it from the open door of a car, and towers for over three hundred vertical feet. The face, aptly named the Bastille, presents the appearance of a French castle when seen from the west.

For many years a steel cable was stretched from the top of the Bastille to a point on the opposite side of the canyon, some three hundred feet above the rushing creek. Climbers called the wire "Ivy Baldwin's 5.11 Traverse." Between 1906 and 1948 Ivy Baldwin, stunt man, balloonist, tumbler, parachutist, and circus clown, walked the wire eighty-nine times. He made the last crossing on his 82nd birthday, against the protests of his wife, who threatened to shoot the sand out of his weight bags with a rifle. The wire is no longer there, and climbers who want to repeat Ivy's 5.11 feat have to be satisfied with mere rock climbing.

Immediately opposite the Bastille, on the other side of the canyon, lies the immense sprawling mass of Redgarden Wall. In size, character, and importance in the development of Colorado rock climbing, Redgarden

Wall is comparable to "Cloggy" in Great Britain. Many important developments have taken place on its steep walls. Painted in colors of flame red, and brilliant oranges, and subtly garbed in traceries of yellow lichens, it leans skyward in a formidable series of vertical walls, intricate crack systems, and intimidating overhangs. Pigeons wheel around its upper reaches in dizzying swoops, leading the eye across vertigo-inducing walls. In places, the cliff is six hundred feet high.

Redguard Route

In 1956, four Colorado climbers, Chuck Murley, Cary Huston, Dick Bird, and Dallas Jackson began attempts to climb Redgarden Wall. The cliff, up to this time, had been considered impossible. Its height and

Ivy Baldwin on his low wire.
Courtesy of Eldorado Springs Resort.

78

Right. Redgarden Wall showing Redguard Route.

Left. The difficult section of the Birdwalk on the first pitch of Redguard Route (5.7).

obvious steepness had deterred attempts. The existing hard routes in the area, the Northwest Passage and the Northwest Overhang on the Maiden, were both relatively short climbs, relying on direct aid. As the group examined Redgarden Wall for possible weaknesses, they were anticipating applying the new direct aid techniques to this larger face.

The first pitch of the line they chose was a tricky sequence of slightly off-balance moves up a series of deceptive looking slabs and small ramps. They looked easy from below, but a noticeable lack of protection and the off-balance nature of the climbing made them tricky. Dick Bird led this section, and the following steep crack. The pitch has since become known as the Birdwalk, named after his ascent. On two separate occasions the three reached a point some 600 feet up the wall, but were stopped by the final section, a steep face with small hand and footholds.

On their successful attempt they recruited Dale Johnson, hoping that his additional experience might help them crack the final pitch. As Dale had not been on the climb before, the other three insisted that he have the honor of leading the difficult first section, and encouraged him with good natured comments as he struggled with its difficulties. On reaching the final pitch, Chuck Murley decided to "give it one last go," before Dale tried. He surprised everyone by climbing straight up it. They decided to call the climb Redguard Route.

This climb in 1956 was advanced by Colorado standards. It followed a technically difficult line up an impossible looking cliff. The difficulty of the climbing was sustained, with hard sections of free climbing to be dealt with on each pitch. The modern grading of the climb is 5.7, and it is generally recognized that the Birdwalk is the most difficult pitch. It is likely that the first ascent party was stopped by the final pitch more because of the unnerving nature of six hundred feet of exposure, than by the actual technical difficulties. They had expected sections of direct aid when observing the climb from the ground, but were pleasantly surprised to find a continuous line of cracks and holds, enabling the complete route to be climbed free. Their successful ascent opened up Redgarden Wall to rock climbers of following years, and it was to become the most intensively climbed rock face in Colorado in the years following 1956.

The North Face of Hallett Peak

Ray Northcutt was a rock climber from Boulder who began his climbing career while doing military service with the mountain troops at Fort Carson in Colorado Springs. There he had made the acquaintance of Harvey Carter, and the two had climbed together. Northcutt was noted for his dedication to physical fitness and followed a rigorous schedule of running and calesthenics in preparation for longer climbs. He would run a

Chuck Murley, Dale Johnson and Dick Bird on top of Redgarden Wall, after the first ascent of Redguard Route. *Courtesy Dick Bird.*

minimum of a mile each day up a steep mountainside, and included 100 chin-ups in three sets as part of his training routine.

Northcutt believed in being in the best possible shape and spent a good deal of time working out on boulders in addition to running and calesthenics. Climbing boulders as practice for longer climbs had begun at Fort Carson, where military climbers called it "trick climbing."

Ray Northcutt was one of Colorado's masters at bouldering. His running and calisthenics kept him in top shape, and some of his trick climbs are still used by modern climbers.

In 1956 Northcutt and Harvey Carter decided to attempt to climb the North Face of Hallett Peak. This nearly 1,000 foot high rock wall close to Longs Peak in Rocky Mountain National Park was comprised of steep buttresses of vertical rock. A route had been done on the face already, but it ascended a moderate chimney between two of the buttresses. The main buttresses were unclimbed.

To Northcutt and Carter in 1956, the main face of Hallett Peak must have presented a forbidding prospect. It was high, steep, and sombre due to its gloomy north-facing aspect. The height of the mountain, 12,713 feet, added the potential perils of lightning and high mountain storms as factors to be considered.

In comparison to the existing routes on the East Face of Longs Peak, the buttresses of Hallett Peak seemed steeper, were less broken, and appeared to offer more sustained, technically-difficult rock climbing. The two were suitably impressed and prepared for a serious and demanding climb.

Their first attempt took them part way up the west buttress. Some six hundred feet from the ground, they found themselves on a steep slab beneath a large horizontal overhang. Northcutt drove in a thin vertical piton, "only to see it bend over like a piece of tinfoil."[1] To climb back down would have been perhaps even more hazardous than to continue. He continued upwards, feeling that his one scanty protection piton did not allow a margin for mistakes. His account continues:

So, up I went. There just wouldn't be, there just *couldn't* be any mistakes. Continuing upward along a wall dealing not in footholds and handholds but in minute edges and fingerholds, I neared the top and stood but a few feet beneath the slab. I raised my right foot, placing an inside edge on a rounded, minature wrinkle. And as I took lateral pressure from the extremities of my right hand, I straightened my right leg, elevating myself to a position almost level with the lip of the slab. Slowly, I relaxed my left hand, swung it in an arc above my head, and at last, although not seeing it, I felt the prominence

of a solid but somewhat scanty hold on the slab above. Feeling I had this one behind me, I released my right hand, and slid it along the wall to secure another hold above. Suddenly a terrifying sensation pierced every fiber in my body. My right edge had given way, leaving me hanging by the fingertips of my left hand. Aghast, I glanced down the rope at my partner on his narrow ledge below, and saw on his face an equal look of apprehension. We both knew that this thin, white bond of nylon would do neither of us any good. His belay anchor had driven very poorly, and we had absolutely counted on my getting in an intermediate piton. Almost frantically I searched the rock for another edge. Finally, after what seemed like an eternity, though it was only a matter of seconds, I found one, regained my perch and practically shot up to the slab above.[2]

After this hairy incident, route-finding problems and the difficulties of the climbing caused time to run out. Preferring not to spend a night on the face, the pair rappelled down. Returning to the face on July 28th, they felt that their previous experience would give them a head start, and that the climb was feasible in a single day.

Reaching the overhang which had almost seen his demise, Northcutt took tension from the rope and was able to skirt its west lip and lodge himself in a tight overhanging chimney. This chimney led to a roomy ledge, and the major difficulties of the climb were behind them. They moved rapidly up the final three hundred feet of easier rock, spurred on by the rumble of thunder to the west, which indicated that the fair weather was coming to an end.

The ascent of this climb by Northcutt and Carter in 1956 was a major accomplishment. The psychological problems which the two climbers had to overcome were formidable in 1956. But, as often happens in the history of climbing, subsequent ascents were to be a somewhat different story.

Northcutt published the story of the climb under the title, "A First Ascent on the North Face of Hallett Peak," in the 1959 *American Alpine Journal*. The California climber Yvon Chouinard read it and was intrigued at the prospect of such a major north face in Colorado. Northcutt's account had left little doubt as to its difficulties. Chouinard, who had been involved in some of the most difficult climbing in Yosemite Valley at that time, felt that it was worth a trip to Colorado.

Chouinard hiked up to the foot of the face with Ken Weeks in July, 1959. After Northcutt and Carter's ascent in 1956, the route had acquired quite a reputation. Arriving in mid-afternoon, Chouinard felt it would be a good idea to climb a couple of pitches that evening, and leave fixed ropes to give them a head start the next day. This was a commonly accepted practice in California in those days prior to ascents of big walls in

The North Face of Hallett Peak showing the Northcutt-Carter route (III,5.7). *W. T. Lee U.S.G.S. photo.*

Ray Northcutt (top) and Harvey Carter (bottom) on the first ascent of the Northcutt-Carter route on Hallett Peak in 1956. *Courtesy Harvey Carter.*

Yosemite Valley. The two started climbing at four in the afternoon. The first two pitches went very quickly and with no real difficulty. They decided to go on a little further, as the climbing still seemed reasonably easy. Moving rapidly, they kept going, and to their surprise, reached the summit at 8:00 p.m. that same evening. The entire climb, on which they had planned to spend the whole of the following day, had taken a total of four hours! Their experience on the big walls of Yosemite Valley and their superior technical ability at that time had enabled them to make their way up the face without being overawed by its reputation or by its steep appearance. Also, Chouinard and Weeks followed a more direct and slightly more difficult line, avoiding a long traverse to the left which Northcutt and Carter had taken in 1956. Subsequent events have shown that Chouinard and Week's time of four hours is about average for two competent and experienced climbers. Northcutt himself returned and climbed the route in about four hours at a later date.

Some years later, the Northcutt-Carter was climbed solo by Layton Kor in a total time of ninety minutes! Kor free-soloed most of the route, but trailed a climbing rope from his waist and tied it off for protection to a piton at the most difficult sections. With Kor's solo ascent, the North Face of Hallett had progressed through three classic stages: an impossible climb—the hardest climb in the area—an easy day's outing. These three stages had been widely recognized in Europe and had been applied to a number of once so-called "impossible climbs."

Northcutt and Carter's route on Hallett Peak was a major achievement in 1956. Using a criterion of difficulty which is directly related to the number of unknown factors involved in a particular climb, their ascent in 1956 was a major tour-de-force and set the scene for future developments. The ascents of the North Face of Hallet Peak, and of Redguard Route in Eldorado Springs Canyon, opened the doors to the most intensive period of technical rock climbing that Colorado had ever seen.

REFERENCES

1. Ray Northcutt, "A First Ascent on the North Face of Hallett Peak," *American Alpine Journal,* Vol. II, No. 2, 1959, p. 235. 235.
2. *Ibid.*

Part III

THE GOLDEN AGE

Layton Kor. *Larry Dalke.*

THE SIXTIES

Don't fall now or we'll both go!
Layton Kor to any number of
partners during the sixties

It has been said that the sixties were the golden age of Colorado rock climbing. This description is based on a delicately balanced relationship between individuals and events; on a complex mixture of myth spiced by sufficient fact to lend the substance of plausible reality; on a flavor of wildly improbable new climbs made possible by the pioneering examples of Hornbein, Johnson, and Northcutt; and by the appearance of a small group of new figures possessing tremendous technical ability and daring, coupled with that rich complexity of personal idiosyncrasy which is the very stuff of legend. It was a time when the electric energies of a handful of new climbers acted as catalysts to spark reactions between personality and the flow of historical events which, firework-like, have left only blurred retinal after-images for later generations.

From the point of view of precise chronological accuracy, the decade of the sixties really had its origins in 1956. The pioneers of the late 1950's climbed out from under the inhibiting psychology exerted by the most massive Colorado rock faces and showed that with a modicum of technical ability, a dash of optimism, and a reasonable sprinkling of good luck, anything, literally anything, was possible. This message was transmitted to the climbers of the sixties, some of whom served their apprenticeship in the years prior to 1960. Restraints of both technique and psychology, which had previously inhibited advances, disappeared. The doors were thrown open for a flood of energy to be loosed on the mountains, the like of which Colorado had not seen before.

Bob Culp has written, "Never before (in Colorado) had there been a group of climbers who were making climbing a way of life."[1] Prior to the sixties, climbing had been a sport and a weekend activity. A number of climbers emerged during the late 1950's for whom climbing was to become a way of life. Many climbers take this approach for granted in the 1970's. In 1960 it was new.

The "sixties" is a concept rather than a precisely defined chronological period; more a state of mind than a sequence of years. To those who know Colorado climbing, mention of the sixties often stimulates a particular facial expression. The eyes close slightly and assume a far away look. Romance, laughter, wildness, joy, sadness and a sense of glories past flit by. At risk of disturbing those readers who place a high premium on chronological accuracy, the term "the sixties" will be used with this connotation for the remainder of this chapter.

Three Months to Live

During the middle 1950's there was a group of climbers active in the Boulder region. This group included Cary Huston, Dallas Jackson, Stanley Sheperd, Dick Bird, and Dale Johnson. In 1956 a tall, gangly youngster named Layton Kor began to hang around the peripheries of this group of hardened rock climbers. At meetings in the Sink, a local tavern, around tables in the University cafeteria, and during chance meetings at Gerry's, the local climbing equipment store, his ears would prick up when the latest climbing was mentioned. Kor was apparently too shy to directly approach the local hard men, but would listen intently to their discussions of the latest climbs. Soon, rumors began to trickle back to the group about a crazy individual who had been seen climbing solo on the rocks of Boulder Canyon and Eldorado. It was Kor. Within a short time members of the group were placing bets among themselves on how long he would live. Three months was the longest that even the most optimistic of them gave him. Before long it became apparent that Kor possessed unusual rock climbing ability. He was tall, six-feet five inches, strong and agile. In those early days his predominant characteristic seems to have been an absence of fear. After his initial hair-raising solo climbs, Kor was hooked. Rock climbing became the central driving force in his life. During the following ten years he was to become the most influential figure in Colorado's rock climbing history and to pioneer the most remarkable series of technical rock climbs the state had ever witnessed.

The Bulge (5.7). The leader has just clipped into the bolt placed by Kor on rappel in 1957 and is about to make the crux moves.

The summer of 1957 was Kor's second year of climbing. He had climbed many of the existing routes and was primed to attempt a major new line. One day he was solo climbing on the rocks of Eldorado Springs Canyon and became stuck. He could move neither up nor down. Two climbers happened to be passing by and one of them, a law student named Ben Chidlaw, dropped him a rope and rescued him from his precarious position. Shortly after this incident, Kor took Chidlaw up the now classic Redguard Route. For some time Kor had been eyeing a possible new line on Redgarden Wall, to the right of Redguard Route, and had made one unsuccessful attempt on it. The following day he persuaded Chidlaw to accompany him on a second attempt. Chidlaw remembers that they anticipated having a difficult time, but that Kor "just romped up the face and we were back in Boulder by 10:00 a.m." The line which Kor chose picked its way for hundreds of feet up a remarkably blank section of wall, singularly lacking in cracks and other prominent features. It was improbable, and presented open face climbing in highly exposed positions. Undaunted, Kor flowed his way up the wall, chatting encouragingly to Chidlaw, who felt somewhat overwhelmed by the whole business. At the crux, an unprotected 5.7 bulging section of rock, Chidlaw had to shout up to Kor to "stop talking and concentrate on the climbing." The crux passed by uneventfully after this admonition and Kor's first major new route was established. They decided to name the route The Bulge, descriptive of the crux pitch. Shortly after this first ascent, Kor rappelled down the route and drilled in an expansion bolt to give protection. The crux moves were graded 5.7 with the bolt, and the route still inspires respect in modern climbers due to the exposed climbing and the lack of protection.

The Bulge was an early example of a talent for which Kor was to become noted during later years: his ability to examine a cliff and to pick out a line of ascent. He refused to be daunted by sections which looked impossible from the ground, and he possessed a rare intuition for sensing the presence of hidden lines of holds on apparently blank walls. Many of Kor's climbs are masterpieces of route finding. Those who climbed with him have said that he just seemed to "know" where a climbable line existed. This sixth sense for the existence of a line on an improbable-looking cliff has long been recognized as one of the key characteristics of pioneer climbers. In Kor's case, he possessed this ability to an unusual degree and picked out lines on some of the most intimidating rock faces in Colorado.

Subsequent to his ascent of the Bulge, Kor continued his explorations for new routes. His energy for climbing seemed inexhaustible. At first he had difficulty finding people to climb with because he was unknown to the local climbers. Later, as word of his exploits spread, he continued to have difficulty finding partners due to his interest in the most difficult climbs and because of his hair-raising ways of tackling them. Chuck Alexander made the first ascent of Sundance Buttress near Estes Park with Kor in 1958, and commented, "there's a fine line that should be reached where you keep your belayer relaxed and yet let him know that the climbing is hard. Kor could never find this line. He always struck terror into the hearts of his belayers."

The First Ascent of T.2

In 1959, Kor picked out a possible line on a steep face to the left of Redguard Route in Eldorado Springs Canyon. The proposed line led directly to the summit of the second tower at the top of the wall. He invited Gerry Roach, a youngster who had not been climbing for long at that time, to accompany him. Roach's account captures the flavor of climbing with Kor in 1959:

"Want to go climbing tomorrow, Gerry?"
"Sure, Layton, what's up?"
"Uh, just a route in Eldorado. I'll pick you up at four a.m."
"Four a.m.! Must be some route."

The other climbers in the room all gave me looks of impending doom. They obviously knew something I didn't but, in my 18-year-old enthusiasm, I paid no heed.

At 4:30 a.m. Layton's car roared into Eldorado. "Damm, it's still dark." "Watcha expect, Layton, it's the middle of the night." We sat in the car for awhile and at the first hint of dawn we were off.

"Hey, this is Redguard." I protested. "Just wait," was all Layton said as he disappeared upwards.

The first three pitches sailed by in dim confusion and finally in the light of day we started the fourth pitch off the upper meadow. As Layton moved up, lichens tinkled down through the air well away from the rock. We were into it now. Higher up Layton got into trouble. I had followed him many times but had never seen him so gripped. He did some incredible stems that I knew my mere 6'-2" could not duplicate. As soon as I reached the same spot Layton announced, "If you can't make it up in 30 seconds I'll start hauling! This route's gotta go!" "Thirty seconds? Jesus!" I looked around frantically for a hold, found one, pulled up and had just about worked out the crucial combination when Layton hollered, "Time's up!" "Wait, Layton, I'm making it!" Too late. With a great "This route's gotta go," Layton began hauling on the rope. I came up sputtering and protesting but Layton could only think about the fifth pitch.

He tiptoed across a difficult traverse and nailed a steep crack. As I followed, Layton employed another tactic—he launched into an incredible nonstop patter: "Atta - boy - just - keep - inching - along - grab - that - knob - great - move - hang - on - just - keep - inching - along."

At the top of the fifth pitch a rack of biners and

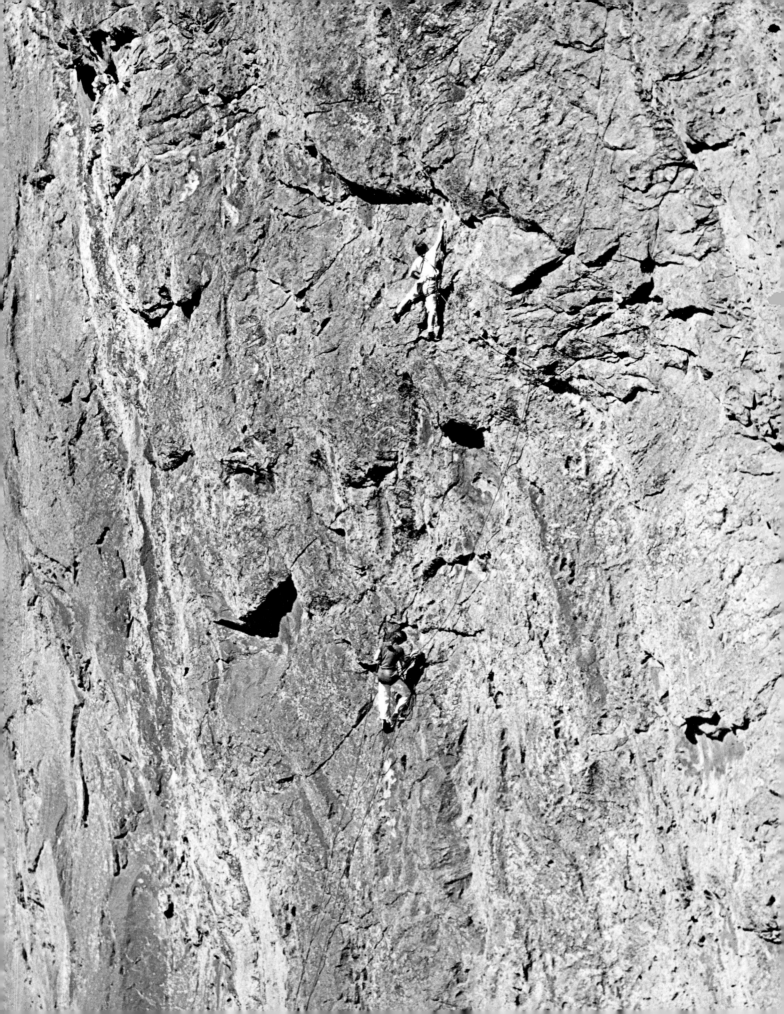

The crux move on the Northcutt Direct Start to the Bastille (5.10). The climber uses a hidden foothold and makes a long reach to a sloping hold.

The Sixties

hardware jammed behind a large flake. Layton became furious and yanked so hard that the entire flake system we were on shook and shook. As I pondered our anchors the rope slipped away and jammed 50 feet below. I lowered Layton and he free climbed back up the steep crack on finger jams; an impressive display.

Higher, after Layton had run out 80 feet of rope, I suggested that he place a piton. He did, but I was able to pluck it out with my fingers. "Yeah, well I didn't want you to get too worried."

At the overhanging exit off the ramp we had our last great struggle. Layton used an aid pin and made a long move from high in his stirrup. I could either make the move or retrieve the pin, but not both. Layton held me on tension while I removed the pin, but the struggling and stretch in the rope left me hanging free in a horrible position. A great thrashing ensued and finally Layton lowered me to the ramp. We repeated the entire process but it was just a replay of the first time. After a second great thrash the piton had to be left behind.

As we shook hands on top it began to dawn on me what we had done. T2 was open.

After its first ascent in 1959, T2 (for Tower Two) became a favorite classic climb. Kor and Roach started by climbing the existing first three pitches of Redguard Route, and it was at a later date that an independent start was added, to make the whole climb separate and distinct.

Ray Northcutt and the First 5.10

During 1959, Ray Northcutt continued to develop his rock climbing technique and maintained his high level of physical fitness. He was competitive, as many climbers are, and one day in 1959 was at the foot of the Bastille in Eldorado Springs Canyon. "See that crack," said one of his companions, pointing to a thin vertical crack some seventy feet high, "Layton free climbed it the other day."[2] This was enough for Northcutt. Tying on to the end of the rope, and with his informer as belayer, he set off climbing the crack. Through his mind kept going the words, "If Kor can do it, so can I." Using two pitons for protection, he was able to make a difficult series of free moves and finally reached the easier section of the Bastille Crack proper. At this point, his belayer informed him that he had been tricked, that Kor hadn't free climbed it, and that he had only said that to get Northcutt going!

This pitch subsequently turned out to be the first pitch in the Boulder area to receive a 5.10 rating, and to maintain that rating through the 1970's. Northcutt's ascent in 1959 was an event ahead of its time. No other lead justifying a 5.10 rating was to take place until well into the 1960's.

It is possible that Northcutt's ascent of the direct start to the Bastille was the first 5.10 lead in America.

The first California 5.10 was Dave's Deviation at Tahquitz Rock, put up by Tom Frost and Joe Fitschen in the spring of 1960. The first Yosemite 5.10 was the upper pitch of Crack of Doom by Chuck Pratt and Mort Hempel in May, 1961. Northcutt's direct start to the Bastille is only a short pitch close to the ground, but it had a firmly established 5.10 rating even in 1977. Indeed, its difficulty had become so well established by 1977 that some climbers of the seventies questioned if Northcutt's lead in 1959 had actually been done completely free. In 1976, when interviewed, Northcutt remembered the climb clearly and stated that he had indeed climbed the crux moves completely free; testimony to his high free climbing standard in 1959.

The Diagonal

In 1958 Northcutt and Dale Johnson had made application to the Park Service for permission to climb the Diamond and were turned down. The Park Service ban applied only to the Diamond's main face, however. Below Broadway, and to the right of Stettners Ledges, was a massive expanse of blank rock as big as the Diamond. Northcutt spotted a thin crack system slanting its way up the face in a diagonal line, and felt that there was the prospect of a route. Northcutt says, "I just kept my mouth shut and didn't ask for permission to try it." He calculated that if he asked the Park Service, they would probably say no, but felt that the ban explicitly referred to the Diamond, giving him a justification should he be challenged during or after an attempt on the "Diagonal" route on the lower face.

Northcutt's first attempt on the Diagonal was with George Lamb in August, 1958. They climbed far enough up the slanting crack system, over a large arching overhang on direct aid, for Northcutt to become

The East Face of Longs Peak showing the Diagonal.

convinced that the route was possible. In September of that year Northcutt was living in Boulder and met Kor. They climbed together during the fall, and Northcutt found Kor attentive and interested in his story of the attempt on the Diagonal. Northcutt and Kor agreed to attempt the Diagonal again the following summer. During the spring of 1959, they climbed together regularly and were in good shape by the time the summer months arrived. On the first weekend of July, they made their first attempt and were able to follow the slanting crack system for a number of pitches. The summer of 1959 was very wet and the cracks were running with water, making the climbing difficult and necessitating a good deal of direct aid. In the early afternoon a storm came in, and it began to rain heavily. The line they were following was exposed to stonefall, from Broadway and Upper Keiners, and the rain washed down a number of rocks. As the rocks went bouncing by, Northcutt and Kor decided that the face was no place to be. They retreated but left fixed ropes to their high point.

The following weekend, Northcutt and Kor returned to the face and prusiked back up their fixed ropes. Three more pitches up wet cracks took them to a point two-thirds of the way up the face. Ahead of them the nature of the rock changed, became tighter and more compact, and the crack system they had been following became shallow and less satisfactory for piton placements. To the right, a system of holds and small ledges offered promise of a traverse line. Northcutt led across the traverse, which involved some difficult free climbing.

This section of rock was to become the focal point of a controversy among Colorado climbers in following years. Northcutt said afterwards that he had free climbed the whole way across. Subsequent ascent parties had to resort to a rappel to avoid a blank slab at the end of the traverse, and there was no clearly substantiated account of a second completely free ascent. Northcutt was in amazingly good shape in 1959, and he had climbed the 5.10 direct start to the Bastille the same year, which supported the possibility that he had completely free climbed the traverse.

In 1960, Dave Rearick and Bob Kamps climbed the first sections of the traverse, which included 5.9 moves, but were unable to free climb the smooth blank slab at the right side while making the second ascent of the Diagonal. Later, Larry Dalke and Pat Ament had a similar experience. Further speculation was created by a published photograph taken by Kor which showed the start of the crux traverse, with Northcutt carrying a pack. If the traverse had been climbed completely free, it would have been very hard, not the kind of leading to

attempt carrying a pack.

Considering the expertise of Rearick and Kamps, and of Dalke and Ament, their judgment of the feasibility of climbing the blank slab could not be dismissed lightly. During the 1960's and 1970's the topic stimulated regular discussion among local climbers, and Northcutt's "free" ascent of the traverse assumed legendary proportions.

Rearick and Kamps, and Dalke and Ament, reported similar experiences at the blank section. Forty feet down, and slightly to the right, they had both noticed two drilled bolts in place. A slightly diagonalling rappel took them to the bolts. The bolts had certainly been placed by Northcutt, since no one else had climbed the route prior to Rearick and Kamps, and they matched other pairs of bolts which Northcutt had placed for anchors lower down the face.

When interviewed in 1975, Northcutt remembered that an afternoon storm had caught him and Kor just as they were approaching the right side of the traverse. They left fixed ropes in place and rappelled down to the foot of the face. A few days later, they returned, prusiked back up their ropes, and completed the climb. Northcutt said he got off the fixed rope forty feet lower down from the point from which he and Kor had rappelled and had placed the two bolts which Rearick and Kamps were to find later. From this point, he and Kor pulled down their ropes and continued the climb. The questionable forty feet, which none of the later parties had been able to free climb, had been avoided by the rappel off the face. In Northcutt's mind, he had indeed free climbed the whole of the traverse, but the section which had stopped the later parties had been avoided.

The fact that Northcutt did not free climb the last few feet of the traverse in no way detracts from his achievement. The Diagonal was a tremendous climb, and one which has held its reputation well to the present time. The high standard of free climbing required, and the objective dangers from water and stonefall, combine to make the Diagonal a respected and infrequently repeated route in 1977.

Bob Culp recollects hiking into Chasm Lake on the day that the Diagonal was completed and hearing an excited party ahead crying, "Northcutt and Kor are down from the Diagonal!" He had no idea what that meant, but soon a couple of strange looking characters came stomping triumphantly down the trail. Culp remembers Kor, "tall and gangly—dressed in ridiculous knickers that came above his knees, socks that never reached them, and a tiny red beret perched like a beany on his head, was friendly and replied to questions. He waved his ice axe vaguely in the direction of the East

Face and shook his head over the difficulties of the climb." Culp describes Northcutt as being "small, muscular and compact," and says, "He looked the part of the mountaineer. His clothes had just the right authenticity and he wore his red beret at a jaunty angle."[3] (A few days later Culp bought a red beret of his own.)

Culp has written, "The Diagonal was Northcutt's climb. He conceived it, and led most of it. It was the hardest climb in Colorado at the time."

Shortly after completing the Diagonal, Northcutt dropped out of climbing completely. The Diagonal was his masterpiece, culminating a decade during which he had become an acknowledged master in Colorado climbing. He had hoped to be able to make an attempt on the Diamond, but following events were to frustrate that ambition.

The Diamond

In 1954 Dale Johnson, after extensive preparation, had been refused permission to attempt the Diamond. Likewise, an application by Dick Pownall, who was later to become a member of the 1963 American Mount Everest Expedition, was turned down in 1955, even though Pownall had arranged for a well-equipped support party from Fort Carson to accompany his party in case of emergency. Johnson and Northcutt had made formal application to the Park Service in 1958, submitting photographs, ability certificates, and detailed plans. They, too, were refused permission. In 1959, the Californians Chouinard and Weeks, eager to

pirate the first ascent from under the noses of the Colorado locals, secretly sneaked up to Broadway, without asking the Park Service for permission, and bivouacked below the wall. A major storm moved in before they could begin climbing, and they were compelled to beat a retreat.

In 1960, the year after Northcutt's successful ascent of the Diagonal, the Park Service relented and simultaneously issued application blanks for a Diamond attempt to all parties that had previously expressed interest. Johnson contacted Northcutt, but he had not climbed seriously since the Diagonal the year before and felt that he was not in good enough shape to make an attempt. As Johnson searched for a companion, two California climbers also received application blanks.

The two Californians were David Rearick and Bob Kamps. They had both climbed extensively in Yosemite Valley. Together, they had made the fifth ascent of the Steck-Salathé route on Sentinel, and Rearick had made the third ascent of the North West Face of Half Dome with Royal Robbins. Visiting Colorado for the summer, they had just made the second ascent of Northcutt and Kor's route, The Diagonal, on the lower East Face. They had the experience and the psychological confidence to commit themselves to a multi-day climb on the Diamond.

At this time, Colorado climbers were dependent on soft steel pitons imported from Europe. These pitons, especially in the smaller sizes, were relatively weak, and became bent and distorted easily after they had been hammered and removed from cracks a few times. Rearick and Kamps had brought out from California a

The Diamond. Rearick-Kamps route (D.1.) marked.

David Rearick, Bob Kamps, and Bonnie Kamps, are feted in the Estes Park rodeo parade after their successful ascent of the Diamond. *Denver Post photo*

The East Face of Longs Peak
and The Diamond.

selection of prototype hard steel chrome-molybdenum pitons which Yvon Chouinard was manufacturing. They came in a wider variety of sizes than the soft steel pitons, with "knife-blades" for hairline-thin cracks, and "bong bongs" for cracks up to five inches wide.

In a letter written to Dave Rearick in 1955, shortly after Dale Johnson had been refused permission, Jack Rensberger, a friend of Rearick's, had outlined a plan for climbing the Diamond. In this letter he acknowledged that Dale Johnson was an expert in engineering his way up blank sections of overhanging rock with expansion bolts, but felt that there were sufficient cracks to make a climb feasible without resorting to bolting. "Bolts were the main basis of (Johnson's) theory, and they felt it was impossible any other way," he wrote in his letter. He continued, "As soon as the route I've decided on (many times easier and requiring only pitons and two four-inch wedges) is tried by any good climber, the Diamond will be conquered." This letter, written in 1955, was prophetic. In 1960, after checking out their climbing record and their equipment, the Park Service gave Rearick and Kamps permission to go ahead with an attempt.

A condition of the permission was that the pair had to arrange both a primary and a secondary support party in case of emergency. The primary support party had to actually be on the mountain, in the vicinity of the Diamond. This group consisted of Jack Laughlin, Charlie Roskosz, Dean Moore, Charles Alexander, and Gary Cole. Members of the Rocky Mountain Rescue Group, led by Gordon Stocker, were available on call as secondary support.

It was drizzling steadily as the group fixed ropes in the North Chimney leading to Broadway. The fixed ropes were to make it easier and safer to carry the climbers' equipment up to Broadway and the base of the Diamond. Rain continued that evening, and the climbers spent the night in the shelter cabin at Chasm Lake. The next day, Monday, the first of August, dawned cold and windy. But it had stopped raining, and Rearick and Kamps headed up the fixed ropes to the foot of the wall. In the rather matter-of-fact report which they prepared for the Park Service, they described the start of the climb as:

> The actual climbing began at 9:30 a.m. on August 1. The first pitch, 140 feet, is easy free climbing. The second pitch is moderate to difficult face climbing on sound rock, leading to an overhang slanting to the right. The third pitch involves direct aid to ascend the right edge of this overhang, and ends on a grass-covered platform with a large (loose) boulder, easily visible from Chasm View. The fourth pitch starts up the inside of the corner above, gaining 30 feet by difficult free climbing until direct aid is necessary. Easy "nailing" brings one up to the

conspicuous six-foot overhang above, and it was passed with a single piton. Increasingly difficult nailing is encountered in the wide grass-filled crack leading from here up to the Ramp. On the first ascent this section was being drenched by water falling from the chimney near the top of the Diamond. The highest point reached August 1, was about 80 feet below the Ramp. [4]

A bolt was placed to reinforce the poor belay stance, and the two climbers rappelled down to Broadway for the night, leaving fixed ropes up to their high point.

After spending a comfortable night on Broadway, they prusiked up their fixed ropes early the next morning. The next four hundred feet of the wall leaned outward and the rock changed for the worse, becoming loose and fractured. A stream of water spattered down from the top of the face, but thanks to the overhanging nature of the rock, the two were climbing behind the falling water.

Two pitches higher they found a small ledge measuring two feet wide and seven feet long. After climbing one more pitch above the ledge and arranging a fixed rope, they settled in for the night. Rearick's laconic comment as they settled into this tiny aerie was simply to state that the temperature was about forty degrees, and that their down jackets kept them comfortable. A surprisingly casual notation, considering the exposed nature of their perch, and the fact that they were the first two climbers to be this high on the wall after many years of contemplation of the climb's feasibility.

With the exception of the top pitch, which contained several large blocks of ice, the next day's climbing proved relatively straight-forward, and they reached the top at 1:15 p.m.

Several hardy newspaper reporters had made it up to the top of Longs Peak to interview the successful climbers, and as they descended they met others en route who had been defeated by altitude at various levels. While on the face, Rearick and Kamps' ascent had been followed by daily gripping accounts in the local newspapers and on radio, and a half-page account of the adventure appeared in *Time* magazine. After the climb, Rearick and Kamps received a "hero's" welcome in Estes Park and found themselves star attractions in the summer rodeo parade. As an interesting aftermath, there also appeared a spate of accounts by newsmen who pointed out the exhaustion and suffering they had experienced to watch and photograph the climb. In some accounts, it appeared that their adventures made the actual climbing of the Diamond seem child's play by comparison!

The ascent of the Diamond brought to fruition that first gleam of anticipation experienced by Frederick

Chapin as he observed the East Face of Longs Peak from Chasm View in 1870. Its successful ascent by Rearick and Kamps in 1960 was one more dent in the concept of the impossible. Undoubtedly, many old-timers in 1960 thought to themselves, "That's it, what more can they do?" But rather than the ascent of the Diamond being an ultimate, it was to prove to be only the beginning of a series of events in the 1960's in which, once again, the concept of the impossible was seized roughly by the scruff of the neck and shaken up so as to be unrecognizable.

Layton Kor - the Early Sixties

Layton Kor's old Ford was a familiar sight near Boulder and on Colorado highways during the early 1960's. He usually drove at sixty m.p.h. along the straights, over hills, through turns, and probably through the narrow gate of Eldorado Canyon as well.

In 1960, Kor developed a "strange lung disease" and departed for a starvation diet at a Texas sanitorium. On his return to Colorado he had lost forty pounds, looked like an emaciated skeleton, and was a confirmed vegetarian. Culp has written that seeing him lustily devour two huge heads of lettuce in rapid succession on bivouac ledges was a unique experience. "Lotsa energy in lettuce!" he would mutter between gulps. With the existence of his lung disease well established, he regularly prevailed upon his climbing partners to carry all the gear up to the base of the climb. Once there, Culp says, he would perk up, say he felt really good all of a sudden, grab the equipment, and lead off at breakneck speed.

By 1960, Kor had already completed a number of new ascents in Eldorado Springs Canyon. These had included The Bulge and T.2, the West Buttress of the Bastille, and the Northwest Corner of the Bastille. In 1960 he roped in George Hurley to attempt another new route on Redgarden Wall. The line they eventually climbed followed a steep crack system and included a formidable crack-chimney pitch. Hurley has written of the first ascent:

> When Layton Kor and I first climbed the Grand Giraffe, we thought we were on an extremely hard, maybe even a desperate climb. To some extent the desperate quality was part of Layton's style. He liked to wonder aloud about the human possibility of whatever we were doing. "It's awful," he'd say, or "Don't fall or we'll both go," as he leered down a hard lead. Usually he was just having fun but on the chimney pitch of the Grand Giraffe I was not laughing.
>
> Since the time of the first ascent of the Grand Giraffe attitudes have changed. In 1960, Kor and I actually enjoyed stepping on a piton. During the second lead we wanted to move back left into the main crack. There were

Layton Kor (6'-5") gives a ride to Norman Mulligan (6'-4") on top of Devil's Tower in 1957. Baker Armstrong facing camera. Ben Chidlaw back to camera. *Courtesy Baker Armstrong.*

George Hurley leading the first pitch of the Grand Giraffe (5.8). *Courtesy George Hurley.*

Moving around the second bulge of the off-width crack on the third lead of the Grand Giraffe - the hardest free crack in the Boulder region in the early sixties (5.9).

hand holds but no visible footholds. A Simond piton made a wonderful little ledge. On a later ascent we found an almost invisible foothold hiding under lichen just where it ought to be. The desirability of free over aid climbing was not as clear then as it is now.

The rule that "the leader never falls," was still a rule which took precedence. We even gave lip service to the. idea that the leader should be able to climb down whatever he climbed up.

The name we gave our new route, The Grand Giraffe, was a take-off on the Grand Jorasses and a way of debunking ourselves and our efforts in a canyon in the foothills of the gentle Rockies. We looked to European climbs with awe and reminded ourselves that Eldorado was a practice area, a klettergarten. It was only later, after we had climbed in Europe, that we realised that Colorado climbs deserved serious respect.

The Grand Giraffe was an important climb in 1960. For a number of years afterwards, the fourth pitch was the hardest free crack in the area. The crack pitch was graded 5.9 in 1977. After making the first ascent with Kor in 1960, George Hurley was to go on and become a leading climber of the sixties and the seventies. In 1977 he was leading 5.10 climbs, and still turning out new routes. Hurley was a quiet, unassuming figure, easy to overlook against the more extroverted characteristics of his contemporaries, but his remarkable persistence over the years made him one of Colorado's most experienced rock climbers.

If Buhl Thought That, So Did We

One of the problems facing a beginner in Colorado was that there never existed a regular congregating place for climbers. During the late fifties and early sixties, the Sink served this function to some extent, but it was only occasionally frequented by a small number of climbers. Colorado never had the equivalent of Camp Four in Yosemite Valley, or the Padarn Lake Pub in North Wales, where large numbers of climbers could be found on a regular basis.

Bob Culp suffered from this problem. He started climbing during the summer of 1959 and says that he was somewhat limited initially by the lack of a partner. "I had taught myself to climb from European books and always climbed solo— unaware that there was such a thing as an American rock climber, since I hadn't seen any in my scrambles."

In 1960 Culp made the acquaintance of Layton Kor and was introduced to the inner sanctum of experienced rock climbers in the Boulder region. Kor and Culp climbed together in Eldorado and were delighted to recognize a mutual fanaticism. They had both read Herman Buhl's *The Lonely Challenge*. Buhl had said that a climber must solo if he were to realize his potential. Culp has written, "If Buhl thought that, so

Looking up the first lead of the Grand Giraffe.

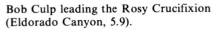
Bob Culp leading the Rosy Crucifixion
(Eldorado Canyon, 5.9).

did we." Kor soloed the Bulge and the Northwest Passage and Culp also soloed the Bulge during this period. "Soloing to us meant climbing without a rope," Culp writes. "A fall would have been disastrous."

Over the years, Culp has become one of the acknowledged wise men of Colorado rock climbing. He has climbed almost everywhere in the state and has a tersely humorous style of recounting his adventures, both verbally and in his writings. He owns a climbing equipment store and runs a small climbing school and guide service in Boulder, called The Boulder Mountaineer. His store is one of the few places where one can obtain reliable current information on local rock climbing developments.

Culp had a number of near tragedies during his early climbing days. On one occasion he was standing near the top of a rock pinnacle in Gregory Canyon which he had climbed unroped. He noticed a perfect crack in which to try out the new Joe Brown hand jam, about which he had recently been reading. Just as he inserted his hand in the crack, the ledge on which he had been standing spontaneously collapsed. His hand, which had apparently been poorly jammed, popped out and he fell over backwards, passing the sliding remainders of the ledge. Landing on another ledge a little way below, tumbling debris rained onto him. Bruised, bleeding, and amazed that he was still alive, he limped and crawled back to his car and drove down to the University hospital. No bones were broken, but he spent a week in a hospital bed.

A short time later, another near tragedy almost robbed Boulder of this inspiring figure. Culp was climbing a new route near Boulder Falls and was leading the second pitch. He climbed up to a point above his belayer where, had he fallen, he would have cratered on the ground one hundred feet below. He continued, unable to get any protection in, and reached a point where he could no longer climb up. He tried several times to no avail. The hideous realization dawned upon him that he had exerted so much energy that he could no longer climb back down to a resting spot. Terrified, and fully aware of the consequences of a fall, he hung on, clutching the rock until his arms were in such intense pain that he could no longer stand it. Announcing that he was coming off, his fingers loosened on the holds. As he slid down he felt something holding him by his waist. The jacket he was wearing had somehow caught on a tiny nubbin of rock! His arms too weak to support him, he rested his full weight on his jacket, slowly regaining his strength. Rested, he was able to pull up with his arms and to place a runner on the nubbin to stand in. The crystal turned out to be only a quarter of an inch thick, but was enough to hold the runner. The rest, and the use of the runner, enabled him to step up to a point where he could reach good holds and finish the lead.

The Northwest Face of Chief's Head

During 1961, Culp made a number of first ascents with Layton Kor. Ruper in Eldorado Springs was done in one three-hour "blast" and has since become one of the most popular routes in the canyon. The same year, Kor and Culp headed up to Rocky Mountain National Park to make an attempt on the massive unclimbed Northwest Face of Chief's Head. Fricke's guidebook description of the climb they made reads, "This is one of the most challenging climbs in the area. The wall is smooth and featureless with only a few black water streaks and an occasional small flake or corner to indicate route possibilities." The face is over a thousand feet high, in a remote situation, and on a high alpine peak. Kor and Culp's ascent in 1961 was, for many years, shrouded in mystery. The face did not receive a second ascent until the summer of 1975 — fourteen years later! Culp's account of this climb, portrays their adventure well:

The northwest face of Chief's Head was one of the biggest unclimbed walls in Rocky Mountain Park when Layton Kor pointed it out to me in the winter of 1960. Its remote location and forbidding appearance had discouraged attempts to climb it.

Kor was excited. "The best thing left in Colorado" he boasted. "It'll take everything we've got to get up it! It's got to be climbed!"

We prepared for the climb with uncharacteristic care. During the cold, snowy months I sent away to the Dolt Hut for a collection of CCB pitons which we thought might work better than the Simonds and Army Angles we normally used. We made sporadic attempts to get into shape by climbing ropes in the CU field house and traversed the university buildings to strengthen our fingers. These sessions usually ended up with our searching the library for climbing books or photographs we might have missed.

One day at the gym we watched the wrestling team working out and Layton suggested we give it a try. After a few minutes of threshing about I was ready to call it quits but Kor was still raring to go. We were approached by the wrestlers, who seemed to be fascinated by the commotion we had caused. I waved them on to Layton. What followed was an incredible melee that left everyone rolling on the mats — those not actually wrestling were convulsed with laughter. They could do nothing with

The Northwest Face of Chief's Head. Approximate line of Kor-Culp route marked. *Lew Dakan.*

Layton Kor (right) and Bob Culp contemplating the Northwest Face of Chief's Head at the time of their successful ascent. *Huntley Ingalls.*

Top: Kor leading on the first ascent of the Northwest Face of Chief's Head. *Bob Culp.*

Bottom: Culp seconding on Chief's Head. *Layton Kor.*

him! He had no wrestling experience but possessed an abundance of energy. I remember him frantically leaping about trying to dislodge a young man with a death grip on one of his long legs who gasped, "Just like trying to pin a giraffe!"

My first close-up view of the climb was not very encouraging. It was early June and the face was running with water. The wall loomed dark and ominous with smooth rock that seemed crackless. Kor had stayed behind at Black Lake to shake the last lingering effects of an illness and had sent me ahead with all the gear and instructions to take advantage of the light and pick out a good line. It was impossible to pick out a real line so I invented an imaginary one right up the center.

Next morning as we surveyed the climb Kor's only comment was, "Looks good as any."

With some uncertainty I began climbing. Although there were seldom any cracks, the rock was fantastic and little holds seemed to sprout under my fingertips. The rope reached to a convenient ledge. The route above was uncertain but that was Kor's problem for the moment.

Pausing just long enough to grab the hardwear he was off. He had completely shaken the previous day's lethargy and was impatient to get on with it. "Move your belay down to the end of the ledge," he shouted. "I'm gonna need all the rope I can get."

Somewhat reluctantly I untied from my anchor. By the time I had re-established the belay most of the rope had been taken up. "Good flake up here," I could hear him shouting as he banged in a pin. Clipping in a stirrup he leaned back for a view of the route above. "It's gonna go—it's gonna go!" I could hear him humming happily as he moved out of sight.

Seconding the pitch gave me a preview of what was in store above; consistently difficult climbing on good but small holds with little protection. One piton driven upside down under a flake had protected the lead.

As I approached him Kor began getting me ready for the next pitch. He always preferred to lead and had been known to try to psych out his partners so he could get all the pitches. "You're gonna love this next part." I could hear him gloating. "Perfectly smooth." "No holds at all." "You might get in some protection about fifty feet up." On and on.

As I started off it dawned upon me that his predictions were absolutely accurate. Reaching up at arm's length I was barely able to get fingertips on a small edge. Working my feet up on friction I pulled up. Above, about six inches further than I could reach was another tiny nubbin. Maybe with a lunge? I decided against it and stepped back to consider other alternatives. There seemed to be none. Kor was getting restless. After all we were wasting time with most of the wall above us. "OK Layton, you give it a try," I relented.

Moments later I was trying to get tied onto the belay anchor with Kor already half way to my high point and climbing rapidly. Without hesitation he pulled up on the small edge, shot up an incredibly long arm to the high nubbin, and stepped neatly up. "Good holds up here," he remarked, as he began an upwards traverse to the left which ran out the rope without a single piton.

Groaning inwardly I cursed myself for not leading the pitch. At worst I would have faced a relatively short

fall. Now if I came off I was in for a pendulum halfway across the wall. With clenched teeth and pounding heart I pulled up. The nubbin looked impossibly high, but from the extreme of a thumbtip mantle I was just able to reach it. It was good. I gradually calmed down before rejoining Kor.

"You're gonna love this next one," I could hear him beginning.

The climb progressed. Kor was a genius at routefinding. Or maybe he was uncommonly lucky. Perhaps it was just that he had the commitment to climb through whatever he encountered. Probably it was all three. At any rate, although the difficulties and uncertainties persisted, we were soon halfway up the wall. It was here that we encountered the crux.

It was Kor's lead. The rock above looked blank. Nothing new. He moved up a few feet and placed a shaky pin behind a small flake. "Probably ought to put in a bolt," he fretted, but decided against it when he thought he could see a small crack above. A few minutes later he had half the rope out and the crack was nonexistent. "This is serious up here," he shouted, "get ready. Get ready!" Standing on a ledge barely big enough for both feet and tied to a questionable anchor, I was in no mood to think of catching a 150 foot fall.

Layton Kor was a unique phenomenon. It has been my pleasure to climb with many superbly talented rock climbers but never, I think, with any who possessed the qualities of Kor. To be sure, some may have been technically better but none had the animal energy that would come bursting out to see him through the worst situations.

From my ledge I could see him spread-eagled above, finger and toe tips touching the rock. He rarely paused; just long enough to scan the rock above and then he was moving on. Such was his commitment that he was able to bring to bear the full focus of his immense drive without even entertaining the idea of retreating.

Eventually came the dreaded words. "Sorry about this but the rope won't reach. You're gonna have to come up a ways."

It wasn't so bad on my end. The climbing was reasonable, but I knew Kor was in a difficult spot. If he came off while I was climbing?...."Oh, well," I tried to convince myself, "It's Layton. You're probably safer here than on the drive up."

Kor made it safely to a ledge. I followed what had been for him a totally unprotected and even unbelayed lead that may have been hard 5.9. "I really feel good today!" Kor chortled.

There was a lot more to come but nothing desperate. One false start high on the wall required Layton to climb down with me directing his feet to tiny holds. An apparently blank area that had us worried suddenly developed a perfect piton crack that ran to the end of the difficulties. By that time we hardly needed it.

We used three pitons for aid and placed three bolts for belay anchors in crackless rock. The famous CCB pitons had been of no use whatsoever.

We were met by our friend Huntley Ingalls, who had soloed the north ridge to take pictures. At the summit, in the fading light, we had one final surprise. Kor was hopping up and down in excitement. "Roberto, get up

Kor high on the crumbling limestone walls of Glenwood Canyon. *Steve Komito.*

here! You've got to see this". There to the south was a great wall that neither of us had known about: the east face of Mt. Alice. Kor lingered for the better part of a minute to enjoy the view. "Now that has got to be climbed," was his parting comment.

Billy Westbay and Dan McClure made the second ascent of the Northwest Face of Chief's Head fourteen years later in 1975. They reported 5.9 and 5.10 climbing and confirmed that the ascent of the face by Kor and Culp in 1961 had indeed been an epic achievement.

Glenwood Canyon

During their ascent of the Diagonal, Kor and Northcutt had spent a good deal of time talking, and daydreaming, of making a trip to the Dolomites together. During 1960, Kor began training with

The walls of Glenwood Canyon.

determination for the proposed trip. Finally, when it came time to depart, Northcutt couldn't make it and Kor decided to go alone.

The locals waited for his return, expecting to hear tales of spectacular feats. They were disappointed when Layton reappeared with stories of living on beer and cinnamon rolls, being arrested in Innsbruck for camping in the city park, and generally being unable to communicate with anyone.

On his return to Colorado, he found Glenwood Canyon, with towering limestone walls, often overhanging, and frequently horribly loose. Kor revelled in this situation, both from the satisfaction of treading where no climber had previously ventured, and from the knowledge that the walls were similar to the Dolomites. Unfortunately he had difficulty convincing partners of the particular joys of the area. Whenever he was able to

talk climbers into accompanying him, usually one visit was enough. Each returned wide-eyed, mumbling of unbelievable horrors, and vowing never to return.

Bob Culp was one of those whom Kor talked into visiting the Canyon. They drove down on a weekend and climbed three short routes the first day. Kor spotted a big overhanging wall in a side canyon, and they embarked on it the second day. Culp remembers that it was "dangerous and difficult...it had some hard aid and some free climbing on bad rock that was 5.9." Kor led up the face and stopped at a small ledge high on the wall. Culp climbed up to him, and his recollection of the following moment gives a good insight as to why Kor's partners were frequently reluctant to return to the Canyon. "I climbed to Kor," Culp says, "and the ledge was just a piece of rock stuck onto the wall with mud. Kor's anchor was a single piton hammered into the mud

106

Huntley Ingalls jumaring up to Kor on their
attempt to climb the "Mudwall." *Courtesy
Huntley Ingalls.*

The Sixties

between the ledge and the wall! It was absolutely
sickening. I just wanted to get off it before the whole
thing collapsed.'' It seems reasonable to expect that this
incident, and Culp's reaction, might have dampened
Kor's ardor, but this was not the case. Culp continues,
"The interesting thing was that all the time we were
climbing, we were looking off to the left to where there
was an overhanging mud wall. It was just appalling
looking; six hundred feet of solid overhang with little
bits of crumbling rock falling off spontaneously. As
soon as we got back to the ground, all Kor could talk
about was climbing it.''

Culp and Kor returned to Boulder, and Kor
embarked on a search for a partner for the mud wall.
Eventually, he talked Bob LaGrange into accompanying
him. LaGrange was a two hundred pound giant noted
for his erratic approach to rock climbing.

A shared joke among local climbers was the question
of what would happen if anyone ever had to catch
LaGrange in a leader fall. Roger Raubauch, one of the
lesser known but colorful climbers of the time, settled
the question. One day he came into Gerry's, the local
equipment store, beaming from ear to ear. Producing
his hidden hand from behind his back, he revealed a
mangled and bandaged mess. "This,'' he proudly
announced, ''is the hand that caught Bob LaGrange.''

LaGrange agreed to accompany Kor on an attempt on
the Glenwood Canyon mud wall. Kor led the first pitch,
kicking down loose rocks as he climbed. It was too
much for LaGrange. They called off the attempt and
departed, leaving a fixed rope up to the highest point.

Kor was undeterred. He attempted to persuade a local
rock climber named Tink Wilson into going back with
him. Tink recalls that ''some hunch told me not to go.''
Next, Kor approached Huntley Ingalls. Huntley,
lacking Tink Wilson's instinct for self preservation,
agreed. He recalls, ''I'll never forget it. While we were
walking up to the cliff there was a stone fall and rocks
came cascading down the face. Kor turned round and
said very provokingly, 'Don't pay any attention to that.
That don't mean anything.' It was just crazy to climb
the thing.''

Huntley's faith in Kor withstood this first test, and he
accompanied him on the route. The two prusiked back
up to the high point which Kor had reached with
LaGrange, and with Huntley established on the ledge,
Kor set off on the next pitch. The difficulties continued,
grew worse, and the quality of the rock did not improve.
Dolomites or no, Kor eventually realized that he was
chancing things, and, to Huntley's relief, called a
retreat.

Kor was to do other routes in Glenwood Springs
Canyon in later years, including a major overhanging
wall in a side canyon with Larry Dalke, which they
called Bearpaw. Generally, however, the Canyon has
not been popular with Colorado climbers. Lurid stories
of the bad rock encountered on these first ascents served
to keep people away. In recent years, climbers from the
Aspen area have done further exploration and report
excellent new routes on a number of buttresses of
igneous rock which intrude into the sedimentary
limestone.

ELDORADO ADVENTURES

Outer Space

In 1961 Kor climbed a new route angling right from
the top of the second pitch of the Bastille Crack in
Eldorado Springs Canyon with Steve Komito, a local
elf, famous for his big grin. The climb made its unlikely
way up some exceedingly steep and somewhat rotten
rock and depended mainly on direct aid. Komito, at
five-feet-four inches, and Kor, almost a foot taller,
must have made a comical pair. Komito recounted the
details of this climb in a tape-recorded interview:

> It was interesting the way it started. It was in the
> summer of 1961 while I was in summer school in Boulder,
> and that was the first year I had started to do some of the

better climbs with some of the better climbers. I hadn't
met Kor. One night at a party I remember a friend of
mine pointing out to me that the great hulking man over
there was Layton Kor. I remember asking my friend why
he looked so angry. The reply was, well, his climbing
partner had just pooped out on him and he was angry
because he had a new route picked out that he wanted to
do. I'd had a few beers and felt very strong and brave. I
remember crawling over to him on my hands and knees,
because I was pretty well plastered, pulling on his cuff
and saying, "Mr. Kor, Mr. Kor, I'll climb with you
tomorrow." And God, he just picked me up. He was so
happy he just picked me up and said, "Have you ever
done any climbing?" I said, "Oh, a little bit." He said,
"Have you ever done any artificial climbing," aid
climbing they called it in those days. I said, "No, but I

think I can learn.'' So right then and there he took me away from the party and took me home with him because he wanted to make sure I didn't get away. He put me to bed in his trailer and then he set the alarm. It was unbelievable. He set the alarm for four in the morning! It was still dark when we got up. He wanted to get an alpine start to do this God-damn route in Eldorado! My most vivid recollection is of Kor feeding me cantaloupe at 4:30 in the morning saying, ''We've got to get an early start, this will take all day,'' and dragging me down to Eldorado just as the sun was coming up. We did the first two pitches of the Bastille crack. I remember my hands were cold and numb even though it was midsummer because it was early in the morning.

He said he'd show me how to do aid climbing, that he'd lead the pitch and all I had to do was come up and clean the pitons after him. Most of my climbing with Kor was pretty much like being a bucket on the end of a rope, because I was actually light enough that he could pull me up. He'd pull me to the next higher piton. I'd clip a stirrup into it and then go back down to the next lower piton and hang upside down while he took my weight, and knock it out. He could reach so far between the pitons that I had no possible way of reaching them. I mean he was so giant and I was so short.

Kor joked one time that I was sort of a piton retriever machine. He'd just pull me up and then lower me back down and then I'd knock them out. I never became a very good climber because all I ever did was knock out Layton's pitons. He would smash the damn things in and then it was your problem to get them out and you had hell to pay if you didn't. Of course, in those days, there was no thought of ecology; there weren't that many climbers. I'd shout up, ''Layton, Layton I can't get this piton out.'' And he'd shout back, ''Knock the rock apart if you have to.'' We never bothered to think about it. It was just like people using up oil ten years ago; there was so much of it nobody really cared. So far as defacing a rock, it was something you didn't bother to think about. It was more important to get out the pitons.

Kor and Komito felt that the exposed nature of this new route on the steep upper rocks of the Bastille deserved an evocative name. They decided to call it Outer Space.

Komito's statement, ''I never became a very good climber because all I did was knock out Layton's pitons,'' is true in the sense that his name does not appear in the guidebooks as the leader of new routes. But, over the years, Komito has become one of the landmarks of Colorado climbing, second in importance only to the Colorado sun in brightening the local scene.

Steve Komito. Jolly cobbler of Estes Park.

During the sixties, Komito's home was a crash pad for scores of passing climbers, and many aspirant hard lads shared his hospitality. Admiring Roy Holubar's independence in his equipment business, Komito wanted likewise to become his own master and set up shop as a bootmaker in Boulder. His store became a crossroads which every climber eventually visited, and it hummed with the sound of sewing machines and climbing gossip. The same is true today. Komito's shop, now in Estes Park, is one of the real nerve centers of Colorado climbing. The famous, the obscure, and the eager beginner all troupe in and out, well-shod with footwear and inside information, stepping a little brighter and livelier from contact with Komito's jolly good humor.

The Naked Edge - First Attempts

During the late 1950's and early 1960's, a climber named Stanley Sheperd was active in the Boulder region. He was a small, wiry fellow, of intellectual bent, known for his high level of energy and his outrageous puns. Sheperd says of himself during the early sixties, "I was getting fairly good, on my best day I was about as good as Kor on a bad day." Sheperd aspired to do major new climbs, but lacked the push of contemporaries such as Kor. He writes, "We were under the influence of the slow drama of Ray Northcutt's great project, The Diagonal, and were very slow ourselves. We would do the first couple of leads of a climb, come back to Boulder and tell everybody who would listen how hairy it was, and wake up a day later to find out that Kor had gone out and done it in a couple of hours."[5] Summarizing his activities during this period, Sheperd writes, "My ability to visualize a climb and to name and publicize it far exceeded my ability to get up." Sheperd is probably a little too modest about his climbing ability, and his first ascent of a climb called Athlete's Feat on Castle Rock, even though it involved a good deal of direct aid, was impressive for 1961.

Standing and surveying Redgarden Wall one day, Sheperd imagined a line running up the exposed corner of one of the wall's most magnificent buttresses. He had recently been reading a lurid novel. He climbed the route in his mind, without leaving the ground, and gave it the same name as the novel: The Naked Edge. This climb was to become the scene of many dramas during following years, and its development typified major advances in technique and style. In 1961, shortly after Sheperd's imaginary ascent, Bob Culp and Jack Turner made the first of many attempts on the Naked Edge. Culp led a long thin crack. The nailing was straightforward and easy, and they graded it A.1. At the

The Bastille - Eldorado Canyon. (1) Bastille Crack. (2) Northcutt Direct Start. (3) X-M. (4) Outer Space.

top of the crack, Culp placed two bolts for a belay at the bottom of a steep slab. Turner climbed past and attempted the slab, but was turned back. Culp had a similar experience and also retreated. Subsequent to Culp and Turner's attempt, Stanley Sheperd and Bob Boucher made an attempt. They, too, were able to climb the first crack on aid, but were turned back by the slab.

Kor heard about the attempts and press-ganged his "piton retrieving machine," Steve Komito, into accompanying him. They nailed the first crack without trouble, and Kor headed over to the right side of the slab which had repulsed Sheperd and Boucher, where he found an incipient crack. After some tenuous nailing, Kor found himself "in-extremis." Komito recollects that "Kor was shrieking that he was going to come off at any moment and just clean me right off the slab. I was petrified!" Somehow Kor managed to lower himself back down to a ledge, and the two made a dishevelled retreat. The time had not yet arrived for the Naked Edge to be climbed.

"Climbers Rescue Youths Off Wall"

During 1961 Kor worked his way through many climbs, and many partners. With Jack Turner, on a snowy Christmas day, a new route unfolded on

Laybacking three-quarters of the way up the notorious Ruper Crack (5.8).

Redgarden Wall, involving steep climbing and direct aid. Turner wanted to call it the J-C Crack, but Kor prevailed and the climb was named the Rosy Crucifixion. The following day, a struggle with low temperatures and a steep corner-crack system involving hard free climbing and some aid had Turner and Kor living escape fantasies of warmer climates. Turner suggested naming the route Rincon, an area in California noted for ocean, and warm sun, and surfing. The contrast with winter Colorado appealed, and Rincon it was.

Shortly after the first ascents of Rosy Crucifixion and Rincon, Jack Turner was sitting at home, toasty warm, on a cold and snowy winter evening. The phone rang. It was Kor:

Turner, we gotta go climbing.
For God's sake why?
There are a couple of kids stuck up on the Yellow Spur. The Rocky Mountain Rescue just called. We gotta go and get 'em.

Kor picked Turner up and lurched his old car down to Eldorado Springs at a speed which turned the gently falling snow flakes into horizontal bullets. The place was a zoo. The Rocky Mountain Rescue was there. Everyone and his friend seemed to be there. Chaos reigned. Hours had been spent discussing the situation. Possibilities had been examined and discarded. A monstrous eight-foot diameter searchlight bathed the scene in eerie yellow light, revealing only snow flakes. "Come on, Turner," yelled Kor, exuding confidence, and charging up the hillside. At the foot of the cliff, a moment was spent tying into the rope, and Kor disappeared into the gloom, swimming his way up a snow-filled chimney-crack system (The Dirty Deed). "O.K. Turner," he bellowed from 150 feet up. Turner followed, kicking and struggling his way up the snowy steepness. A traversing ledge led across the cliff from the Dirty Deed chimney to the top of the first pitch of a climb called the Yellow Spur. Two shivering kids from Boulder High School, sixteen years of age, huddled in the dark on the snow-covered ledge. The *Rocky Mountain News* the next day boasted the banner headlines, "Climbers Rescue Youths Off Wall."

The youngsters were Larry Dalke and Pat Ament. After their meeting on the snowy ledge of the Yellow Spur, Kor, Dalke and Ament became regular climbing companions.

During the spring of 1962, Ament was taking it easy at home one afternoon when the telephone rang. "Ament, you gotta get down here right away. Bring all the money you can get hold of." It was Kor. "What's up, Layton?" responded Pat. "There's somebody here

Redgarden Wall. (1) The Yellow Spur. (2) The Grand Giraffe. (3) Ruper. (4) The Rosy Crucifixion. (5) Le Toit. (6) Kloeberdanz. (7) T.2. (8) The Naked Edge. (9) Diving Board. (10) Redguard Route. (11) Genesis.

selling Chouinard equipment. It's incredible. Bring all the money you got.'' Ament immediately phoned Dalke. The two of them pooled all their money, about a hundred dollars, and shot off down to Kor's trailer. They were soon the proud possessors of a selection of Chouinard pitons. Their new toys included solid thick-bladed pitons called "bugaboos." Ament recalls that "bugaboos were our favorites." Previously, they had only had European soft steel pitons, blades for thin cracks, and angles for wide cracks. Bugaboos proved ideal for cracks of intermediate widths and seemed particularly suited to many cracks in the Boulder region. Chouinard's new pitons were much harder than those previously available. Chrome-molybdenum was mixed with steel to produce a hard alloy capable of

being hammered into a crack and removed up to a hundred times without deformation. Additionally, Kor, Dalke, and Ament were able to purchase extremely thin pitons called "knife blades," as well as the fabled "rurps." Rurps were the tiniest of pitons, about the size of a razor blade, intended for hairline cracks. Chouinard's "Realized Ultimate Reality Piton" would just about hold a climber's weight, provided he didn't do anything radical, like coughing.

Ament remembers that, "Rurps assumed almost magical significance for us. We'd go screaming down to Eldorado in Layton's old car. He'd look across at me and say, 'got the rurps?' — 'Gosh, Layton, no. I thought you had 'em.' Around we'd spin, bald tires squealing, and tear back to Boulder to get them.

Without the rurps we just couldn't make upward
progress on new routes. Psychologically, we just had to
have them along, even if we never used them.''

X - M

In 1962, shortly after purchasing their new Chouinard
equipment, Kor picked Ament up and they went
hurtling down to Eldorado Springs Canyon with Kor's
usual haste and abandon. "Climbing with Layton,"
Ament recalls, "was such a traumatic experience. You
never knew if you were going to come back alive or not.
Getting there in Kor's old Ford was half the danger of
the climb."

Once in Eldorado, Kor led the apprehensive Pat along
to the foot of the steep face of the Bastille. He had
picked out a line which led up the cliff towards the
higher pitches of Outer Space. Ament's tape-recorded
account tells of their adventure:

> It was a fiasco for both of us. The head of my
> hammer flew off and landed on top of somebody's car.
> Layton was screaming at me. I was standing there trying
> to figure out how to get the pitons out without a hammer,
> and here comes the haul line down the cliff with Layton's
> hammer tied to it, swinging across the wall around the
> corner, missing my head by about two inches.
>
> I was so terrified that it was all I could do to get up. I
> didn't know anything about direct aid, and had a
> desperate time seconding the first pitch, because I
> couldn't reach Kor's pitons.
>
> At the belay ledge, he clipped some rurps on me and
> said, "This is all you'll need for this pitch." I reached
> over and tapped a rurp in and said, "I can't believe this is
> gonna hold me." He said, "Sure it'll hold you." I said,
> "You sure?" He said, "I'll show you." So we changed
> belay for a minute and he went out and stepped right up
> on it without testing it. Didn't know if I'd placed it well
> or not. "See, they hold!" He was about two hundred
> pounds. I said, "Oh my god!" I was terrified that I'd
> have to catch him if it gave way and he took a fall.
> Catching him was a major feat. He came back, and up I
> went placing rurps.
>
> The day before we did the climb we'd been to see a
> science fiction movie. It was about rocket ships going up
> into outer space. The name of the ship in the movie was
> Rocketship X-M. We were heading up directly to Outer
> Space, so it seemed very appropriate. We decided to call
> the route X-M and laughed hysterically about it.

X-M became a firmly established hard climb after its
first ascent in 1962. For Kor, it was just one more of a
string of new direct aid climbs. For Ament, it was one of
his earliest experiences with hard direct aid under the
tutelage of Kor. He learned a great deal from Kor
during these early experiences, and later in the sixties
was to emerge as a talented climber in his own right.

Larry Dalke: Early Experiences

Over the years, Larry Dalke emerged as the most

enigmatic figure of the 1960's. His talents on rock, both in free climbing and direct aid, were amazing. In comparison to Kor and Ament he was quiet and reserved. His ability for climbing steep rock at speed was unsurpassed. Bob Culp states, "He was the fastest climber on artificial I have ever seen. . .Dalke in a burst of genius was something to behold." Dalke's ascents were made all the more remarkable by his frequent lack of awareness of how desperately hard a particular move was. Culp writes, "I well remember Dalke with his high pitched voice shouting down uncertainly, inquiring, 'Where's it get hard?' just after negotiating some dreadful spot or other."

During the early sixties, Larry Dalke also learned from Layton Kor. High up on Redgarden Wall was an eye-catching overhanging buttress of rock. Dalke accompanied Kor on an exploration of this buttress in 1962. Larry confesses, "I just didn't know what we were getting into when we started it." They climbed up Redguard Route to the base of the main overhanging section, and Layton nailed a steep crack which led up to a cave. The quality of the rock was poor. Larry recalls, "I remember sitting in the cave up there and thinking it would never end. I was huddled way back and Layton was pulling great blocks off as he went through the roof. He led both pitches and I followed trying to bang his pitons out." The steeply overhanging nature of the route inspired them to call the climb "The Diving Board."

Sometime prior to the ascent of the Diving Board, Kor had been walking along the base of Redgarden Wall with Bob Culp. A massive overhanging roof runs the whole length of one section of the wall. Kor and Culp had already made one route over the roof, which they had surmounted using direct aid, and which they had called "Le Toit" (The Roof). (Both Kor and Culp, inspired by Buhl's book, were enamored of route names that had a European flavor.) As they walked along examining the roof, Culp recollects:

We were just wandering around looking for places to go. We found one place where there was obviously a line. Kor went bobbing up and climbed up free to underneath the roof. He pounded in an old piton and he had put in one other piton way down below. He was hanging on to the piton with one hand, leaning out looking at the crack, and it came out. There was a big bellow, and he came flying down, head first. He fell all the way from the ceiling to within about a foot from the ground (Approximately thirty feet). The second piton was just barely high enough to stop him. I saw him coming and in those days you were supposed to give dynamic belays, but I figured probably I'd better not. I stopped him as fast as I could, and it hurt him. Kor was funny about tying onto the ropes in those early days. Sometimes he would have great enormous knots that he had made up. He would forget how to tie his slings. He would tie them in

overhand knots; just take the two ends of the sling, tie it in an overhand knot, and then open it up as a loop. He had been hit in the stomach with a balled up knot when he fell, and felt so sick that we just lay around there on the ground for a while.

Kor later returned to this scene with the unsuspecting Larry Dalke. Rather than having his enthusiasm dampened by the fall, it had served only to make Kor all the more determined to finish the route. More careful this time, Kor led across the roof on direct aid and took up a belay in slings. The next lead involved some complicated direct aid climbing via a twenty-five-foot traverse and a twenty-five-foot straight-up crack. They were both impressed by the difficulty of the aid on this pitch and gave it an A.4 grading. Kor was working in Denver at the time as a bricklayer for the Kloeberdanz Construction Company. They decided to call the route Kloeberdanz, and the name has since mystified many climbers.

The First Ascent of Genesis

In 1962, the year following the ascent of the Northwest Face of Chief's Head, Bob Culp, along with Jack Turner, became involved in the first ascent of a spectacular direct aid route in Eldorado Springs Canyon named Genesis. In the summer of 1962, Turner had accompanied Kor to Yosemite and together they had climbed the Steck-Salathé route on Sentinel. During the remainder of their stay in the Valley, Kor and Turner climbed with such well known Yosemite climbers as Ivon Chouinard, Tom Frost, T.M. Herbert, and Royal Robbins. When they returned to Boulder, they had developed what Huntley Ingalls termed a "fighter pilot" mentality. Namely, they were prepared to push themselves much closer to the edge of their limits than ever before, and they were much more willing to take the risk of a fall.

Turner had climbed a number of difficult direct aid routes in Yosemite, including El Cap Tree Direct with Robbins, which had involved a good deal of A.4 nailing. On his return to Boulder, now the proud possessor of Chouinard rurps, he set about looking for an unclimbed line on which to apply these new techniques. His first attempt on a steep overhanging wall to the right of Redguard Route with Francis Raley involved a thin, twenty foot expanding flake. Turner had trouble with the flake and faced the traditional problem that, as he drove in his next piton, the lower one fell out. Eventually he solved the problem by means of a number of old-style long Simond pitons. These he was able to insert gently behind the flake without exerting sufficient pressure to cause it to expand. At the top of the flake he placed expansion bolts and established a belay. The next section of thin, incipient

The Sixties

Looking down the Red Dihedral. The leader is just starting the crux second pitch which traverses left beneath the overhang.

cracks turned him back. After a number of other attempts on the route, Turner returned with Bob Culp. He had told Culp how difficult the flake was to nail, so Culp promptly free climbed it and found it surprisingly easy. Turner succeeded this time in leading up the shallow cracks above the flake, which involved some very thin moves on rurps. Culp led a final easy pitch to the top to complete the route. The first ascent was graded A.5, but subsequent ascents, as often happens with thin aid climbs, deepened and widened the original rurp cracks, and the climb became much easier. In 1962 Genesis was the first route in the Boulder region to receive an A.5 guidebook rating.

The Naked Edge

In 1962 Kor's interest in the Naked Edge, which had repulsed he and Komito in 1961, was rekindled. Kor, accompanied by Culp, was able to force a route via the incipient cracks between the slab and the overhang. This pitch was solid A.4. at the time of Kor's first ascent, but later became much easier as subsequent ascents deepened hairline cracks at the thinnest section. Kor and Culp continued upwards but were unable to find a line up the steep final edge; they finished the climb via a dihedral slightly to its left. Kor returned in 1964 with Rick Horn and was able to follow the line of the Edge all the way to the summit. The Naked Edge has become one of the great classic climbs of Colorado since its conception in the mind of Stanley Sheperd and its successful first ascent by Kor and Horn. In later years, significant developments which epitomized modern free climbing were to be played out on its steep walls.

The Red Dihedral

High on Micky Maus Wall above Eldorado Springs Canyon, Kor spotted a long overhanging dihedral on a wall of striking red sandstone. Accompanied by Dalke and Mayrose, he climbed the route using continuous direct aid on the two long crux pitches. A hanging belay in slings at the top of the dihedral was the take-off point for the final pitch underneath an enormous roof. Dalke remembers that they did the climb on a cold January day and that he was wondering if they would have enough time to finish it. "Paul Mayrose and I were hanging in that sling belay for an awful long time," he recollects. Kor led under the roof on direct aid and found it extremely hard. Insecure pin placements behind loose flakes gave difficult and dangerous nailing. A fall would probably have sent Kor, splat, into the opposite wall of the dihedral. Kor eventually made it over the roof and was soon shouting, "Come on." Dalke, mid-way up the pitch, was horrified to hear him yelling,

"Better hurry, Dalke! The rope's rubbing over an edge. It's gonna cut you off if you fall!" Once again it was Kor's perverse sense of humor and Dalke's panic-stricken rush to be saved from iminent death was unnecessary. They called the climb the Red Dihedral. Dalke remembers that Kor placed one expansion bolt under the roof. Later climbers, unable to emulate Kor's skill in direct aid, have added more expansion bolts until the climb now sprouts a total of three, making the crux pitch far easier than on the first ascent.

During the early years of the 1960's, Kor's direct aid routes, such as The Naked Edge, Nord Wand, The Red Dihedral, and the Eldorado roof routes, were among the most difficult in the country. After climbing the North America Wall in Yosemite in 1973, Jimmy Dunn whimsically commented, "It was good practice for the harder aid routes in Eldorado."

The Black Canyon of the Gunnison

In 1960, Bob LaGrange had returned from a sight-seeing trip to the Black Canyon of the Gunnison. Bubbling over with enthusiasm, he showed Layton Kor color slides of massive granite cliffs bigger than either of them had climbed before. It was just the kind of place they had been looking for. A few days later the pair assembled their equipment, drove to the Canyon, and completed the first ascent of a 1,700 foot route on its south rim.

In 1963, Kor visited the Logan Mountains with Royal Robbins, Dick McCracken, and Jim McCarthy, and they put up a new Grade VI route called Proboscis. In 1963 Proboscis had a reputation for being the hardest big wall climb on a remote mountain in North America. Shortly after returning from Proboscis, Kor, McCarthy, and Tex Bossier embarked on a new route on Chasm View in the Black Canyon. The 1,700 foot route took three and a half days and involved two bivouacs. The crux pitch high up the wall consisted of a series of large overhangs through a section of bad rock. Kor, after studying the overhangs for a while, turned round to Bossier and McCarthy and in an ominous voice said, "I think I'd better lead this pitch. I'm not married." The pitch took him eight hours, and he was later to say that it was one of the most difficult artificial pitches he had ever climbed. After the climb, McCarthy said that it was more difficult than Proboscis. By 1976, the route had not received a second ascent.

In 1964, Kor returned with Larry Dalke, and they were able to climb a new route on the south face of Chasm View in the Black Canyon. Kor later wrote, "This is one of the most difficult climbs in the area, comparable with the north face of Sentinel Rock via the Steck-Salathé route."

The Black Canyon of the Gunnison.

119

The Painted Wall, showing the approximate line followed by Kor, Dalke, and Culp, on their unsuccessful attempt.

One of the most spectacular formations in the Black Canyon is a 2,500 foot cliff called the Painted Wall. White veins of pegmatite zigzag through purple granite and gneiss, giving the Painted Wall its name. Fractured by centuries of weathering, the rock is loose and unstable, and much of the wall overhangs.

In 1962, Kor had climbed the northern arete of the Painted Wall with Jim Disney. In 1967, he climbed the southern arete with Larry Dalke, Wayne Goss, and Mike Covington. On both of these climbs, Kor was able to look over onto the main face of the Painted Wall and to contemplate the possibility of a route. In 1967 Kor, Bob Culp, and Larry Dalke made an attempt on the Painted Wall. The result was an epic of major proportions.

Starting up the center of the wall from the top of a large grassy terrace, they immediately encountered rotten rock, worse than anything they had previously climbed in the Canyon. After a number of difficult, loose pitches, they arrived underneath a massive overhang. Culp recounted the next few hours in a tape-recorded interview in 1975:

> The ceiling went way off to the left and then up. It was Kor's lead. He went nailing around the overhang and was busy on the pitch for two or three hours. Dalke and I were hanging in slings dozing and freezing....a storm was moving in, and it was getting late on in the afternoon. It was a long pitch, continuously overhanging, and ended up nowhere, just at a couple of pins on more overhanging wall. Kor had done two or three rurp placements in a row. In some places he had done sky hooks in a row. It was a fiercely difficult artificial pitch.
>
> When my turn came to jumar, there was no rope left to lower me out. Kor had run out the full length of the rope around the corner, leaving me with about a thirty foot pendulum. I put my jumars on, tied the pack on, turned off my mind, and jumped. I took a fantastic pendulum and ended up way out from the rock. There I was hanging on the rope with Kor cackling down, "You should see the expression on your face."

The next section of the wall looked worse—rotten and continually overhanging. Dalke led up a little way and said he didn't think it would go. Kor made an attempt and after an hour had made little progress. Reluctantly, he allowed Culp and Dalke to convince him that perhaps retreat was the prudent thing, and they prepared to rappel. Culp's account continues:

> The sickening thing was that, to get off, we had to rappel from the two bad anchor pins clear to the end of the hauling line, which ended up twenty feet from the wall. From there, the plan was to pendulum in underneath a big ceiling, and we had no idea if it could be done. Kor took off first. We just hung there watching. He rappelled down, then disappeared under the ceiling. He pendulumed back out, and then he swung back under and grabbed onto something, apparently a pin, and eventually secured himself. It was one of the most horrifying descents I've ever made.

Later, Kor returned to the Painted Wall with Larry Dalke. They attempted the face again, but problems with disintegrating bolt drills led them to abandon the attempt. In the late 1960's, Wayne Goss and Rusty Baillie made attempts on the Painted Wall, but were also unsuccessful.

THE EAST FACE OF LONGS PEAK

Second Ascent of the Diamond: The Yellow Wall

By the summer of 1962, Kor had an impressive string of new climbs behind him. His experience on the Diagonal with Northcutt, and on the Northwest Face of Chief's Head with Culp, had given him a taste for new routes on big alpine faces. In the summer of 1962, he decided to try for a major prize: a new route on the Diamond.

After going through the lengthy check-out process, Kor, Bob Culp, and Jim McCarthy were "certified" by the Park Rangers as fit for an attempt on the wall. Approaching the face, both Culp and McCarthy went down with a virus. Rather than abandon the attempt after all the preparation that had taken place, Kor roped in Charlie Roskosz, a member of the support party. Roskosz's wife didn't even know he was on the face until she read about it in the newspaper a day later! The climb was successful, and Kor and he reached the summit of Longs after one bivouac on the face. On his return, Roskosz was hauled up before the local magistrate and received a fine for his unauthorized ascent.

Prior to the attempt, a five page application form provided by the Park Service had to be filled out. Each climber, and each member of the support party, was supposed to personally sign the form. Culp had been designated with the responsibility of seeing that the form was filled out. Rather than going to the trouble of tracking everyone down, he had simply forged all of the names. After the successful climb, as Roskosz was being taken to task for having "illegally" climbed the wall, someone informed Culp that the Rangers were wise to his forgery and that he had better go along and clear the matter up before they banned climbing on the Diamond altogether. Inside the Chief Ranger's office, Culp launched into a feeble series of excuses and was doing his best to explain the forgery, when, in mid-sentence, he noticed an expression of blank incomprehension on the Rangers' faces. Culp was never sure afterwards if he had been tricked, or had misunderstood the situation, but it turned out the Rangers had no suspicion at all of his forgery! Hastily covering up his mistake, Culp mumbled some inanities and left the office red-faced.

Jack of Diamonds

In the summer of 1963, Kor made a one-day ascent of the Rearick-Kamps route on the Diamond with Royal Robbins. Two days later, this pair put up a new route on the Diamond, also in the incredibly fast time of one day from Broadway, over the summit of Longs, and down to the shelter cabin at Chasm Lake. They called the new route Jack of Diamonds. Royal Robbins described their experiences in an account which arrived, after two years of anticipation, in January 1977—only a few weeks before this book went to press:

Dear Bob,
You asked me to reminisce a bit about the first ascent of Jack of Diamonds which Layton Kor and I did in the summer of 1963. I remember that summer fondly. I was doing lots of climbing, was fit, and Liz and I had saved enough money to travel and climb as we pleased. I spent a lot of time around Boulder that year, making the most of the rich lode of climbing opportunities offered by the eastern Rockies. I climbed in Eldorado and Boulder Canyons, fell off Ament Routes on Flagstaff, couldn't get high enough to fall off Gill Routes in the marvelous Split Rocks, scrapped skin on the Owls and Sundance, and came to grips with the prince of Colorado walls, the Diamond of Longs Peak.

It's a long but lovely walk up to Chasm Lake. I remember more the loveliness, at this distance, than the length. Embedded in my memory are pictures of the pines and twisted aspen, the fresh stream bubbling downward, the wildflowers, and, up high, the meadows and lakes. It has always been a wonder to me that the Colorado Rockies, which appear so desolate, barren, and dry from a distance, can present to the visitor such an abundance of alps, wildflowers, lakes, and streams.

There were a number of parties camping in and about the stone shelter at Chasm Lake when Liz, Layton and I arrived. We were ambitious to make the second ascent of

They Scaled the Sheer Face of Longs Peak

Charles Roskosz, 26, left, a University of Colorado student, and Layton Kor, 24, of Boulder, right, a part-time bricklayer, became the second team in history Sunday to scale the Diamond face of 14,255-foot Longs Peak in Rocky Mountain National Park. They spent 19 grueling hours, rode out a hail storm and survived a slip which plummeted Kor a few feet before his safety rope checked him to conquer the sheer cliff face. (See story on page 1.)

Denver Post Photos by Lowell Georgia

Top. Kor leading on the one-day ascent of D.1. *Royal Robbins.*

Bottom. Robbins emerging at the top of D.1. *Layton Kor.*

D-1, because of its reputation as a Yosemite wall in an alpine setting, and also simply because the Rearick-Kamps route was an elegant line up a stunning face. We were doubly ambitious, for we hoped to get up in a day.

I knew there was no one in the country, perhaps in the world, at that moment, with whom I stood a better chance of climbing the Diamond in one day than with Layton Kor. He was fast. Kor, in fact, had never developed the knack of climbing at any speed other than flat out. He was always in a hurry, and climbed every route, even the most trivial, as if he were racing a storm to the summit.

Climbing with Kor, one could not remain unaffected by his tumultuous energy. It was stressful, because to climb with him as an equal required that one function at the limit of one's abilities. Layton was ever alert to a weak moment, and perceiving one, would pounce with the ever-ready phrase, "Maybe I should take this lead?"

Kor was a phenomenon. He was the first climber to break the hegemony which Californians had long enjoyed in Yosemite. Until Kor arrived, it was folk wisdom among Yosemite climbers that *everyone* who came there—no matter how they might star on their home ground—*every* climber on his first visit to Yosemite suffered a decline in his personal estimation of his climbing worth. Yosemite would inevitably take the piss out of the arrogant visitor. This was mostly due to the peculiar nature of Yosemite climbing, which tended toward holdlessness and strenuousness. But Layton wasn't daunted. He astonished us all by his ability to immediately do the harder routes in the Valley, and in record time as well!

I had great respect for Kor, and this would grow during our ascents of the Diamond. But, more than respect, I liked Layton. He was a climber's climber, which is to say, he didn't play to the crowd, and he climbed for the right reasons, that is, to satisfy himself. He wasn't the sort of fellow to step on a piton and later claim a free ascent, because to him that would be utterly pointless. It wasn't what others thought of his climbing, but what *he* thought, that counted.

Layton was certainly highly competitive, and inwardly driven to make an impact upon climbing history. His list of first ascents of technically difficult rock climbs, both free and aid, is perhaps unmatched by any American climber. But Kor was one of the very few highly competitive climbers who never criticized the efforts and achievements of others. He was interested in action, life, joking conversation, and plans for the next climb. In fact, although he never talked about religion, Kor was a sort of natural Christian, generous when others were wrong, and not in the habit of finding fault with his neighbor. There was one exception to this. I once heard Layton express scorn for a Coloradan who had made a tasteless bolt route up one of Kor's favorite sandstone spires in the Utah desert.

During the afternoon of July 12, Layton and I left the shelter cabin and trod the fine brown granite along the south shore of Chasm Lake. We were soon on Mills Glacier and then followed Lambs Slide to Kieners Traverse, which brought us to North Broadway, and a several hundred foot descent to our bivouac at the base of the Diamond. It was comfortable, and our sleeping bags assured a good night's sleep.

Our ascent went smoothly, except for a ten-foot fall when Kor pulled an aid pin. The icy chute at the top of the wall provided interesting variety to what was otherwise a straightforward, if difficult, technical rock climb. That Rearick and Kamps had climbed this route with only four bolts was evidence not just of their technical competence, but even more of a stern, anti-bolt discipline which had its roots in Yosemite climbing at that time; a discipline which, though occasionally violated, would later prevail in American mountaineering.

According to Bob Culp's prodigious memory, we did D-1 in sixteen hours. Sounds about right. At any rate, we reached the refuge before dark.

After two days rest, we were back on Broadway, this time by way of the five-hundred-foot North Chimney. This approach was shorter, but not without its dangers. We climbed it unroped with packs, and at times I felt we were engaged in a daring enterprise. There were several unpleasant passages, and at the top a steep section of loose rock. Layton swarmed up it, but I was thwarted by a hold out of reach. Kor, seeing my distress, lowered a vast paw which I gratefully clutched and used to reach safe ground. I excused myself with thoughts of a heavy pack and lack of reach, conveniently forgetting how often shorter climbers than I had managed stretches where I deemed a long arm essential. Hoping to avoid a bivouac, we started even earlier than we had on D.1. I remember Kor swarming up the first pitch, pulling off a great block of loose rock which crashed down the North Chimney.

One of the lovely things about an east face in the high mountains is that the morning sun so quickly takes the night chill from the air. For a while, everything seems warm, secure, and safe. Hard to imagine suffering from the cold in such a place. Quite different from Yosemite, where the breezeless morning sun is an enemy. But mountain weather is ever fickle, partly because we are ever foolish, wanting to believe it is being nice just for us, when it is just one of her inconstant moods.

By noon, the winds were being rude and clouds swirled overhead. Now, to lead was a pleasure and to belay a cold hell. Not that either of us fiddled about on the leads. We were competing against each other, yes. After all, each of our lives was given to climbing, and we both wished to excel. In this sense, each of us was an obstacle in the other's path, or so it seemed. In this sense we *were* competing—but our cooperation was far more important. Thus, it is off the mark to say we climbed the Diamond rapidly because we were competing. It is more accurate to say we climbed fast in spite of the running dog of competition which raced with us to the summit.

The East Face of Longs loses its benign aspect when the sun disappears westward. The wind brings numbing cold to fingers and cheeks, and snow whirls about. Discomfort is intensified when one is in a hanging belay, becoming impatient even with the speed of Layton Kor.

I quote from a note about the ascent which appeared in the 1964 *American Alpine Journal*: "Racing against the setting sun to avoid a bad night in slings, Kor led the last pitch, a long, strenuous jam-crack. On my last reserves I struggled up this final pitch, topped the Diamond, and shook the hand of a great climber."

It was a long walk down. Mile after mile through the night I paced steadily behind Kor, through the Boulder Field—which seemed an enormous area. Kor showed no signs of weakening, and I forced myself to thrust my legs forward, long strides trying to match his. I wouldn't weaken. I would keep up behind this natural force that wouldn't slow down. Aching feet, legs, back. Mind numbed, but there was the light of the shelter; crowded, sordid, smelly, but warm and welcoming. I well remember Liz, but, oddly, I can't recall booze. Ah, I have grown so sophisticated that I can't imagine a climb like that with a walk like that, not being followed by wine, as well as love.

What's Gonna Happen if We Get Stuck? The Diagonal Direct

When Kor climbed the Diagonal on the East Face of Longs in 1959, Northcutt had been the driving force. With the second ascent of the Diamond behind him, Kor felt that it might be possible to follow the main crack line of the Diagonal to Broadway, rather than taking the long traverse to the right two-thirds of the way up the face. In 1963 Kor spent a week climbing on the lower East Face of Longs with Tex Bossier. The pair climbed a number of new routes, including Grey Pillar and Crack of Delight, and felt in strong shape. They decided to attempt the direct finish to the Diagonal. Bossier's tape-recorded narrative tells of the desperate adventure this was to become:

I had dropped out of school and had a job as a hod carrier working for Kor. He just loved to shout, "Hey, mud." (You're supposed to bring the mortar, so my name was mud.) We decided we were going to try the direct finish on the Diagonal. I had expected the thing to be tremendously difficult from its reputation, and we

The East Face of Longs. (1) Diagonal Direct. (2) Yellow Wall. (3) Jack of Diamonds. (4) Enos Mills Wall (First winter ascent).

treated it as such. I was very apprehensive. We were using direct aid where we didn't need to in the lower sections, but there wasn't any really extreme climbing. We were climbing very fast.

Going over the overhang wasn't anything as bad as I had expected. I had all these horror visions in my mind....It was a little bit messy because there was water coming down it and we had to climb through it. A thing that slowed us down was bolt chopping. When Northcutt first climbed the Diagonal, the only pitons around were ex-army, and he placed a lot of bolts to make things secure. A lot of them were belay bolts. I was kind of irritated at Kor doing this. I just wanted to say, "To hell with the damn bolt, let's go!" He had "style" in his mind in those days. If a bolt was there and it wasn't supposed to be there, then you were supposed to get rid of it.

We got to where the traverse started. Didn't take us too long to get there. About four hours. We could have done it in three hours, had we been less cautious and not spent time bolt chopping. Right there, a storm came in. It started to rain. We talked about it, and under the circumstances it looked harder to do the traverse than to go straight up. We also thought it wasn't going to be that bad, and we didn't want to go down, but the nature of the climbing changed dramatically. The face became scooped out with boiler plate slabs, and the cracks were very shallow.

The storm was really getting bad. Rain was severe. We still thought we were better going up. We had a feeling about the difficulties of retreat and thought it was safer to continue. Water from the upper part of the wall was channeled down the crack system. It was coming down the rope and ending up in my swami belt, just like a water spout. I was freaked out. Then it started getting cold, but we were committed. It was getting later and later and we were making extremely slow progress. It started to turn into snow, and ice, and the wall started to freeze up. Fog also was coming down. Kor was off somewhere above, and we couldn't even see each other. It was extremely cold by this time. I would go into uncontrollable shivering and cramps on the belays. I had the feeling that if we didn't get off the climb that day, I'd

Tex Bossier.

never be able to live through it.

It turned into a full-fledged, full-blown storm. There was a Ranger with a telescope on Mt. Lady Washington, and he said it was a hell of a storm. We just weren't prepared for the conditions. We didn't have equipment for it. We didn't have any bivouac gear. We had down jackets, but they were completely soaked before the temperature dropped. We had no idea where we were in the fog. I have no idea how difficult the climbing really was. We were really scared. The conditions were so bad. In the guidebook they mention Kor getting knocked out of his stirrups by an avalanche. That's true. He was leading one of the scooped-out sections. I heard this hollering, and screaming, and cursing. "What's going on!" I shouted. We were enshrouded in fog and I couldn't see him. It just knocked him straight out of his stirrups, backwards.

We started leaving pitons in place. We didn't even clean the last pitch of the climb. We just left everything. I kept thinking, "What's gonna happen if we get stuck? Who is there to come and rescue us?" We just had to keep going. I thought, "There's only one person in the whole of the United States who can get me off this climb, and I'm with him! If I get stuck, that's it."

Kor belayed me to Broadway. We got the pack up and were going to coil the haul rope. Part of it was over the edge, down the face, and it got stuck! Kor said, "To hell with it!" That was unprecedented. Never in my whole climbing career had I even considered abandoning a rope...and all the pitons? I wasn't arguing though.

We started to traverse Broadway. There are some hairy-assed spots on Broadway. I knew Kor was pressed. He led off on a traverse. There was freshly fallen snow over previous icy snow. He sank in up to his knee in the new snow. There was one steep place, fifty to sixty degrees. The ledge was very narrow, with the Diamond above you and that whole lower wall below. Kor nailed in a piton for a belay and said, "On belay." Crossing in his footsteps, I got about half way across when some of the snow gave way and I half fell over backwards. One leg stayed in the step. I was on my back with my head looking down the lower wall. The whole panorama of the face went by as I fell backwards. I expected to go shooting off into space and take a horrible pendulum across to Kor. It was in slow motion. Everything was on film through my eyeballs. But one of my legs stayed. I got straight up and went over to Kor.

.....He's got one knife blade in, that you could take out with your fingers! That you could take out with your fingers, for God's sake! I was about eighty feet horizontal to him when I slipped. I said, "God, Layton. This thing would just never have held." "I know, I know," he said. He said that when he saw me fall over backwards, his heart just went into his throat and he knew we were both dead. It wasn't as though he'd looked for the best belay. He just found the first place and stuck in a knife blade. He knew it was inadequate, but that was the situation. I said, "Look, if the belays are going to be like this, should we stay roped?" "Yes," he said, "we stay roped."

"O.K.," I said, and we took off again, making our way over to Alexander's and Mills Glacier.

Obviously, we were in an emergency pressure situation, and we were not performing according to the accepted rules of climbing. This wasn't the "adrenaline rush" that people talk about in climbing. This was the

The support party at the Chasm Lake cabin prior to the first winter ascent of the Diamond. *Layton Kor.*

constant pumping of adrenaline the whole time. "You gotta go, you gotta move. Time's running out." The feeling was that if you let down in any way you just wouldn't make it. It was a momentous thing for me. I've never in my whole life had anything like that happen to me, before or since.

We got down to the shelter and the storm lasted for days. Next day we looked up and could see the wall. It was encased in ice. It was completely frozen over. If we'd been up there, we'd just have been a goddamned icicle along with everything else. I said to Kor afterwards, "I don't think I would have made it if we'd had to stay the night up there." Kor replied, "Yes you would. You'd have made it if I had to stay up all night and beat on you with my hammer." But the way he said that, I also had the feeling that he didn't know for sure whether he would have made it or not.

Kor and Bossier had experienced the full brunt of the bad weather conditions which Northcutt had so feared during his attempts on the Diagonal in 1958 and 1959. Events proved that his concerns were justified. The relatively low angle of the Diagonal (it leans back at approximately eighty degrees) had put Kor and Bossier right in the path of water, snow, and rocks coming down the face from Broadway and the Notch Couloir. The Diamond, in comparison, was relatively safe. Its overhanging walls deflected any falling debris out beyond the range of climbers. After stories of Kor and Bossier's epic filtered down, the Diagonal Direct did not receive a second ascent until Michael Covington and Billy Westbay repeated it in 1975. They found the climbing hard, and found Kor and Bossier's pitons in the last pitch up to Broadway—silent witnesses to an epic of years gone by.

The Diamond: First Winter Ascent

During the winter of 1966, Layton Kor made a trip to Europe and became involved in the attempt led by John Harlin to climb a direct route on the North Face of the Eiger in winter. Harlin was killed during the attempt while jumaring a fixed rope which broke. Kor was greatly distressed by Harlin's death, and on his return to Colorado his attitude towards climbing vacillated between disinterest and his old well-known enthusiasm. Shortly after Kor's return to Colorado, Wayne Goss asked him if he was interested in making a winter attempt on the Diamond. Kor and Goss had climbed together occasionally since 1964, and Goss had learned much from Kor during his beginning years. By 1967, Goss had developed into an expert climber in his own right and had become interested in the possibility of a winter ascent of the Diamond. Climbers had long talked of this possibility, but no serious attempt had been made.

Kor said he was not interested in trying the Diamond in winter, especially after his Eiger experiences, and

Goss teamed up with Bob Culp for an attempt on Christmas Eve, 1966. They reached Broadway and established a bivouac. The next morning they heard over the two-way radio they were carrying that a big storm was moving in, and that three youths who had attempted to climb Longs the day before had not returned. Abandoning their attempt but leaving their equipment on Broadway, Goss and Culp eventually found the three, frostbitten after a night out, and helped them down the mountain.

Later that winter, Goss and Culp managed to persuade Kor to join them in another attempt. Kor's account of the successful outcome, entitled "On The Granite Wall," was published in *Trail and Timberline* in 1967, and is reprinted here in its entirety:

We arrived at the shelter cabin about 2:30 p.m. on March 4 to find superb conditions dominating the

Traversing Broadway on the winter ascent.

surroundings below the East Face of Longs Peak. Bob Culp and Wayne Goss, my two ropemates, standing nearby agreed that to call this winter climbing, when conditions were almost summer-like, was a bit unfair.

Close behind was our helpful support party, consisting of Dany Smith, John Pinamont, and Tom Ruetz, all members of Boulder's Rocky Mountain Rescue Group. It was thanks to them that the crushing loads with our climbing gear had reached the cabin.

After a short rest, we watched the openings in the mist give us a view of the colorful, vertical Diamond. Happy with the prospect of a winter first, we all dug into the monumental task of shoveling snow out of the cabin. Before long, steam rose from the cookers and soon hot soup, meat, and pots of warm drinks kept us happy until the cold drove us deep into our sleeping bags. As usual I had trouble sleeping, and to add to my misery the wind picked up and the howling noise remained all through the night. By morning six inches of snow had fallen and our winter had returned.

Before feeling the effects of our light breakfast, we left our support party and began hiking through the fresh snow to the bottom of the East Face. An hour later we ascended Lambs Slide and were at the beginning of Broadway. Culp, who had not been feeling well up to this point, became most uncomfortable with a sore throat. Knowing this was no place for anyone who was ill, Bob left immediately for the shelter cabin. Wayne and I roped up at this point; to go any further without protection would have been unwise. After the first rope length of traversing we could see that the white band we were on was little more than a steep bank of unstable snow. At the end of every lead we were forced to burrow deep into the snow to reach rock for piton anchors. After about two hours of dangerous wading and one close call with an avalanche which sloughed off inches below us, we reached our bivouac site below the Diamond. It was very late so we began digging out a cave with a cooking pot as we had dropped our shovel during the traverse of Broadway. Cold and near-darkness kept us at a fair pace till finally we reached the rocky floor and large amounts of "Bivvy" gear left by Bob and Wayne on an earlier attempt. After sorting out the mess and rigging a hammock above the bivouac to keep out the storm, we retired to our bags completely spent. Again our cooker sent out the blue flames which promised much-needed food and liquids. After our snack, sleep followed. Around three o'clock, a piton which supported the hammock above gave way—leaving us half-buried in the new snow. Once again our soup pot was put to work and peaceful rest seemed hours away.

The morning arrived too soon and the weather was still quite bad. We gobbled down some food, stuffed our packs full of gear, tied on the 150-foot ropes, and worked our way through the snow to the beginning of our new route 100 feet away. The climb began with mixed climbing across steep slabs plastered in snow. Our very first rope-length took us an hour and a half and ended on a tiny stance in the middle of nowhere. As we were directly above the north chimney the powerful wind from the bottom of the East Face funneled up the walls carrying sharp snow crystals which forced us to put on our ski goggles.

Wayne quickly led the next pitch, climbing up a slippery groove well over 70 degrees. After he had

anchored the ropes and pulled up the packs, I prusiked up, removing the pitons until we both shared the same ledge. Still no improvement in the weather, and our two-way radio which the Park Service had been kind enough to lend us, promised even worse conditions for the next day.

Preferring to try again in a day or so (after all, who could want to climb in bad weather?) we were soon on our way down the wall, leaving fixed ropes behind us until we had reached the easy snow slope at the bottom of the north chimney.

The next couple of days we spent at the shelter cabin, mostly listening to the transistor radio and eating. The weather remained windy and cold, and our food supply dwindled till finally we all packed out toward Boulder for fresh supplies.

Just a day later Wayne and I returned to Longs. We spent the entire day hiking from the parking lot until finally the last fixed ropes carried us to our bivouac on Broadway. The weather had improved considerably and our bivouac that night was quite fun. We rose early the next morning convinced we would get our wall and soon were together at the beginning of the ropes.

I snapped the prusik handles (mechanical versions of the prusik knots) onto the fixed line, applied my weight, and watched loose snow free itself from the long red rope leading to our high point. After finishing the diagonal struggle I slid the handles down the rope to Wayne and soon we shared the tiny perch, where days before, bad weather had forced us to retreat.

After organizing our equipment we ascended the third rope-length of the climb. This vertical step, which was entirely artificial, ended on a mossy ledge in a snow-filled corner 130 feet above. Several sound anchors gave mental rest as Goss rapidly nailed his way up another exciting pitch deep into unknown terrain. An occasional gust of wind and the feather-like snow that followed made us happy with our warm clothing. After Wayne had rigged another sling belay 80 feet above, he hauled up the packs, while I removed the belay pitons which provided security on the dangerously steep wall.

It was always nice to be moving, for while in motion the warmth seeped through our systems and chased out the cold and misery we endured on the silent stances. About noon I began the fifth lead of the climb. This airy experience followed a wide crack on the edge of a 100-foot pillar. I had nearly reached its top when a protruding piton tore a large hole in my down jacket. Unable to stop, I continued struggling up the bad-width crack until some small footholds provided rest. The now-useless down spiraled like falling leaves toward Goss, who hung in slings 75 feet below. It was very late in the day when I left the comfort of a two-foot ledge on top of the pillar and began hammering long pins deep into the 90-degree wall. If we were lucky a bivouac ledge awaited us at the end of the lead.

One hundred feet up, the rock became rotten and the smooth diagonal overhangs stopped all progress. I was trying desperately to place a piton on my left, when the tiny angle holding my weight popped out and a terrifying 20-foot plunge into the dusk followed. When it ended I was swinging upside down squinting toward Goss, whose bright smile showed it had been an easy catch.

I quickly climbed hand over hand up the rope, drove a larger piton into the same crack and once again studied

Goss on the Diamond - note the north wall hammer. *Layton Kor.*

Kor seconding. *Wayne Goss.*

the traverse to the left. A thin sling hooked over a tiny knob held my weight, while I nervously placed a poor piton upside down beneath the roof. Using this for balance, I left the little security I had and tiptoed on the very edge of my double boots across a slab which ended in an overhanging snow-filled corner. It had turned completely dark as I hung from my tortured fingers, placing several pitons to secure the belay.

"Lightning" Goss, who was in remarkable shape, removed all the pitons in just a few minutes, and soon headlamps cast out two beams halfway up the Diamond.

"Just above is the bivouac," I told Wayne, not really sure of anything except how lousy I felt. As Wayne belayed I sighted along the flickering light, which cut into the darkness, yielding a 1½-inch crack. Three aid pitons put me on a small snow shelf 15 feet above Wayne and

with the last of my energy I stamped out a small ledge in the snow. Again I placed the necessary belay anchors and began hauling up the packs which felt like three mail bags full of lead. Soon a bright shower of sparks lit up the large piton on which Wayne was hammering, and before long he pulled out the last piton of the day. I slowly worked my way into the sleeping bag while Wayne, without a word, dug through the packs removing food, cooking gear, and other items we would need for the night. After joining me in idle comfort, he fired up the stove to provide us with the only food we could consume, hot raspberry Jell-O.

Even though we had to remain sitting all night, it was warm, reasonably comfortable, and we only woke up occasionally to change positions. Morning arrived with the sun gods and their yellow warmth which we

Kor at the bivouac. *Wayne Goss.*

thankfully absorbed along with more hot Jell-O.

Stiff swollen fingers kept us from smiling as we sorted out the mess from the night before. After things were a bit straightened out, more pounding, which inserted our metal spikes, carried us up a huge overhanging openbook above the bivouac. One hundred and twenty feet up I crawled into another sling belay, a position which was overhanging Goss and the bivouac site by 10 feet. We carefully nailed the last 70 feet of the openbook up, to, and over a three-foot roof; then belayed 30 feet above in slings from a horizontal crack system. This thin and

Goss on the summit. *Layton Kor.*

brittle crack cut all the way across the Diamond to the well-known table ledge. The view at this point was quite spectacular as everything below to Broadway was overhanging.

Artificial climbing on the Diamond in winter, as we were finding out, is a slow and delicate process, and our snail-like pace was almost sure to provide us with another "bivvy" on the wall. The next rope-length was even more rotten and every well-placed piton sent granular, red rock dashing all over the mountain. After I had climbed another 130 feet, the last 10 of which consisted of a horizontal traverse on "spooky" knife blades, I set up the fifth hanging belay of the climb. While Wayne removed the pitons I viewed the crack system 40 feet to the left where I had joined the master of technical climbing, Royal Robbins, on a one-day ascent of the wall.

Once again darkness set in and as our headlamps were giving us trouble, we almost expected a night in slings on the blank wall. Both Wayne and I agreed to make the top if at all possible, as we were still worried about the unsettled weather. Fifty feet above, another large roof provided a strenuous ten minutes and a spectacular view into the depths. Above the overhang the crack widened and an occasional free move was needed to eliminate the use of expansion bolts as our biggest pitons (4 inches) were not large enough. After many minutes of struggling with rope slings and my headlamp cord I somehow managed to force several pitons deep into the icy crack, setting up the last belay of the climb. Wayne soon shared my position at the hanging "spaghetti gardens."

After a few minutes rest we changed places and I led into the night with a blinking headlamp until the wild blast of the wind told me it was all over. We arrived at the top of the wall at about 10 p.m. and bivouacked on the spot. The wind kept us awake most of the night and our short walk to the summit of Longs the next morning was a tiring, breathless undertaking. Even that was soon over and I shook hands with my tremendous partner for the first winter ascent of the Diamond—an experience we would long remember.

The winter ascent of the Diamond, via a new route, was a tour de force for Kor and Goss. It was to turn out to be one of Kor's last major climbs.

End of an Era

By 1967, during a decade of phenomenal climbing, Layton Kor had firmly established himself as Colorado's leading rock climber. After his early beginnings, scrambling solo on the rocks of Boulder Canyon and Eldorado, his climbing talents had earned him international recognition, and the name Kor evoked respect throughout the climbing world.

Kor's legend was based on more than technical ability on rock. At six-feet-five-inches, he literally loomed over his contemporaries, radiating nervous energy. His companions felt his strength and experienced his compelling psychological drive. Culp has written of Kor's sheer "animal energy" which would see him through the worst situations on the rock face, and which would also inspire caution and respect in those with whom he climbed.

During his travels, Kor gained a reputation as one of climbing's most colorful characters. His boisterous manner, lusty good humor, and steady supply of ribald jokes were well known.

Given this panoply of characteristics, Kor could easily have become a disliked and feared figure. His strength was prodigious and gave him the potential to deliberately, or inadvertently, abuse those with whom he climbed. Yet, invariably, Kor's contemporaries remember him with admiration, with love, and, above all, with respect. He frequently took them to the brink of disaster, but, like any good father telling a young son a horror story, he could always transform the horror to pantomime, and assure a happy ending.

The key to Kor's paradox lies in the fact that his sterner characteristics were balanced by a constant, underlying quality of childlike glee. Paradoxically, despite his oaths and crudeness, Kor was a perpetual innocent. His toothy grin, raucous laughter, and sheer delight in the exuberant expression of his physical energies, softened him and made his potentially overwhelming qualities lovable.

Of his more forceful characteristics, those who knew Kor well during his climbing years say that he frequently exhibited the qualities of a man possessed. A driving inner tension gnawed at him. His way of escaping from this sensation was to be active in a way which totally occupied his mind and body. His climbs, pushed to the limit of the possible, served this function well. On belay ledges his tension would mount amidst inactivity, and he would begin to explode. Once the climb was over, he was rarely satisfied, and would soon become keyed up and wired to go again.

In 1967, shortly after the Eiger tragedy, Kor began to reconsider his involvement in climbing. Harlin had possessed tremendous strength, both of will and body. Kor could not imagine anyone that strong dying. The realization of Harlin's death hit him hard. Also, after ten years of high standard routes, Kor's interest in climbing was naturally waning.

By 1968 it was becoming clear to Kor that climbing offered only a short-term solution to his driving inner needs. He confided to friends that climbing was becoming a dead-end road.

Those who knew Kor closely in 1968 say that he regretted and felt guilty about some of his escapades. A small-town boy originally, and a bricklayer by trade, Kor lacked sophistication during his early climbing years. His climbing had taken him to many parts of America, to Yosemite, and to Europe. It was a giddy whirl of new experiences. Charismatic, he was attractive to women, and his affairs became an important part of his legend. In Yosemite, and at the Vagabond Club in Leysin, Switzerland, drugs were commonplace. Like many others during the sixties, Kor experimented.

Kor had originally come from a religious family, and in 1968 he found himself attracted to religion as an alternative to climbing. He became interested in the Jehovah's Witnesses. In the summer of 1968, Kor climbed a last route in the Black Canyon of the Gunnison with Bob Culp. The two spent the night on the bivouac ledge discussing spiritual matters. Shortly after this, Kor was to forsake climbing and become a devoted Jehovah's Witness. Colorado climbing lost the individual who had been the major driving force of the sixties. Culp has written, "The image of Kor's rangy figure striding to and fro from the Sink, arms waving excitedly, with a troupe of eager young climbers in his wake, and his, 'Roberto—there's this fantastic wall I've spotted that's *got* to be climbed...' will be what I remember longest."

REFERENCES

1. Robert Culp, *personal communication,* 1976.
2. Ray Northcutt, *personal communication,* 1976.
3. Robert Culp, "Boulder Rock Climbers: Faces of the Sixties," *Trail and Timberline,* November, 1970, p. 239.
4. David F. Rearick and Robert F. Kamps, "Report of the First Ascent of the Diamond," in Paul Nesbitt, *Longs Peak: Its Story and a Climbing Guide* (Colorado: Out West Commercial and County Printers, Inc., 1972), p. 50.
5. Stanley Sheperd, *personal communication,* 1973.
6. Layton Kor, "On the Granite Wall," *Trail and Timberline,* 1967, p. 102.

Bill Forrest.

BIG WALLS IN THE SEVENTIES

I usually prefer climbing with a partner, but sometimes I have an irresistable desire to "find" myself through the solo experience.

Bill Forrest (1970)

During the 1960's, Colorado climbers employed the traditional repertoire of techniques for dealing with extended climbs on big walls. These included direct aid with etriers and pitons; sophisticated hauling systems to move heavy supplies up overhanging rock; the use of jumar ascenders to speed up ascents; and ingenious methods of arranging hanging bivouacs on multi-day climbs. The Diamond on Longs Peak was the main focal point for big wall climbing in Colorado during the 1960's.

The Diamond - Solo

In 1970, a Denver climber, Bill Forrest, made plans for the first solo ascent of the Diamond. Forrest was an ex-school teacher who had developed a small climbing equipment manufacturing business. Over the years, he had developed tremendous experience in big wall climbing and had a particular reputation for being at home on bad rock. Rusty Baillie once said of Forrest, "He could arrange safe anchors on an overhanging talus slope." Forrest's liking for big walls had led him to make a number of new ascents, including a six-day ascent of the East Face of Shiprock. He had done a number of routes on the Diamond during the late 1960's, and in 1970 planned to make the first roped solo ascent.

Forrest's preparations for his solo ascent of the Diamond were kept confidential. He told only close friends of his intentions. His preparations completed, he carried all of his own equipment in to the face.

Forrest's solo ascent was a bold venture. It involved difficult A.3 nailing and a poorly protected 5.8 off-width crack high on the face. His account of the climb is given here in its entirety:

Solo ascents have been an accepted part of European mountaineering for some time. The solo climbs of Herman Buhl and Walter Bonatti are a small but significant part of modern climbing literature. But until Royal Robbins soloed El Capitan's Muir Wall, it appeared that the prevailing attitude among American mountaineers was that it was a foolhardy and dangerous activity—always to be frowned upon. Robbins' solo

effort rocked the boat. Physically, mentally, and technically prepared for his climb, he succeeded and quite justly gained praise and approval from even the staunchest anti-soloists. Robbins' success lent perspective. His epic ascent fostered a new solo concept—"Man is free to develop his full potential." Apparently, this concept is the keystone of the 1970 Rocky Mountain National Park regulations which, for the first time, legalized solo climbing.

Secretly, I have enjoyed solo climbing for some time. I usually prefer climbing with a partner, but sometimes I have an irresistible desire to "find" myself through the solo experience. Being along in the mountain crucible can lend a vital, yet rational dimension to the sport. When soloing, the keen sensations experienced while climbing with a partner are intensified. Using a hold, testing a piton, choosing the route—critical moves and decisions—become super-exciting and meaningful. There is an absolute premium on successful execution. And successful execution is largely a matter of preparation. Solo climbing demands the utmost in preparation.

I started to prepare for the Diamond solo as soon as I heard that it had been legalized. I was curious to see if I could do it, and wouldn't be satisfied until I had tried. The idea of soloing one of America's finest high-altitude walls via a new route would certainly guarantee some high adventure.

As I hiked up the Longs Peak trail toward Chasm View on the morning of July 23, I felt prepared. For weeks I had gotten myself into and out of every solo climbing situation that I could think of. My mind, body, technique and equipment were together—I felt ready to take care of myself on the wall, and planned to have some fun. But lugging my eighty-pound pack up to Chasm View wasn't fun—at times it seemed absurd. Under the imposing wall, I thought of myself up there—alone with my big bag—and the whole scheme appeared ridiculous. That was the plan—to do it as my own thing—no outside help. Because the plan was so beautfully simple, it became less ridiculous, more worth doing. I hustled my bag and body to the bivouac cave on Broadway by late afternoon.

On Friday, I climbed four pitches up the Yellow Wall route and set up a hammock bivouac. The day's climbing had been good for me. I knew that I was going to go ahead with the climb; I liked it. It kept me busy all the time—leading, descending, cleaning, and hauling. I worried some about the weather, it seemed too warm that night, and I was concerned about the new route ahead, but I was tired and fell asleep quickly.

Long before dawn, I was awakened by a terrible roar

Top. Bill Forrest topping out on the Diamond on his solo ascent. *Don Briggs.*

Bottom. The Diamond showing line of Forrest's solo climb.

Right: Bill Forrest and Kris Walker with t[he] equipment they used to climb the Painted Wall, which is behind them.

as an avalanche of rock cascaded down the north chimney. Sparks shot through the darkness and the mountain seemed to groan and lurch, but my anchors held and the bottom didn't rip out of my hammock. I couldn't get back to sleep, and I hung in the chilly breeze waiting for the beautiful sunshine.

Saturday was one of the most memorable days of my life. It started with salami and then a very exposed free traverse. It was cold and windy, but I climbed the traverse with surprising confidence and then nailed up to a very exposed belay at the base of my new route. Thirty feet of easy nailing brought me to an evil crack—too wide to jam, too narrow to chimney. I cursed, prayed, chickened out, and finally got with it and struggled. I didn't dare lose my composure, but it was awfully awkward. I fought and flailed. That crack took my best, but once up it, I was glad I was there; it added zest to the route. Above the crux, the crack narrowed and offered fun nailing and nutting to table ledge, which I reached just before dark.

That night I was full of confidence; not even a bad storm could keep me from getting up the remaining pitches. I kept telling myself to be cautious, to keep making the right moves. The lights of the big cities on the Great Plains glittered and winked far below me as I sat on my little ledge. I was so close to turning an idea into a reality that I almost got choked up and sentimental as I made a meal of peanuts and oranges in the dark.

On Sunday morning, I climbed three pitches to the top of the Diamond. There were a few bad pins and I had to make a small pendulum to get to an exit crack, but everything went smoothly despite occasional snow flurries. As I was working up the last few vertical feet, I heard a voice. It was my friend, Don Briggs. I broke my solemn rhythm and lunged for holds and then the hands of that wonderful friend who hugged me mightily. Gary Garbert, my long-time desert climbing partner, soon joined us. Happily united, we scrambled up the talus to the top of Longs Peak. [1]

Forrest's solo ascent of the Diamond was an extension of the tradition which had developed in Colorado during the sixties, employing both direct aid and free climbing techniques on a high mountain wall. His choice to solo the Diamond implied a deliberate re-definition of the normal rules governing big wall climbing, both to intensify his sense of adventure, and to place the outcome of his attempt more in question. Considering the altitude, the difficulties of the approach, and the objective dangers of being caught on the face in bad weather, Forrest's solo ascent of the Diamond was a major achievement, continuing the tradition of Robbins on the Muir Wall.

The First Ascent Of The Painted Wall

In 1972 Bill Forrest and a companion, Kris Walker, turned their attention to the Painted Wall in the Black Canyon of the Gunnison. After the attempts of Layton Kor, Larry Dalke, and Bob Culp in the early 1960's, Rusty Baillie and Wayne Goss had made a number of

Top. Kris Walker seconding the crux 24th pitch of the Painted Wall. *Bill Forrest.*

Bottom. The Painted Wall showing Forrest-Walker route.

attempts between 1968 and 1971. They also were unsuccessful, and the wall remained unclimbed. Forrest had inspected the face at close quarters and had assembled a composite telephotograph which showed its details. He and Walker spent long hours in Denver, poring over the photograph and trying to work out a feasible route. Earlier attempts had involved considerable use of drilled expansion bolts. Forrest and Walker were hopeful that by use of nuts and pitons they would be able to climb the wall without bolts. On Sunday, April 23, 1972, Forrest and Walker camped at the foot of the Painted Wall, after struggling with the steep gullies and the poison ivy for which the Black Canyon is notorious.

That night, Forrest lay in his sleeping bag, contemplating what lay ahead:

> All I could see was this enormous piece of rock towering up into the sky. Every detail was clear in the evening light. I could see huge overhangs everywhere. At the top of the wall was a line of the biggest overhangs I had ever seen. We were pretty confident that we could climb everything else on the wall, but we just didn't know about those overhangs on top. I wasn't sure if we could find a way through them. [2]

Two days of difficult climbing took them to a point eight hundred feet up the wall. On Tuesday afternoon a storm moved in, and when they woke up on Wednesday, snow had fallen. The two hiked out of the canyon, leaving fixed ropes in place. Two days later they returned and spent a day hauling two hundred pounds of equipment, food, and water to their previous high point.

Sunday, April 30th, found Kris Walker struggling with the thirteenth lead of the climb. He touched a large rock which proved to be precariously balanced. The rock moved and began to slide downwards. Walker grabbed it and tried to jam it back into place. "I couldn't get it to stay up there," Walker says. "If it fell, it'd come right down the rope and hit Bill."

> I eased it onto my lap as best I could. I could barely lift it—it felt like a hundred pounds. There was a channel in the wall near me. I thought if I could get it into the channel, it would fall away to the left and clear Bill completely. I yelled down to Bill. He looked up. I let the thing go. [3]

The rock didn't quite make the channel. Instead of going to the left, as Walker had planned, the boulder bounced to the right. It headed directly toward Forrest. "I looked up as Kris called," Forrest says. "I hadn't been looking up before because of the falling rock. I could see a huge rock plummeting down toward me. I thought I was a goner." The rock whistled past him and exploded into fragments a few feet down the wall. Badly shaken, he barely made it up the next three

Bill Forrest leading the crux 24th pitch of the Painted Wall on the first ascent. (500mm. telephoto from opposite rim of the canyon).

pitches, reaching four hundred feet before calling it quits. "It was almost the end of the climb for me," he says.

The next day they reached a point fifteen hundred feet up the wall, and encountered a long, steep crack system containing much loose rock. Stones which the leader dislodged funneled right down onto the belayer. The crack system continued for five hundred feet. They called it Death Valley.

At a point two thousand feet up the wall, just above Death Valley, they found a good bivouac ledge. It was directly under the summit overhangs. Forrest says:

> They looked absolutely enormous. I still had no idea if we could find a way through them. But there was no other way but up. We were too far up the wall to consider retreat. It would have been crazy trying to get down all that loose rock we had climbed. There seemed to be very little chance of a rescue team getting to us if we couldn't make it.[4]

The next day, Wednesday, May 3rd, found Forrest leading the pitch through the overhangs, the twenty-third pitch of the climb. Forrest says:

> This was probably the most difficult pitch I've ever done in my life. I got to a point where I couldn't go any higher. I thought if I tried to go down, all my pins would come out.[5]

He decided to use a pendulum to traverse to a more climbable area. Swinging across, he saw that he was too low. Somehow he had to get higher. Finally he decided to drill a hole for a skyhook. This was the only hole drilled on the entire climb, and the skyhook enabled Forrest to gain a knife-blade crack. Two more pitches took them to the top of the wall.

Their first attempt took three days, and the final push, after the storm, had taken five days: a total of eight days for the climb. The length of time taken and the difficulties encountered justified giving the Painted Wall a Grade VI rating. It was certainly the most serious and demanding route of its kind in Colorado, and its ascent in 1972 by Forrest and Walker was an outstanding accomplishment in big wall climbing.

REFERENCES

1.   William Forrest, "Solo on the Diamond," *American Alpine Journal,* 1971, p. 285.
2.   William Forrest, "First Ascent of the Painted Wall," *tape recorded interview,* 1972.
3.   *Ibid.*
4.   *Ibid.*
5.   *Ibid.*

Part IV

THE FREE CLIMBING ERA

David Rearick. *Pat Ament.*

FREE CLIMBING
- THE SIXTIES

The lure of the first is strong.
Royal Robbins

During the early years of the 1960's, Layton Kor had become expert at sophisticated direct aid, but a number of his early climbs also included difficult, and sometimes poorly protected, free climbing. The Bulge in 1957, though only 5.7, was audacious and involved long, unprotected run-outs. In 1960, the Grand Giraffe presented a crack pitch of formidable difficulty. In 1962, Kor, accompanied by Huntley Ingalls, climbed a difficult mixed route called Psycho. The first pitch involved direct aid over the roof which ran along the base of Redgarden Wall. With Ingalls belayed in slings at the top of the first pitch, Kor free climbed an unprotected 5.9 traverse along the lip of the roof. For years this pitch was notorious for its unprotected difficulty. (A bolt placed by Pat Ament and Larry Dalke on the second ascent made the pitch somewhat more secure, but a fall would still have left the climber dangling in space below the roof.) Black Jack (5.10) was another example of Kor's free climbing ability. In the high mountains, the Northwest Face of Chief's Head consisted primarily of hard (5.9) free climbing.

Generally, however, climbers during the early sixties tended to view short climbs as preparation for longer routes in the high mountains. Speed was at a premium, and they just would not bother to spend extended periods of time working on difficult free moves when a hard section could be quickly nailed. Also, with much virgin rock available and new routes waiting to be done, there was little incentive to work on free climbing existing direct aid routes.

Kor was the dominant influence on Colorado rock climbing during the early years of the 1960's and was central in determining acceptable style. Most other climbers of the day followed his example and used a mixture of free and direct aid techniques as situations seemed to require.

Dave Rearick

During the early 1960's a number of events occurred which were outside of the mainstream, and which hinted at the shape of things to come. Dave Rearick had become well known for his first ascent of the Diamond with Bob Kamps in 1960. In many climbers' minds, the Diamond ascent firmly established him as a big wall man, specializing in direct aid. However, Rearick was responsible in the early 1960's for refining free climbing on small cliffs in the Boulder region, and for developing further the concept of free climbing as a worthwhile end in itself. He had climbed extensively in California with Royal Robbins and Chuck Pratt, and his free climbing ideas were based on these experiences. A graduate student, later to become a professor of mathematics at the University of Colorado, Rearick's rational mind enjoyed imposing restrictions which precluded the use of direct-aid, and he found satisfaction in patiently working out free moves on unlikely looking sections of rock.

In 1962, Rearick and Bob Culp went out one day to do a normal mixed free-and-aid ascent of T.2., the route established by Layton Kor and Gerry Roach in 1959. The finger crack on the fourth pitch possessed a number of fixed pitons. Clipping into these for protection, Rearick began climbing the crack without using aid. Once over the hard part, he began to think about pushing the complete route free. Rearick returned and placed a bolt in the lip of the first overhang to provide protection for a free climbing attempt. He says:

> There used to be a talus spike sticking up from the ground beneath the first overhang. We took that as a starting point. We would stand up on it to start, which was a big advantage, because standing on that you could reach buckets which aren't reachable anymore except by strenuous pull-ups and little handholds. Culp and I worked on it and Lee Harrel was there. We were trying it any old way, mostly from the top of the talus spike, and weren't making it. Harrel was fooling around downhill from the talus spike and he said, "Let's try it here." I happened to have the rope on so I said, "OK, I'll try it." I took an overhead belay through the bolt and got up over the hardest part on small flakes which have altogether disappeared now. Just as I went over the edge, I grabbed a big chicken head which pulled off. I didn't fall, managed to hold on, and got up. Then Bob Culp also did it with an overhead rope.
>
> As soon as possible, maybe one or two days later, we

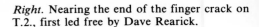

came back to do it all free before anybody else. Culp was having an off day so I led three of the hard sections, the bottom, the fingercrack, and the top.

Rearick's description contains an interesting phrase, "As soon as possible......we came back to do it all free before anybody else." Rearick was not intensely competitive, but the idea of bagging a first free ascent did add a little spice for him.

Prior to the development of free climbing during the 1960's, competition was a relatively minor factor in rock climbing and was only occasionally expressed in the bagging of new routes. Routes such as the Diamond and the Naked Edge were real prizes. First ascents carried the most kudos, but no one cared particularly about the manner in which they were done. Just to get to the top, by virtually any conceivable means, seemed amazing. Free climbing brought with it a more refined set of parameters, within which climbers could compete with themselves, in terms of answering the question, "Can I do this pitch without resorting to direct aid?" and which enabled them to more precisely compare their efforts to those of others. Factors such as resting on protection between moves, lowering off from protection, placing protection on direct aid prior to making free moves, and taking short falls in attempts to make free moves, became progressively more important. Stylistic restrictions became refined amidst an ongoing debate which has continued into the modern era of the 1970's.

Shortly after his free ascent of T.2, Rearick, accompanied by Pat Ament, embarked on an ascent of the Yellow Spur on the west of Redgarden Wall. Layton Kor and Dave Dornan had climbed the route first in 1959, using direct aid on the first and sixth leads. Rearick was able to find free climbing alternatives to the first aid pitch, and in so doing was to open Ament's eyes to the real possibilities of free climbing. Ament says that Rearick was his most influential mentor in these early days. "Rearick was so different from Kor," Ament says, "very slow and meticulous." Ament himself was to develop free climbing in following years, and acknowledges Rearick's influence.

Free Climbing in the Mid-Sixties: Royal Robbins

Rearick had picked up his notions on free climbing at Taquitz and Yosemite, in the company of Robbins and Pratt. "Robbins really invented the free climbing game," says Rearick. Sardonic, witty, a specialist in groan-inducing puns and sweat-inducing free climbs, Royal Robbins possessed a superb gamesmanship approach to rock climbing. Competitive by nature, he delighted in measuring his abilities against the best

Left and right. The West Buttress of the Bastille (5.9). A favorite climb in Eldorado Canyon. (First ascent in 1959 by Layton Kor and Carl Pfiffner).

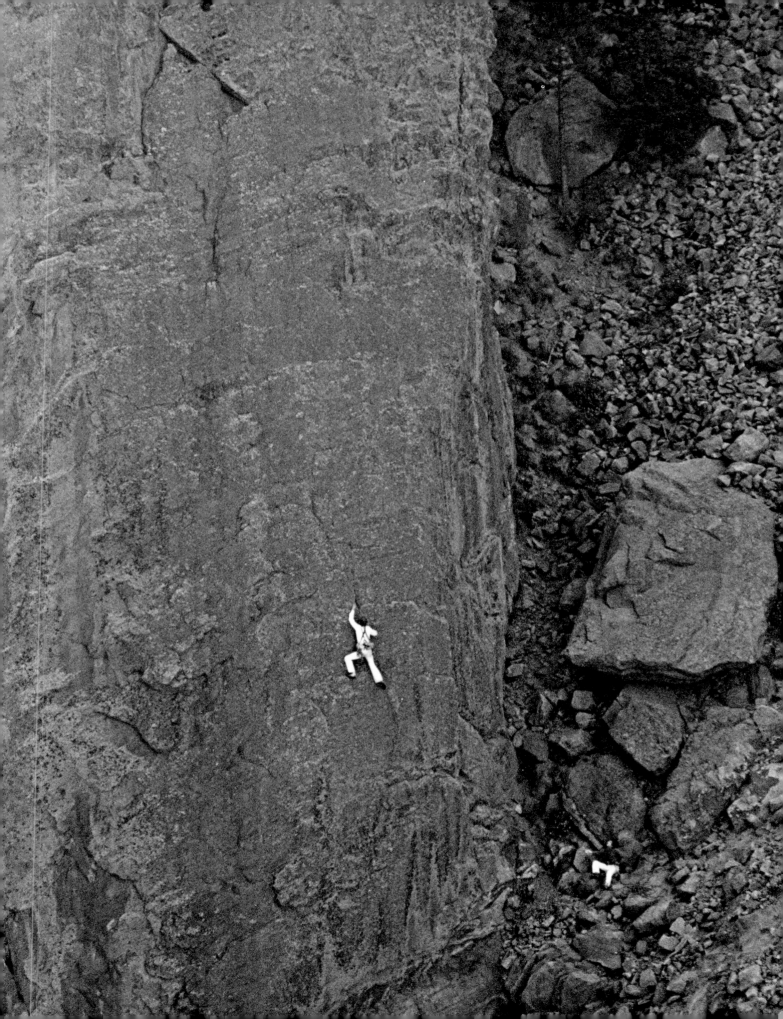

Top: Royal Robbins on Ruper. *Pat Ament.*

Bottom: Liz and Royal Robbins. *Pat Ament.*

standards of the day, either by free climbing classic routes which had previously depended on direct aid, or by seeking out new routes. Rationally appreciative of the benefits, and the drawbacks, of competition, he had little taste for its harsher overtones. He thrived in competitive situations which motivated him to give of his best, while at the same time implicitly throwing down the gauntlet to say, with a grin, "Try and better that, if you can."

The summer of 1964 was Robbins' big year for free climbing in Colorado. He teamed up with Pat Ament to make a series of brilliant climbs which were considerably more advanced than existing free routes. They decided to attempt to free climb Country Club Crack on Castle Rock in Boulder Canyon, a route which had first been climbed by Ted Rouillard and Cleve McCarty in 1956, mainly on direct aid. The climb followed a left angling crack system, slightly overhanging, and led up to a pronounced overhang just below the top. Dave Rearick had made an unsuccessful attempt to free climb the route and had reached a point part way up the cracks, but he had had to resort to direct aid below the roof. Ament felt that the route could go all free and decided to "sic Royal on it."

Robbins climbed the first few moves on aid, clipped the rope into a carabiner, and descended. With overhead protection he was able to free climb the difficult starting moves of the route. He was then able to free climb the cracks and a few moves over the roof. The last few feet resisted his efforts, and he used two pitons of aid to gain the last eight feet of difficult climbing. Even with the use of pitons for the final few feet, his ascent was a remarkable demonstration of tenacity and free climbing expertise.

Shortly after climbing Country Club Crack, Robbins completed a number of other free routes on Castle Rock. These included a free ascent of Athlete's Feat which included three 5.10 pitches and two 5.9 pitches. It was the most sustained and difficult free climb in the Boulder area in 1964. Robbins also led free ascents of two other difficult climbs on Castle Rock, the By Gully, and The Final Exam. While he was leading the Final Exam, Robbin's wife Liz was sitting at the base of the cliff carving a piece of wood. Robbins looked down and grinned, "Now Liz, don't bewhittle my efforts."

During the summer of 1964, Robbins paid a visit to Estes Park. A route on Sundance Buttress, first climbed by Layton Kor and Jack Turner in 1962, attracted his attention. Robbins was able to free climb the route, which consisted mainly of crack climbing up a steep granite wall. He took four or five leader falls at the crux pitch, a four-inch crack which went out around a roof. His mastery of granite cracks and his willingness to take

Left. Strenuous hand jams high on the second lead of Country Club Crack. It is important not to over-protect this pitch, to avoid problems of rope drag at the difficult section over the roof above.

Right. The last few feet of Country Club Crack which defeated Robbins on his free attempt in 1964. (The crack here is too wide for finger jams and too narrow for hand jams. A knee lock was discovered on a later ascent, which enables the leader to rest before making the strenuous final moves.) Pat Ament made the first free ascent of Country Club in 1966.

Above. Moving through the crux moves on the second pitch of Athlete's Feat.

Left. Laybacking the strenuous second pitch of Athlete's Feat - the most demanding free climb in the Boulder region at the time of Royal Robbins' free ascent in 1964.

The crux crack on Turnkorner from which Robbins took a number of short falls before making the first free ascent in 1964.

leader falls enabled him to free climb the route, which had previously been called the Kor-Turner route. After the first free ascent, Robbins, a dilettante of word games as well as rock climbs, renamed it Turnkorner.

In 1963, Kor and Paul Mayrose had climbed the classic Crack of Fear on the Twin Owls, also close to Estes Park. The ascent had involved direct aid, and on the second pitch Kor had placed three expansion bolts from precarious perches on six-inch bongs. Shortly after climbing Turnkorner in 1964, Robbins, with Dave Rearick and Dan Davis, attempted to make the second ascent of the Crack of Fear and was hopeful of being able to free climb the route. Rearick set off leading the first pitch with his left side in the crack. Robbins, who had not climbed the crack before, called up to him, "You won't stand a chinaman's chance if you don't get yourself properly oriented." It turned out that the crack was indeed easier if climbed with the right side in. On the difficult second pitch, Robbins was able to free climb most of the way, but had to employ two aid pitons at a difficult bulge where the crack jogged to the left.

The first all-free ascent of Crack of Fear did not take place until 1966. Jim Logan was a skinny young kid who had not been climbing for very long, though he had recently managed to lead the Final Exam (5.10) on

Turnkorner high on Sundance Buttress above Estes Park.

Strenuous off-width climbing on the first
pitch of the Crack of Fear (5.9).

Right. Jim Erickson leading the second pitch
of the Crack of Fear. He is in approximately
the same position as the climber in the photo
to the left.

Castle Rock. A California climber, Chris Fredericks,
who had led the Crack of Doom in Yosemite earlier that
summer, arrived in Boulder and was hot to try a free
ascent of the Crack of Fear. On the basis of his lead of
the Final Exam, Logan was introduced to Fredericks as
"a 5.10 climber," in such a way that it appeared he had
been running up and down 5.10 routes for years.
Unknown to Fredericks, Logan's previous crack
climbing experience was zero. That evening, Dick Erb
demonstrated the finer points of crack climbing
technique to him — in his living room!

Fredericks was successful in leading all of the Crack
of Fear free, with bongs for protection. Sitting on the
belay ledge at the top of the second pitch, he could not
see Logan seconding, but he could hear a pounding
noise. Logan was so small and skinny that he had been
able to chimney inside the crack which normal sized
people had to climb on the outside with akward arm
bars. He was pounding out the bongs from inside the
crack! Descending after the climb, the young Logan felt

The Twin Owls showing the Crack of Fear.

The bolt ladder on the final pitch of the Yellow Spur. Robbins made the first all free ascent of the Yellow Spur in 1964, but traversed left below the bolt ladder, which was later led free by Larry Dalke (5.9+).

exuberant and proclaimed,

"Boy! 'I just can't wait to get back to Boulder to tell everyone.'' ''Now Jim,'' responded Fredericks patiently, ''that wasn't why we were doing it.''

Logan was later to return to the Twin Owls as an experienced crack climber in his own right and make the first free ascent of Twister, a 5.10 crack which had previously been climbed on direct aid.

It later turned out that the section of the Crack of Fear which Robbins had been unable to free climb, the section where the crack jogged left, had actually been free climbed by Kor on the first ascent in 1963. Robbins had attempted to use standard crack climbing technique, with the side of his body wedged in the overhanging crack. Kor had moved outside of the crack and had used its edge as an undercling, with his feet in opposition against the wall, which made it somewhat easier.

Even though Robbins missed out on the first completely free ascent of the Crack of Fear, his free ascent of Turnkorner and the routes he had done on Castle Rock were the most impressive spate of short, difficult free climbs the area had ever witnessed.

Castle Rock is composed of granite, the rock on which Robbins had most frequently climbed in Yosemite, and most of his difficult free ascents in Colorado consisted of difficult crack climbs, in which he had gained tremendous experience in Yosemite. This experience, coupled with what Pat Ament has termed, ''his tremendous ability to push himself beyond normal limits,'' enabled Robbins to significantly advance free climbing standards in Colorado in 1964.

Granite cracks were Robbins' forte, but his skill was not limited to crack climbing. He made a free ascent of the Yellow Spur with Pat Ament during 1964, which involved climbing of a completely different nature. Dave Rearick had been successful in free climbing the first direct aid pitch of the route, but he had resorted to pitons near the top. Pat Ament says of Robbins' ascent of this section, called the Piton Ladder, ''Royal went straight up in a couple of minutes, clipping in to the fixed pins and saying, 'Hm, can't be more than 5.7 or 5.8'. . . . I thought, Jesus! This guy must be everything that Rearick says he is.''

The most significant difference between Royal Robbins' approach to free climbing in 1964 and that of Colorado climbers, was his willingness to push his standard to the limit, including being willing to take repeated leader falls, close to protection. Generally, Colorado climbers at this time were very conservative about falling. Robbins demonstrated that short leader falls could be taken safely, and that by these means free ascents of a new level of technical difficulty could be accomplished.

Pat Ament

By 1966, Pat Ament was in his best climbing shape ever. After his experience with Rearick and Robbins, he had applied himself to free climbing and was primed to attempt new free leads of his own. In 1964, Robbins had been the motivating force and had done most of the leading. Ament had accompanied him, apprentice-like, belaying patiently, watching carefully. They had a lot in common. "Royal likes chess and puns and blowing ego trips with his own," Ament wrote in his autobiography. So did Ament. "He is the first climber I have met as competitive as myself." Robbins joined Bob Dylan and Ivy Baldwin in Ament's gallery of archetypal folk heroes.

In 1964, with Bob Boucher, Ament had made the first ascent of a new route on the Diamond which they called the Grand Traverse. It was the longest route on the Diamond, and their first ascent took two days. Also, on the East Face of Longs, he made the third and fourth ascents of Northcutt's demanding Diagonal route, once with Roger Raubach and once with Larry Dalke. In other parts of Colorado, Ament put up difficult new routes in the Royal Gorge, Glenwood Springs Canyon, and the Black Canyon of the Gunnison. Close to Boulder, he had climbed regularly with Kor and Dalke and had put up a number of hard aid routes of his own, including Evangeline, Temporary Like Achilles, Apple Strudel, Fire and Ice, and Centaur. As his aspirations toward free climbing grew, Ament began to work out on local boulders and became one of Boulder's leading experts.

By 1966, Ament was evolving out of his apprentice role with Kor and Robbins, and he was looking for a way to carve his own particular notch on the Colorado climbing scene.

On a summer day in 1966, Ament again found himself in the company of Royal Robbins. The two were joined by the English climber, Don Whillans, who was visiting Colorado, for a day of climbing in Eldorado Springs Canyon. The three climbed the now classic Ruper on Redgarden Wall, and then wandered over to a small, detached rock at the west end of the Canyon. The back of the rock overhung steeply and was split by a crack, called Supremacy Crack. Ament had made a number of previous attempts to climb the crack, and had succeeded in climbing it once before with a top rope, but had never succeeded in leading it.

His account, entitled *A Brief Supremacy*, describes the first ascent:

Ament at nineteen - "Climbers disdain me, take shots at me. But not as cheap as mine at them." *Larry Dalke.*

The legendary and controversial Supremacy Crack has a history which may be amusing and perhaps slightly gratifying to climbers who are intrigued by the origins and lore of such extremes. The discovery of Supremacy Crack must be credited to Dave Rearick. A morning in 1965, he showed me the diabolical, twenty-foot slit.

We drove up the canyon, past the main climbing area of Eldorado, to the provocative hidden crack piercing the south side of a quartzite slab. Dave had a grin on his face instead of the usual austere look. In his mind he was seeing me swing off the crack on his old, white, hopelessly frayed Diamond rope, about which he was sentimental.

We arrived underneath the overhanging crack and dislocated our necks studying it. Dave scrambled the easy way to the top, doubled the rope down from a piton anchor, returned, and had me tie-in. He sat down with the rope around him, half knowing the route would go, half hoping I'd burn off some youthful energy proving it. A fall meant a sixty-foot swing above the river, and the bottoms dropped out of our stomachs when we thought about it. Instructed to practice the swing in order to get rid of the fear of it, I made a move upward, reluctantly, glanced with wide eyes at Rearick's happy face, was overcome with a weak, hysterical sensation, and let go. I was like a ball of gum spinning slowly away from him on a long strand of hair. When it was his turn, Dave much preferred climbing up and jumping off to giving the crack a serious attempt. Every kid sooner or later finds a rope to swing on—Tarzan style—across a river or imaginary gorge. This kid Rearick was in his thirties.

For the most part, Supremacy Crack was a place to play. We never thought of leading it or of doing it "in style." We scarcely gave it a "best effort" and did not consider it a failure because we were able to do a third of it. There was no reason to believe that it would ever be respected by climbers. Part of the reason I brought other climbers to look at Supremacy and try it with me was that it was fun. It was a conversation-piece, something to laugh or wonder about. Bob Culp held the rope, yawned, and laughed, as I played. Tex Bossier tried to motivate me with ravings that what was happening was incredible.

I was never really good enough to do the climb until my mental attitude toward it changed. Instead of viewing it as fun, it became a fevered, exotic dream, a priority for me with a certain oozing charm, and with Roger Rauback belaying I found myself mesmerized to the rock, struggling, applying a certain integration of mind and touch, and succeeding. Roger's face seemed to get red and puffy as he exclaimed, somewhat belatedly, "You did it!"

The crack immediately developed a reputation in Colorado and in other areas of the United States. While actually surprised by this, I was at the same time proud to have made the first ascent.

About a year later, after climbing Ruper in Eldorado, I brought my two companions to Supremacy. It was a hot afternoon, and a lot of people with equipment were wandering around the canyon. My companions were both better climbers than I, and it was my feeling that one of them might enjoy doing the first leading ascent of Supremacy. They were Royal Robbins and Don Whillans.

I expected a day of refreshing humility and was sure that the myth of Supremacy would be dissolved. Whillans hinted that routes like Supremacy were a six pence a dozen in England. On Ruper, he had led both the crux pitches entirely unprotected and exhibited amazing form. On the Ruper crack, the rope from Whillans ran down freely to me and was between Royal and the rock. Royal stood unanchored, and I whispered nervously to him, "If Whillans falls, he'll yank you off." "I'll take that chance," Royal replied.

After the three of us arrived at Supremacy, there appeared a group of tourists and climber spectators ready to witness the absurdity. Whillans elected not to do anymore that day except belay or spread out a blanket by the river and lie in the sun. Royal went a few moves up the crack and placed a nut. It was my first introduction to the use of nuts for protection. He then rather quickly decided that I should lead, since I was familiar with the climb. It was hard to know what to make of Royal's machine nuts with slings through them, apparently the newest of his creative whims. The easiest and most efficient method of protecting such a lead was at hand, but I didn't know it. I grabbed some pitons, a few carabiners, and a hammer!

First to belay, Whillans provided added incentive by keeping a lot of slack in the rope and staring soberly into space. I jammed up the first crux, hung there with one hand half-wedged, placed a piton, clipped the rope through, and lowered to the belay. Whillans gave Royal the rope and went off to lie in the sun. I led past the second crux, hung again by a poor hand jam, placed a second piton, clipped in, and again returned for a breather. By this time, Whillans was flat on his back on his blanket beside the river. After shaking out my arms, I climbed to the high point, proceeded higher, got a third

piton in somewhere near the top, moved back to the second piton, rested briefly there with help from the piton, then went up the remainder of the way to the top. Having upper-belayed the climb the previous year proved to be of little help, since the sequence used now was completely different than any before. It was obviously not a climb one could readily "wire." A few satisfying moments were spent alone at the summit before scrambling down the back way to belay Royal. It was quite a view from the summit with the high country sparkling to the west, with the warm yellow Eldorado walls rising to the east, with green trees and blue sky everywhere and Whillans below showing no signs of movement, undoubtedly drifting into a deep sleep.

Royal followed the crack, only using aid through one section. His showing was as good as (or better than) any of my previous top-roped tries. I had always liked Royal's technique and had been able to learn something from observing it. Here was no exception.

When Whillans was ready to leave America and return to England, he stopped at my house. We traded a few final laughs and reflections about climbing. He speculated that I would never really get much better than I was the day on Supremacy and that no one would have more insight into the depth of that ascent than myself. He was speaking of spiritual things before I was old enough to understand them. I exchanged with him some American currency for a lot of foreign coins which had been a nuisance to him, and he thanked me with a photo he'd taken of Supremacy. I've kept those coins, that lousy far-off photo, and whenever I stumble across them I experience a full range of emotion, remembering the great stimulus, the dizzy unveiling of possibilities, of the '60's.

Ament's lead of Supremacy Crack, though only a short pitch, was a notable achievement in terms of technical difficulty in 1966. After discussion with Robbins, Ament graded the pitch 5.11 in the rock climbers guidebook. It was one of the first pitches in America to receive a 5.11 grading, and was one of the hardest pitches in the country in 1966.

During the remainder of the 1960's, Ament was to devote a great deal of energy to free climbing and was to accomplish a lengthy list of ascents in the Boulder region. These included such difficult routes as Country Club Crack, Super Slab, Tongo, Vertigo, and Super Squeeze, all of which had previously been climbed on direct aid.

During this period, routes that Ament wanted to free climb were beyond the comprehension of other climbers. He had visions of free climbing major direct aid routes, such as the Naked Edge, Outer Space, and the Diving Board, a number of years before they were to become realities.

Ament never clearly defined the style in which he did some of his free ascents. Tending to be vague when questioned, he became known as a controversial, enigmatic, and contradictory character. He would

The Vertigo Dihedral. One of Ament's controversial "free" ascents. He led the first, and most difficult, moves free, but completed the pitch using pitons for direct aid.

regularly moan because the protection was at his waist (and not at his nose), proudly state, "I did every hard move with a pin in front of my face," and then lead the overhanging crux section of the second pitch of the Crack of Doom in Yosemite completely unprotected.

Though many of Ament's free ascents were done in good style, some were done "free" in ways that his critics called cheating. His repertoire of unorthodox methods included climbing the Northwest Corner of the Bastille with Roger Briggs in 1966, using pitons and etriers to aid up and fix protection before making the crux 5.10 moves. On the crux of Vertigo, a steep dihedral high on Redgarden Wall, Ament climbed the first, and most difficult, moves free, but continued up the remainder of the pitch using pitons for aid. On a climb called Gorilla's Delight in Boulder canyon, he was unable to find good protection for the crux 5.9 friction slab and, after scrambling to the top of the cliff via an easier route, brought his partner, George Hurley, up the slab with an overhead rope. All three of these routes Ament recorded as first free ascents. Critics were later to say that Ament had cheated on these pitches. Ament's reply was, "As I was setting new standards, can it really be said that my methods were cheating?"

The degree to which Ament honestly felt that these climbs were valid free ascents, and the degree to which he was engaged in building his own myth, were later to become questions of considerable speculation. Ament was nineteen at the time and eager for recognition. During the later years of the 1960's, his ego became notorious among local climbers. "Climbers disdain me, take shots at me," he wrote in his biography, "but not as cheap as mine at them." His unwillingness to admit details of some of his ascents was to cause him grief in following years, and in a sense he was both a victim of his ego and a victim of the competitive pressures of the free climbing era. Direct aid climbing had peaked, and hard free climbing was the way to make a mark. Robbins had shown him a model of the successful, on-top-of-the-world, competitive climber; but whereas Robbins handled competition with sardonic competence and humorous one-upmanship, Ament, with a nineteen-year-old's hunger for recognition, gilded the lily a little too much—enough to give his critics ammunition. His climbs were hard, "but...." And over the years, the "but" grew larger, fanned by the wind of Ament's own defensiveness. As Robbins has said, "The lure of the first is strong."

Despite stylistic inconsistencies, Ament's climbs in the later years of the 1960's accord him an important place in the history of Colorado free climbing. It is illuminating also to note that many first free ascents of

Left. Beginning the crux section of the Northwest Corner of the Bastille. Th[e] route continues up for fifteen feet and then traverses right to a precarious mantle. Amen[ded] aided up to fix protectio[n] before making the controversial free ascent [in] 1966.

Right. Midway on the cr[ux] of the Northwest Corner. The small hold at the climber's right hand is th[e] infamous mantle hold which has seen many a climber's demise.

Top. Ament at twenty five - climber, poet, dreamer. *Tom Higgins.*

Bottom. Ament on the Smith Overhang - a difficult Flagstaff problem.

the "modern era" of the seventies have also been done in a similarly less-than-perfect style. Ament's sin, if sin is the right word, was only that he did not level about the way he had done some of his climbs. The fact that the word "sin" is in any way applicable, is as much a commentary on the competitive pressures of the free climbing era, as it is on Ament as an individual.

Older, wiser, less hot-headed, Ament in 1976 grinned ruefully and talked of "being the victim of my own ego over the years." A complex mixture of James Thurber and Machiavelli, his ups and downs on the rock face have been accompanied by erratic emotional plunges, from heights of poetic wonderment to bouts of black despair, and he has succeeded in generating more diametrically opposing reactions than any other climber in Colorado. His climbing style may occasionally have been questionable, but there has never been any question about Ament's controversial nature, in which he has delighted. "Those old farts are just jealous," he says of his critics with a grin. His response to his detractors has sometimes taken the form of one of his notorious "black letters"—angry epistles castigating them for real and imaginary offenses. In contrast, he has won the lasting respect and friendship of such well-known climbers as Tom Higgins, Dave Rearick, Steve Wunsch, and John Gill.

Mistakenly identified in climbing literature as a has-been, Ament, as unpredictable as ever, surprised the climbing community in 1976 by getting back in top shape. During that summer he led many of the 5.10 routes in the Boulder area and, on a particularly notable occasion with Bill Briggs, climbed all the 5.10 and 5.11 pitches on Castle Rock in a single day! He also put up a new short climb, Star Span (an overhanging crack reminiscent of Supremacy), of considerable technical difficulty, which effectively repulsed a number of the young hot shots of the seventies later in 1976.

During his climbing career, Ament produced a steady stream of writings, co-authored the rock climbers guidebook, wrote a short autobiography, and published various short articles on climbing subjects. In the same way that his presence has livened up the Colorado climbing scene in the past, one suspects that his pen will continue to do so in the future.

Bouldering: Pat Ament and John Gill

Those "Afternoon Tigers of the Boulder Boulders," stripped of all artifacts save for a pair of tight-fitting shoes and a block of chalk...experts in "low altitude siege climbing," is Steve Komito's apt description of practitioners of the art of bouldering.

Practice climbing on boulders had seen its origins in

Top. John Gill.

Bottom. Gill's one-finger pull up.

Colorado in the "trick climbing" of the military at Fort Carson in Colorado Springs. In Boulder, Ray Northcutt had produced some very difficult boulder problems, as had Corwin Simmons around 1960. Bob Culp had also made quite a reputation for himself as a boulderer, and the story is told of Pat Ament and Larry Dalke attempting a steep overhang on Cookie Jar Rock one day. Culp turned up wearing an immaculate business suit, having just finished work, but wearing a pair of Kronhoffer climbing shoes. After watching Ament and Dalke struggle for a while, he sauntered over and did the move first try, without creasing his suit.

After his free climbing experiences with Robbins, Ament began to work out on boulders more and more. During the mid-sixties, he was to raise standards of bouldering to new levels. The peak of Ament's bouldering came in the years 1967-1969. Flagstaff Mountain near Boulder possesses a large number of boulders, and has long been a congregating place for local climbers. Ament's pioneering of such climbs as First Overhang, Right Side of the Red Wall, The Consideration, difficult routes on Capstan Rock, and many others, represented a new level of this esoteric art. In the company of such experts as Bob Williams, he was able to demonstrate that bouldering had potential as an activity in its own right, rather than serving merely as training for longer climbs.

Ament had heard of a climber named John Gill, who lived in Fort Collins, a town north of Boulder, and who had a reputation as a specialist on boulders. In 1968 he headed up to Fort Collins to seek out Gill and to learn more of his approach. During the following years, Ament bouldered frequently with Gill and describes him as a person of "rare mythical qualities, stature, and bewildering ability." During his attempts to repeat some of Gill's problems, Ament was to frequently "squeeze the initial holds and sigh." He writes, "I could grasp the holds but not the problem." [1]

John Gill has become a legend among rock climbers. Since the mid-1950's, and through until the present day, he has become America's leading specialist in making short climbs of extreme technical difficulty on boulders, particularly face climbs involving minute handholds. During his early days in the military, Gill was involved in gymnastics and trained on a regular basis. As his interest in bouldering developed, he worked out specific training exercises to improve his ability. By intensive training, Gill developed his strength to the point where he could do a one-finger pull. This is a remarkable feat when one considers that few top class rock climbers are capable of doing even a one-arm pull up.

Gill's approach to bouldering was built around concepts of difficulty, style, and technique. He was the

Gill bouldering the left side of the Eliminator at Fort Collins in the mid-70's. *Courtesy John Gill.*

"master" of the small handhold, and he invented a B1 through B3 grading system for difficult boulders. In his article, "The Art of Bouldering," Gill writes, "A climb of bouldering difficulty should involve moves whose fifth-class ratings are at least F.10;" namely, that B1 takes up where 5.10 leaves off. A B3 problem automatically became B2 if successfully done once by anybody. Gill rejected the commonly held notion that bouldering is simply practice climbing for longer climbs, and felt that . . . . ."The boulderer is concerned with form almost as much as with success and will not feel that he has truly mastered a problem until he can do it gracefully." [2]

As Gill refined his approach to bouldering, he developed new techniques. "You should use gymnastics, acrobatics, and aerobatics," he said, "and a good boulder route should almost require the use of these techniques." Gill developed the swinging lieback in the sixties, but made a distinction between dynamic moves and wild lunges, saying, "a dynamic move has to be done with control." [3] Competition has always been a thorny question, with many climbers feeling that it detracts from the value of rock climbing. Gill felt that competition played an important part in bouldering and wrote, "In bouldering. . . .sportsman-like competition plays a valid and appropriate role, especially in forcing the participant to overcome psychological blocks hindering the advancement of his technique." [4]

The following essay, *American Bouldering-An Alternative to the Risk Ethic,* written by John Gill, summarizes his perspective:

The highly competitive atmosphere of contemporary rock climbing has enhanced the pursuit of risk. A large number of climbers accept the premise that a climbing experience is deficient if it fails to demand a mortal commitment under somewhat desperate circumstances. This is the evolving essence of the risk ethic.

Some climbers categorically state that the only satisfactory direction of development for rock climbing lies in the taking of risk, exemplified by the free soloing of difficult and exposed routes. Axiomatic in such a proposition is the faulty observation that technical advancement in rock climbing is no longer possible. Compelling evidence that this is not the case comes from the sub-sport of bouldering—that branch of climbing that has as its twin goals the overcoming of technical difficulty without aid, and the cultivation of elegant form.

Bouldering is essentially severe one-pitch rock climbing, gracefully performed and completely protected. The setting is usually a low rock where a fall would not be injurious. Ascents of higher, more exposed outcrops are customarily protected by top ropes.

In spirit, bouldering is the quintessential kinesthetic experience in climbing. It is the soul of rock climbing: the fascinating acrobatic synthesis of man and rock. It is an intensely personal art form, the measure of its gratification directly proportional to the style and grace of the artist, and the intensity of its impact varying with difficulty.

The emphasis on protection is essential, for as greater levels of difficulty evolve requiring techniques advanced far beyond traditional three point suspension, falls become inevitable, even for the most experienced. In addition, spectacular dynamic techniques that require much practice are now being explored as alternative approaches to established routes. An obvious or intuitive move on a particular pitch might be only moderately hard, but a non-traditional maneuver, something completely aerial for example, might be extremely demanding. Observe that this produces a subtle shift in prominence from the rock to the climber—the climber now uses the rock as apparatus upon which to demonstrate his physical and artistic prowess.

An excellent example is a top-roped overhanging pitch on Beer Barrel Rock near Boulder, Colorado. The talented Bob Williams climbed this route twice—once employing traditional static technique, and once employing a very dynamic and aerial technique in which the climber's body is entirely separated from the rock momentarily. Two names were given to this pitch: Synchromesh and Dynamesh.

As novel and intriguing as the idea of a complete system contained in one small piece of rock at first appears, it is obvious, upon reflection, that there have been numerous sporadic forays in this direction, occurring whenever a pitch has been reclimbed with certain holds declared out of bounds. Commonly this takes the form of intermediate holds being eliminated by tall climbers; on occasion, short climbers, feeling somewhat persecuted, will insist that *all* intermediate holds be *used,* thus (according to tall climbers) terminating the bouldering session on the grounds of aesthetic abuse.

Actually, the basic idea of a one-pitch system has a certain innovative merit, provided the techniques are fundamentally distinct.

Form in bouldering is almost as important as difficulty. Consequently, an awkward although not an exceptionally difficult climb can be a real challenge to a serious

John Gill training - the front lever. *Courtesy John Gill.*

boulderer. A clear parallel exists between bouldering and competitive gymnastics, where style also counts heavily.

The gymnast works to produce a routine which displays elegance, originality, and difficulty. In the relaxed atmosphere of a gymnasium he designs a sequence of stunts that optimize his abilities, occasionally stretching his artistic powers to the point of creating an individual move. Each stunt is practiced a sufficient number of times to guarantee grace and consistency before the difficult process of integration is attempted.

Working under less flexible conditions in a harsher environment, the boulderer, in order to artistically create within the confines of his twin goals, must explore the terrain and must find, concurrently, a pitch and an appropriate style that capitalize on his potentialities. He, too, will practice for the sake of grace and precision.

Bouldering and gymnastics are usually competitive activities. Contemporary gymnastics is an exceptionally formal individual sport in which a performance is rated on a scale of one to ten by a panel of experienced judges. Style, elegance, apparent effortlessness, composition, and difficulty are among the criteria determining a numerical score. There is an internationally accepted three-level scale of difficulty covering most stunts; in the highest category are found impressive feats such as inverted iron crosses on the still rings and double flyaways from the high bar. Judging at a meet is partly subjective (e.g., elegance) and partly objective (difficulty).

Bouldering competition is far more relaxed and informal. There are no appointed judges, and difficulty is the fundamental competitive criterion, with form and style secondary. "Winners" are decided by a simple process of elimination and receive as acknowledgment of their successful efforts the envy and admiration of the other participants.

Competitive bouldering routes are ordinarily of at least 5.10 difficulty. A grading system that has met with some approval rates this minimal level as B-1. B-2 and B-3 are accorded routes of greater severity; B-3 is an objective standard and is awarded routes that have been done only once, although tried frequently by competent boulderers. If eventually a second ascent is made (by anyone), the rating will automatically drop to B-2. There are few climbs of this caliber.

The casual scheme of competition has both assets and liabilities. On the positive side, if all of the participants are good natured, as is frequently the case, a bouldering session can be great fun and can be individually rewarding without laboring under a stringent set of rules. In some, an attitude of self competition may take precedence over competition with others. The therapeutic values are obvious: mental release from worrisome problems, physical exercise that may involve practically every muscle in the body, and the general feeling of well-being that develops in an atmosphere in which objectives are clear and there are no "shades of gray"—one either totally succeeds or fails in his goals. The joys of disciplined motion and accomplishment are realizable in a natural environment isolated, to some extent, from technocracy.

On the negative side, the lack of rigid rules and formal judging denies the participants well defined standings, and the winner a physical reward or public recognition.

Unfortunately, the parallel with gymnastics obscures the variety of appeal inherent in bouldering. For example, bouldering routes, especially potential ones, are frequently referred to as "problems", which, in many instances, relates to the intellectual character of rock climbing. A complicated virgin pitch can be interpreted as a sort of physical chess problem, and the intricacy of its solution may differ markedly from the simplicity of composition of the gymnast's routine, in which most of the moves are traditional and clearly delineated.

Indeed, this puzzle factor may provide great satisfaction for the climber who boulders alone. Self-protection on long pitches can be obtained by using a fixed top-rope in conjunction with a Gibbs' Ascender, thus eliminating the risk factor so eagerly sought by the free-soloer. Obviously, a climber must have great inner-motivation in order to thrive on these non-heroics.

It does not seem too absurd to say that the safe acrobatic association of man and rock in a solitary arena can lead to an almost spiritual realization.

What compels the isolated climber to make the super effort when neither his skin nor his reputation are at stake? Why will he feel dissatisfied with a poorly executed move and repeat it? If the climb is considered training or is to be exhibited to an audience at a later date, the answer to these questions is abundantly (and somewhat disappointingly) clear; but if such is not the case, then the sport possesses a remarkable purity that is not entirely veiled by its competitive aura.

Going a step further, it is possible that severe competition in rock climbing and the direction such competition is taking, coupled with personality conflicts and perennial ethical disputes, will result in some climbers rejecting main stream philosophy and accepting a more personal, transcendental concept of climbing. Unpublicized solitary bouldering can offer access to a spiritual rapport superseding the desire for a reputation or for human companionship.

These lines of thought run counter to the strongly competitive definition of bouldering given previously. Some climbers prefer, instead, a looser definition that stresses potentiality for fun. Others see bouldering as simply practice climbing with no form or substance of its own. The fact that many climbers do not take bouldering seriously in no way imperils its existence. Such differences of opinion that do arise are pleasant parodies of the more acrimonious conflicts that, depending on one's attitude, either plague or vitalize bouldering's big brother. They illustrate the charm of a sport, long in its infancy, that, despite a relaxed and rather fluctuating structure, can be incredibly demanding and delightfully rewarding.

John Gill's climbing career spans the time period 1955 to 1977. At virtually every rock climbing area in America, there are Gill problems that have never been repeated. The brief notation included here gives only an indication of his activities. Interested readers are

Gill bouldering at Pennyrile Forest in Kentucky in the mid-60's. *Courtesy John Gill.*

referred to Pat Ament's biography of Gill, *Master of Rock*, for a complete picture of his tremendous prowess.

Larry Dalke

During the mid-sixties, Larry Dalke began to show his phenomenal rock climbing skill. On a summer day in 1964, he and a companion headed towards a route on Redgarden Wall called the Green Spur. The route had first been climbed in 1960 by Dave Dornan and Dallas Jackson, and the crux dihedral had involved direct aid. Dalke headed up the climb carrying stirrups and direct aid equipment, arrived at the crux dihedral, and just "decided to try and free climb it." He says that he felt surprised that he was able to free climb the dihedral without having to resort to direct aid. This somewhat nonchalant approach was to be characteristic of Dalke during following years. He acquired a tremendous reputation for being able to free climb impossible looking pitches.

In 1965 he returned with Wayne Goss to repeat Kloeberdanz, the route which he had first climbed with Kor in 1962. After climbing the overhang using direct aid, Dalke and Goss found themselves faced by the difficult traverse which Kor had cunningly nailed three years previously. "The reason I led it free... was that I couldn't figure out how to nail it," was Dalke's modest comment in later years. He took three short falls on to an A.4 piton, but was able to successfully free climb the pitch.

During 1966, Dalke was climbing the Naked Edge on direct aid with Wayne Goss. On the last pitch, an overhanging crack, a fixed pin pulled and Dalke took a short fall. Goss has said, "I never saw Dalke scared, only mad!" The fall had just this effect, and Dalke climbed back up to Goss and proceeded to make the first free ascent of the crack in short order.

Later, during 1967, Dalke climbed the Yellow Spur. On the top pitch, where Robbins and Ament had traversed left in 1964, he free climbed straight up past the bolt ladder to make a difficult direct finish. Dalke graded these pitches 5.9. It was not until the 1970's that they received second free ascents, and the term "a Dalke 5.9," usually meaning 5.10 by later standards, came into being.

During this same period, Dalke became interested in solo climbing difficult aid routes and made a solo ascent of X-M on the Bastille, using standard roped self-protection system. He would tie-off the end of the main climbing rope to anchors at the bottom of each

Looking down the crux 5.9 dihedral of the Green Spur, first led free by Larry Dalke in 1964.

Larry Dalke.

piton, and then attach himself to the rope with prusik knots. As he moved upwards, he would slide the knots along the rope. A fall would have resulted in the prusik knots tightening on the rope, hopefully stopping him before he fell too far. At the end of each pitch, he would either rappell down, using a separate rope, or prusik back down the main climbing rope if the rock was severely overhanging. He would then have to prusik back up the rope to recover his pitons. In effect, he covered each pitch three times. His solo ascent of X-M, which depended on a number of delicate knife blade piton and rurp placements, was a bold venture using this system.

The north face of the Matron, the Nord Wand, had developed a reputation as being one of the most serious aid routes in the Boulder area. Kor, at the peak of his expertise, had found it very hard, and had taken a long

The traverse above the Psycho roof (5.8). Kor led this unprotected pitch free in 1962, and Larry Dalke later soloed it.

Entering the off-width crack on the first pitch of X-M.

time and a number of attempts to lead it. The guidebook gave the route an A.4 rating. In 1967 Dalke, using his roped self-protection system, soloed the route in four-and-a-half hours!

Dalke's last major solo ascent was probably the most extraordinary solo climb to take place in Colorado during the 1960's. He soloed Psycho in Eldorado Springs Canyon. A difficult direct aid pitch led up and over a roof to a hanging belay. From the belay, Kor had led an unprotected free climbing pitch along the lip of the roof in 1962. The pitch had become notorious and was solid 5.9. Dalke led the first pitch up to, and over, the roof in conventional manner, protecting himself by sliding jumars along the anchored rope. It was obvious to Dalke that finding places to stand and to slide the jumars would be impossible on the 5.9 face climbing above the roof. He looked it over, trying to figure out what to do. People watching said that he simply pulled up half a rope length of slack, tied off to it, and just went for it. He free climbed along the lip of the roof, making the 5.9 section look like 5.4, with a huge loop of slack rope hanging down from his waist. Dalke's only remark after the climb was, "it was sort of hairy."

In contrast to his tremendous technical ability on rock, Dalke possessed peculiar blind spots. Once, climbing with Tex Bossier on a route which Bossier had climbed before, he called down, "Am I at the hard part yet? Where does the hard part start?" Tex shouted up, "You're at the hard part Dalke, you're right at the crux." Dalke shouted down, "Where does it get easy again?" Dalke's inability to judge the difficulty of moves was one of his noted characteristics.

Another side of Dalke's character was his reverence for the mountains. In a very simple way, he perceived beauty all around him, commented on it frequently, and would make difficult moves to climb around a flower without damaging it.

Off the climb, Dalke at times was another person. His big old B.S.A. motor bike was his other passion in life. He disliked authority and loved to drive the highways at a hundred m.p.h., keeping one eye open for the police.

Dalke's most impressive free climb took place in 1967 when he decided to free climb X-M on the Bastille in Eldorado Canyon. He had previously climbed the route twice on direct aid; once with Kor and once solo. The first pitch was a massive detached flake. In 1975, Dalke recalled, "Originally, I just thought of doing the first crack free. I remember feeling amazed when I got to the top of the flake that I had been able to do it free." At the top of the flake, he was faced with a steep slab leading off to the left, which Ament had led on the first ascent in 1962 using rurps. A bolt had been placed

Larry Dalke making the first free ascent of X-M in 1967.
Courtesy Larry Dalke.

Above and opposite. Mid-way on the unprotected (5.10) traverse on the second lead of X-M. A fall here and the climber pendulums into the pillar below his belayer.

part-way across the traversing section of the slab which, in Dalke's words, "Gave me something to go for." The moves were extreme. It was impossible to obtain protection. He placed a knife blade piton in a thin crack, but felt that the protection it gave was purely psychological. This section was extremely serious. A fall would have resulted in Dalke smashing back into the detached flake at the top of the first pitch. Dalke had the following to say about this pitch and the rest of the climb when interviewed in 1975:

> .....I think I got something psychological in the corner (at the start of the second pitch)—a knife blade or a rurp. I was out there hanging on to the hold before the bolt, trying to get something in. Then it was easy up to the belay, and easy for a ways after that. I got some little things in. I was still free climbing. I went up, and came back, and thought it over; I knew there was a ledge up

there, but you have to commit yourself. It wasn't really a lunge. It's just that once you're up there, you just can't get down, because the sequence of moves up to that point is complicated. When I got there I remember hanging on and just trying to get a piton in at the same time. I can't remember the sequence after that, because that was the worst part. I remembered the next pitch well from the time when I had soloed it. I tried to climb the whole thing pure, and didn't hang on to any pitons. When I came to a resting place, then I would rest.

Larry Dalke's free ascent of X-M in 1967 has become highly respected among rock climbers. Four years were to pass before a second free ascent was made by two young climbers of the seventies, Duncan Ferguson and Jim Erickson. Their report of the technical difficulties and serious nature of the climb served to affirm Dalke's skill and boldness in 1967. In 1977, the climb is still

graded 5.10, with the suffix: "protection difficult."

More than any other single climb of this period, Larry Dalke's ascent of X-M in 1967 has become acknowledged by modern rock climbers as an advanced climb for its time, and one which possessed the characteristics which were to become hallmarks of the most difficult rock climbs of the 1970's—boldness, technical difficulty and seriousness, undertaken in pure free climbing style.

Dalke continued to climb after making his free ascent of X-M in 1967. Later, following conversations with Kor, he, too, was to forsake rock climbing and to join the Jehovah's Witnesses. Fate had led in a strange direction for two of Colorado's greatest rock climbers.

Postscript to the Sixties

During the 1960's, rock climbing standards were pushed to new levels on low cliffs and in the high mountains. From 1956 to 1968, Layton Kor was the dominant figure; his style of free climbing mixed with direct aid where needed was widely adopted by his contemporaries. Climbs such as the Naked Edge, the Nord Wand, and the Red Dihedral were achieved by sophisticated use of direct aid. In the high mountains, routes such as the Diagonal, the Diamond, the Northwest Face of Chief's Head, and the winter ascent of the Diamond, showed that with patience and perseverance, the most imposing walls could be climbed.

Rearick's free climbing efforts in 1962 represented the early beginnings of a line of development in which a set of parameters was developed, and refined, to put the outcome of climbing on smaller cliffs more in question. A pitch which had involved pitons for handholds or for resting was not considered a free ascent, and Rearick was the first climber in the Boulder region to really apply himself to free climbing pitches which had previously been climbed on direct aid. As free climbing developed, progressively more and more limitations were introduced to maintain an element of uncertainty. Style became progressively more prescribed, and with it, the happy-go-lucky approach to climbing which had been a main characteristic of climbing in the sixties began to diminish.

Left. The crux moves on the third lead of X-M. The leader is faced with the difficult mantle which Larry Dalke describes in his account of the first free ascent.

REFERENCES

1. Pat Ament, *Master of Rock: The Biography of John Gill* (Colorado: Westview Press, 1977).
2. John Gill, "The Art of Bouldering," *American Alpine Journal*, Vol. 16, No. 43, 1969, p. 355.
3. *Ibid.*
4. Ament, *op. cit.*
5. Gill, *Op. cit.,* p. 356.

Jim Erickson at age fifteen
(1964).

FREE CLIMBING

- THE SEVENTIES

*Historically, ultimate climbs
have tended to be achieved by
dubious means.*
Jim Erickson (1976)

The main characteristic of rock climbing in Colorado in the early 1970's was a renaissance of free climbing. In much the same way that the earth has become a global village, the 1970's witnessed the phenomenon of the shrinking cliff. Direct aid techniques of the 1960's made new routes on smaller cliffs a foregone conclusion. The outcome was no longer really in question. Given sufficient time, a persistent climber could engineer his way anywhere. The effect of the technology of direct aid had been to effectively cut cliffs down in size.

Direct aid climbing on small cliffs virtually disappeared during the early 1970's. The reasons for this development are complex. Originally, direct aid depended upon pitons driven into the rock to support the climber's weight. When chrome-molly hardware came into general use, elegant climbs were pounded and pulped into scarred remnants of their former beauty. Tom Frost, writing in the *American Alpine Journal* of 1972, pointed out that, due to the repeated usage of hard steel pitons, "on some popular routes it looks as though a jack hammer has been used."

The concept of environmental preservation of rock climbs found ready acceptance among climbers during the 1970's. There were obvious parallels between the concept of rock as a finite resource, and the diminishing nature of many other valuable resources upon which the quality of life depended. Environmental thinking in rock climbing paralleled public awareness of ecology and conservation issues, and the greening of the rock face progressed step by step with the greening of America. Also of major importance, free climbing in good style re-emphasized the aesthetic side of rock climbing which had been overshadowed during the piton era of the 1960's.

In contrast to aesthetic and environmental considerations, free climbing developments also emphasized the competitive side of rock climbing. As style became more prescribed, it became easier for competitive comparisons to be made between different ascents.

During the early 1970's, a speeding up of communication among rock climbers took place which significantly affected the nature of rock climbing. Prior to 1970, events in Colorado occurred in relative isolation. A small number of Colorado climbers paid visits to Yosemite, and such climbers as Robbins, Pratt, and Chouinard made occasional trips to Colorado. Rumors, myths, and legends were exchanged, but precise information was frequently lacking.

In 1967, Pat Ament and Cleve McCarty published the first version of their rock climber's guidebook *High Over Boulder*, and a revised edition was published in 1970. The ascents of the 1960's began to assume more reasonable proportions—still phenomenal, but now described in detail, and possibly within the ability of a new generation of rock climbers.

Climbing magazines played an important part in shaping modern rock climbing. *Summit* magazine, available throughout the sixties, always included some rock climbing information, but was more oriented toward the hiker and the mountaineer. In 1969, the British magazine *Mountain* appeared. Its primary emphasis was technical climbing. During the 1970's, this magazine achieved international circulation. In 1970, the American magazine *Climbing* was first published, and other magazines have since appeared. Information on rock climbing, both internationally and in America, became readily available. New climbs, advanced techniques, sophisticated equipment, and the development of climbing in different areas received coverage. With this ready availability of information, increasing numbers of climbers became interested both in repeating the hard routes of the sixties and in seeking out new ones. There was also the added competitive bonus of seeing one's name listed in the information columns for having made a first ascent. Climbers of the sixties sometimes had to wait a decade to see their names appear in the guidebook. Instantaneous media feedback became a feature of the seventies. Magazine editors became influential opinion shapers and helped to generate a situation in which competitive ethics became a keynote of modern rock climbing.

Equipment was changing rapidly during the late 1960's. By 1970, nuts as an alternative to hammered pitons had come into general use. The use of nuts had its origin in the early days of rock climbing in Britain. Climbers would carry a few small pebbles with them on rock climbs. The principle employed was to slot the pebble into a crack in the rock, so that it wedged firmly at a narrow section. A nylon sling could then be threaded behind the pebble, and the main climbing rope clipped in with a carabiner. Chockstoning of this nature became an art, and British climbers such as Joe Brown and Don Whillans became experts at crafty placements.

In Britain, during the 1950's, a great deal of attention was focused on the walls of Clogwyn du'r Arddu in North Wales, or "Cloggy" as it became known to British climbers. The approach to Cloggy followed a cog railway up a mountain called Snowdon. The story goes that one day a climber picked up an hexagonal machine nut which had fallen off the train and found that it jammed into cracks better than a pebble. During the fifties, British climbers scoured discarded machinery, pirated abandoned cars, and experimented with many strange pieces of old metal. For a number of years, the crux moves on a climb called Kaisergerberge Wall in the Llanberis Pass were protected by a permanently fixed bicycle crank jammed into a convenient crack! Hexagonal nuts were still the preferred favorites, and many loving hours were spent filing out the threads and rubbing the nuts with emery cloth to remove sharp edges. A number of differently sized nuts could be threaded onto slings, giving the climber a wide range of possible placements.

From these early beginnings in Great Britain, the design of nuts has seen sophisticated development. The disadvantage of hexagonal machine nuts was that few cracks had a taper that matched the side of the nut. Subsequently, wedge shapes with tapers matching the more commonly encountered cracks were developed and manufactured in different sizes.

By the early 1970's, nuts had come into generally accepted use, and some climbers preferred to carry neither pitons nor a hammer. The old familiar clang of pitons was replaced by the hardly noticeable thud of aluminum nuts striking against each other as the climber ascended the rock; the actual placement of a nut made no sound at all. Popular routes usually had fixed pitons in place where needed, and it was unnecessary to add new ones. Climbers unable to arrange adequate protection from nuts and established fixed pitons were generally encouraged to direct their energies elsewhere.

During the early years of the seventies, climbers made increased use of gymnastic chalk on their hands to give sweaty fingers better friction. With only small numbers of climbers using chalk, there was no real problem. As the seventies progressed and more climbers acquired the habit, hard routes became dotted with white, and climbing-by-numbers became the style. At each crux, the key holds would be splattered by well-fondled whiteness. The "powder puff kids," as *Mountain* magazine lovingly called them, multiplied like rabbits during a long winter, and popular cliffs began to look like guidebook photographs with white dotted lines tracing routes. The argument that chalk washes off in the rain is fallacious, since it is used most frequently on the hardest overhanging routes where the rain rarely penetrates. Habit forming, the "white bags of courage" became part of the seventies.

Rock climbing footwear saw important changes during the 1970's. Kronhoffer kletterschuhes with ribbed vibram soles used to be the preferred favorites and were excellent for standing on small edge holds. Smooth-soled shoes imported from Europe were to become the most commonly worn rock climbing footgear of the seventies. Called P.A.'s, after the original designer, Pierre Allain, other types included R.D.'s (Rene Demaison) and E.B.'s (Edouard Bordeneaux). As rock climbing increased in sophistication, it became not unusual for climbers to own more than one pair of shoes; a smooth-soled pair for friction climbing, and a stiff-soled pair for edging. The difference in stiffness and frictional qualities between various types of smooth-soled shoes led some climbers to the point of owning four or five different pairs, and there are even a few cases on record of climbers wearing one type on one foot and a different type on the other to obtain maximum advantage on a particular route!

The softer-soled climbing shoes leave black rubber marks on the rock—not quite as disfiguring as chalk—but noticeable on popular routes, creating a potential environmental problem for the future. Some people argue that sophisticated climbing shoes give a form of direct aid, but, so far, the joys of doing hard free climbing in bare feet have been the preserve of only a small number of climbers.

Some climbers are always looking for new tricks to help them get up difficult routes. One of the more innovative ideas came when a climber in Eldorado Canyon was heard to call down to his belayer, "Hey, I've got an idea. Take your shoes off and lay them upside down for a while. The rubber gets soft from the sun and they stick to the rock better!"

The number of Colorado climbers active on high standard, technically difficult rock climbs in the early 1960's could be counted on the fingers of two hands. In the early years of the 1970's, this number swelled into many hundreds. To lead 5.9 in 1960 was sufficient to make a rock climber a legend in his own time. By 1977, leading 5.9 had become commonplace, leading 5.10 was by no means unusual. and an increasing number of

Finger tip laybacking on the first pitch of
Outer Space (5.10).

climbers were finding that 5.11 was within their ability.

Jim Erickson

Throughout the history of Colorado rock climbing, new developments have usually been the result of a particularly gifted individual being able to use the experiences of the past as stepping stones, and by means of special ability, or insight, to create new developments. In earlier days, radical new development was possible; so little was known or had been accomplished. Albert Ellingwood had an unexplored supply of possibilities in 1920. The climbing world was his oyster, and new opportunities abounded for his picking. Even in the early 1960's, Layton Kor was able to blaze new paths, developing a style and a psychology which seemed radically advanced compared to what had taken place before. In more recent years, it has become progressively more difficult for any particular individual to make a mark.

Within this context, the most influential figure in Colorado rock climbing during the late sixties and early seventies was Jim Erickson. Erickson began rock climbing at Devil's Lake in Wisconsin in 1963, when he was fourteen. At the age of seventeen, he led his first 5.10 climb and was obviously a talented rock climber. In 1967, he moved to Colorado to become an undergraduate at the University of Colorado; his major interest was classical music.

Climbing at Devil's Lake was specialized to a high degree. The majority of climbs were face climbs on small holds, and the average height of routes was sixty feet. Arriving in Colorado, Erickson was unable to adjust immediately to more varied types of climbing, and to climbing on larger cliffs. He had to undergo a re-learning process during his first year, and serve an apprenticeship on easy classic routes.

Erickson's first experiences in Colorado were not promising. He had to retreat from a number of established classics, including the first pitch of Redguard Route (5.7). Eventually he "struggled" up the Anthill Direct (5.8), but remembers finding it very hard.

On a summer day in 1968, Erickson embarked on the Bastille Crack, hoping for better luck. The first three pitches went uneventfully. At the start of the fourth pitch, he was unsure where to go next, but saw an old piton sticking out of a steep wall above. "This must be it," he thought, and after much difficulty he was able to climb up to the piton. He knew that the grading of the Bastille Crack was only 5.7, and he felt dismayed that he was having so much trouble. After pondering the situation for a while, he concluded that the wall above the piton was beyond his ability, descended, and

Moving round the corner onto the exposed
upper section of Outer Space on the Bastille.

eventually found a lower angle and much easier corner
to the left of the wall which led to the top of the cliff.
This failure on an old established 5.7 route was another
blow to his confidence, and he began to wonder if the
climbs he had led at Devil's Lake were really 5.9 and
5.10. (The wall which Erickson was attempting to climb
was actually a pitch of Wide Country, a direct aid route
which had never been free climbed! The "easy" corner
which he eventually followed was the actual final pitch
of the Bastille Crack).

A few days later, Erickson returned to Eldorado, and
his eyes roamed over the rocks of the Wind Tower
immediately opposite the Bastille. A large, obvious
crack system caught his eye. Looking in the guidebook,
he found that the name of this climb was Black Jack,
and that it was rated 5.8. The description of the climb
was innocuous: "A short variation on the South Face of
the Wind Tower...rather unprotected and...most
difficult near the end." Still smarting from his
"failure" on the Bastille Crack, Erickson decided to
give it a try. Two hours later he was back down at the
stream again, having failed miserably to make any
headway up the crack. He gloomily wondered if he was
ever going to be able to do any of the harder routes in
the area if he was having such trouble with the easy
ones.

(The story of Black Jack has become notorious.
When Erickson attempted it, it had previously had only
one ascent by Layton Kor and Pete Robinson in 1963.
The 5.8 grading was based on Kor's report of the climb.
By 1970, the climb still had not received a second ascent.
McCarty and Ament felt that it obviously must have
been harder than Kor's 5.8 rating, so they changed the
grading in their guidebook to 5.9. In 1972, Ament and
Erickson published a new guidebook. Black Jack had
still not had a second ascent and was upgraded to
"5.10...poor protection." In 1973, Black Jack
received its long awaited second ascent (Ferguson and
Chelton), and the 5.10 rating was confirmed—a tribute
to Kor's genius in 1963, and a humorous aftermath to
Erickson's attempt during the summer of 1968.)

During 1968 and 1969, Erickson continued to apply
himself to free climbing. After his early failures on the
Bastille Crack and Black Jack, his confidence was
restored when he was able to free climb the Yellow Spur
and the poorly protected second lead of Psycho.

In 1968, Erickson made a trip up to the Shawangunks
and learned that it was possible to free climb apparently
impossible-looking overhangs, in which the Gunks
abounded. On his return to Colorado, he thought he
would try to free climb one of the old aid routes. He
says, "It turned out that there were scores of aid routes
that were within the climbing abilities of many other

Beginning the difficult moves around the roof on the second pitch of Tagger (5.10). The free ascent of this roof by Erickson in 1968 opened eyes to many other overhanging possibilities in Eldorado.

Right. "Barndoor" laybacking on the awkward first pitch of Tagger (5.9-).

Jim Erickson.

climbers in 1968."

Erickson read in the guidebook of a route called Tagger, on the Wind Tower in Eldorado Springs Canyon. The climb went over a large overhang on the second pitch, "with two or three pitons of direct aid." Erickson figured that if only two or three aid pitons were necessary, then perhaps the climb would go free. His experience on the cliffs of the Shawangunks had taught him not to be overly impressed by massive overhangs, and that they could be climbed using free techniques. This proved to be the case on Tagger. Erickson and Jim Walsh were able to free climb the crux overhang.

That same year (1968), Erickson was basking on a sun-warmed ledge in Eldorado Springs Canyon, watching climbers nailing the overhanging section on a climb called Grandmother's Challenge. He looked over and saw that there was an undercling that went straight up through the overhang. "I wondered if it would be possible to go straight up it free, rather than nailing out left up the thin direct aid crack," he says. Using a 2-inch bong for protection at the crux, Erickson was able to free climb the undercling. Afterwards, unsure of himself after his earlier failures that year, he graded the free version 5.9. "I just didn't feel I could climb

Grandmother's Challenge (5.10). One of Jim Erickson's early free ascents.

anything harder at that time," he says. In 1977 Grandmother's Challenge was established as solid 5.10!

The years 1968-1970 were formative years for Erickson. He continued to explore the guidebook for direct aid routes that might succumb to free climbing technique. Rearick, Robbins, Ament, and Dalke had started this trend during the early 1960's, but between 1968 and 1970, Erickson was the only climber in the Boulder area who continued to develop it further. He readily acknowledges, "Many of the climbs I did were obscure." Climbers had assumed that if Kor, Ament, and Dalke had climbed them using direct aid, then they must be impossible to free climb. In some cases, Erickson was to find that this was not true.

In 1969, Erickson free climbed Rincon, the route on the west side of Redgarden Wall originally climbed by Kor and Turner, and again demonstrated his talent for undergrading. He rated the free ascent at 5.9 plus. In 1977, the route had a 5.11 pitch.

During the period 1968-1970, Erickson free climbed a number of other direct aid routes. One of these was a climb called Blackwalk on Redgarden Wall. Prior to Blackwalk, the direct aid routes which Erickson had free climbed had been graded A.1 or A.2, and the aid sections were relatively short. Blackwalk was different. The guidebook gave the route an A.4 rating and indicated that the aid section was long and sustained.

The crux of the first pitch of Blackwalk involved a 5.10 move up a steep headwall protected by bolts. Erickson clipped into the first bolt, and the second, and went for it. Ten feet above his protection he "took the plunge," and his twenty-foot peel dragged his surprised belayer, "Magic" Ed Wright, across the ground at the foot of the climb. Returning later, he was able to successfully make the moves, but his second, Kevin Donald, could not follow. The same thing happened again when he returned with Pitman Orr. Finally, returning with his brother Dave, Erickson led the moves again. His brother was able to second the pitch and to lead the next one.

Psychologically, Blackwalk was a significant climb for Erickson. It was the first A.4 route that he had free climbed. It was becoming more and more apparent that free climbing possibilities had really only begun to be explored. If A.4 on Blackwalk could be free climbed, who knew what else might be possible?

During 1970, two other climbers who were to join Erickson at the forefront of free climbing appeared: Duncan Ferguson and Steve Wunsch. Ferguson was tall, athletic, and practiced yoga. A few months after starting climbing, he led T.2 in Eldorado Springs Canyon, demonstrating a natural talent for rock climbing. The aesthetics of free climbing appealed to

m Erickson laybacking
e strenuous crux of Grand-
other's Challenge.

Left. Finger jamming the crack on the first pitch Rincon.

Right. The crux moves Blackwalk (5.10). Many climbers have turned ba after contemplating the twenty foot run out abc the bolt.

Far Left. The elegant dihedral of Cosmosis (5.9+) in Boulder Canyon, first free ascent by Duncan Ferguson.

Left. Looking down the Cosmosis dihedral.

Free Climbing - Seventies

Ferguson and complemented his life style. That summer, he free climbed his first major route, Cosmosis, a steep overhanging dihedral in Boulder Canyon.

Steve Wunsch had climbed regularly during 1970, and had steadily worked his way through the established 5.9 routes. He was tall, lanky, and had a smooth, flowing style on difficult rock. In 1971, he made the first free ascent of the east ridge of the Maiden, a climb which had had a long history of struggle between bolters and anti-bolters during the 1950's. The crux section was an overhanging wall, previously climbed using three bolts for aid. Royal Robbins had climbed the ridge during the 1960's using only one bolt for aid. In 1971, Wunsch eliminated the aid bolt and was able to free climb the complete route. The same year he made the second free ascent of the Northwest Corner of the Bastille.

During following years Wunsch was to become one of the leading Colorado free climbers, pioneering a number of major routes. His travels over the years took him to Yosemite, the Shawangunks, England, and Dresden. An articulate critic of the climbing scene, Wunsch developed into a key figure influencing free climbing thinking and developments.

The story is told of a long traverse in the Macky pits (a favorite bouldering spot on the University of Colorado campus) which was considered the epitome of difficulty. To traverse once along and back its approximately fifty foot length was considered quite an achievement. Wunsch surprised the regulars on his first appearance by traversing back and forward a number of times with a noticeable lack of effort, and remaining on the traverse for almost an hour and a half. His yoga exercises had given him tremendous flexibility, enabling him to splay his knees out, thereby moving his centre of gravity close in to the wall and making it possible for him to semi-rest on the small finger holds of the traverse. Erickson, who was watching, said, "Wunsch looked as though he could have gone on all day. He didn't quit because he was tired - but because his fingers were in danger of becoming permanently bent into a hooked shape."

The Naked Edge

Events up to 1970 had shown that improbable-looking direct aid routes could be free climbed. In 1971 Jim Erickson, Duncan Ferguson, and Steve Wunsch became involved in an ascent which was to dramatically alter previously held notions of what was possible in the realm of free climbing.

Shortly after Jim Erickson had started climbing in Colorado, he met Pat Ament. Ament's imagination was

strong, and he felt that the Naked Edge in Eldorado Springs Canyon would one day go free. In 1968 this appeared unthinkable and no one, including Ament, had made a serious attempt. As Erickson steadily knocked off harder and harder free climbs, a vision of free climbing the Naked Edge kept returning to him. In 1969, he made a free climbing attempt on the first pitch, a steep finger crack, with Barry Harper and Ed Wright. Reaching a point two thirds of the way up the pitch, Erickson took a short leader fall and retreated. The following year, in the spring of 1970, Erickson made a second free climbing attempt, this time with Kevin Donald and his brother Dave Erickson, with similar results. By 1971, free climbing the Naked Edge had become his foremost ambition.

Jim Erickson wrote the following description of the first free ascent of the Naked Edge for inclusion in this book. It is impossible to convey the audaciousness of this venture in words, but his account gives an indication of its flavor. There is no doubt that its accomplishment opened up a new wave of free climbing in the 1970's.

It is six a.m. on September 26, 1971. Steve Wunsch and I sit wide-eyed in Boulder's IHOP trying to consume enough pancakes and coffee to achieve consciousness. Yesterday we completed the third completely free ascent of Country Club Crack. Today we are poised for an equally presumptuous attempt: the Naked Edge, a spectacular classic regardless of how it is climbed, but to date all the parties to do it have employed direct aid techniques virtually the entire distance. We are to try it completely free.

Memories of previous attempts drift by: three times on aid, two times free, five times failure. No reason today will be different. Steve is excited to try, and needs

Redgarden Wall showing the Naked Edge.

Redgarden Wall. The line of the Naked Edge is
clearly outlined between light and shade.

Right. Stemming off the sharp corner of the first lead of the Naked Edge.

Far right. Finger jamming at the crux on the first pitch of the Naked Edge. Jim Erickson was turned back at this point on his early free climbing attempts. (The climber is in approximately the same position in both these photos).

someone to humor him, and belay.

Mounds of sausage, Swedish pancakes, and coffee coagulate, inhibiting enjoyment of the clear morning air and blue sky. Like stuffed pigs, we waddle up and wander up 200 feet of moderate rock to the start. The first pitch brings memories of pumped arms, lowering on the rope and a ten foot fall. Thankfully, Steve wants to lead it.

Steve climbs upwards, meticulously and irresistibly, to near my previous high point, sets a piton, and lowers down to rest. He smiles beneath his twisted, stringy blond hair, and my hopes begin to bubble. My turn five feet higher, into a critical fixed pin, before I stumble and ride the elevator back down. Only five more difficult feet remain. Excitement boils as Steve climbs up and finesses past my fall with a bridge. When he gets to the belay I burst with happiness. Five minutes later I've followed the strenuous pitch and I'm standing at Steve's side with a grin as wide as Niagara, jumping up and down like a six-year old going to the circus for the first time. Another ten minutes and I've calmed down enough to start climbing again.

Up a beautiful slab, around the edge to a smooth, 20-foot headwall. I carefully reverse moves here for almost an hour, until I unlock the combination to a single 5.10 move. Steve follows and leads the 5.8 pitch above rather easily.

"Here the climbing becomes exposed and spectacular as it moves up the outward leaning edge."

Steve dubs it impossible. I give it a disheartened try, but it is late so down we come, pondering the ultimate metaphysical questions: "Is there life after birth? Sex after death?" Wunsch departs for Yosemite, leaving Achilles brooding.

Sunday, October 3, 1971. 6:30 a.m. I turn off the ignition. A predawn blast of wind shakes the car. I open the door just as another freezing gust hits, and slam it instantly shut. Duncan Ferguson and I exchange nervous glances, afraid that our mutual cowardice might shatter the myth of the hard man. I tentatively turn on the heater. Duncan rationally replies that we could sort our gear in the car. Thank God. We both breathe unconscious sighs of relief. Twenty guilt-ridden minutes later we manage to summon enough courage to leave the security of the car and brave the 50 degree weather. No mere rock-climbers here.

The bottom of the first pitch: I watch silently as sun slowly evaporates the shadows, revealing the crisp colors of the sandstone canyon. We are absolutely alone; a uniquely aesthetic experience. I look at Duncan, then at the spotless sky. Today will be a perfect day.

Climbing the lower pitches, we reach my high point well before noon, and leapfrog protection up the prow into a flared, overhanging slot. My knicker knee rips trying to get in and, after a fall, I lower to Duncan. Next try I make it, and then Duncan makes it look easy. The belay must be one of the most spectacular imaginable, a sloping doormat, suspended in space. For almost an hour we rest, enjoying the insecurity of this singular place.

The final pitch towers still farther above, like the

The second lead of the Naked Edge. From the top of the slab the climber traverses left and is confronted with a 5.10 move. Legend has it that the sharp edge would slice the rope on a fall from this point.

bow of some great battleship, a fitting finale. Strenuous, overhanging finger-laybacking leads around a corner. A severely overhanging hand-crack pierces the prow leading upward thirty feet and out of sight. My forearms feel like melted silly putty as I struggle to rest, shaking first one arm, then the other, light years of emptiness beneath. I have but strength for one attempt.

Ten feet of hand-jams leads to a fixed pin. My hands are sliding like molasses from the crack. I hastily clip in. Ten more feet. Nothing is left in my forearms except dull throbbing. Both hands slip from the crack. The next heartbeat extends for eternity. I instinctively grab the edge of the crack with both hands in a quasi-lieback, pull with everything there is left, and lunge forever for a perfect hand-slot with my left hand. It crunches into the crack and grinds to a stop, ripping skin as my weight puts its strength to trial, preventing a breathtakingly long fall. A few more feet and I'm allowed to rest both arms for the first time since I left Duncan. Ten easier feet lead to the top, where I put in an anchor, tie in, and collapse. Five full minutes pass before I recover the energy to pull up the rope and belay Duncan.

Tainting

Prior to the Naked Edge, Erickson had been progressively refining his approach to free climbing, and the falls he had taken on the fourth pitch had a strong effect on him. Shortly after the successful ascent, he decided that falling and lowering interfered sufficiently to spoil his sense of adventure on new free ascents. He summarized his approach as, "I would try and do nothing which a climber who was soloing could not do." Others had espoused this concept, but it led to major limitations if pushed to its furthest extreme, which was exactly what Erickson chose to do in years following the Naked Edge. He became noted for a particular trait during this period. If he took a leader fall while attempting a first free ascent, or used protection for lowering off, he would not return to try and lead that particular pitch. Erickson was also one of the very few climbers during the early seventies who resisted the temptation to use chalk on hard climbs, even on his first free ascents. Erickson humorously referred to transgressions of his climbing principles as "tainting" during the years to follow.

In retrospect, Erickson felt that his first free ascent of the Naked Edge was made in a style which "humbled the climb," using his later criteria of no leader falls or use of protection for lowering. Even with his reservations, there is no doubt that the first free ascent of the Naked Edge opened up the era of hard free climbing of the 1970's, and paved the way for a series of extraordinary climbs during succeeding years.

Right. The notorious overhanging jam crack on the final lead of the Edge, first climbed free by Larry Dalke in 1966. (Another "Dalke 5.9"). Many modern climbers have successfully climbed the first four leads of the Naked Edge free, only to fail on this strenuous final section.

Chimneying the shallow slot on the fourth lead of the Edge, considered by many to be the crux of the climb.

The strenuous roof at the top of the slot.

Beginning the overhanging layback and jam crack on the second lead of the Diving Board.

A few months after the first free ascent of the Naked Edge, Erickson read an article by John Stannard on piton damage to cracks, which included a photograph of the mutilated condition of Serenity Crack in Yosemite. The ideas expressed reinforced thoughts which had been brewing for some time in his own mind, and he made a decision to climb using only nuts for protection. "You're crazy," Steve Wunsch remarked, "there are going to be some places where you will have to use pins." "We'll see," replied Erickson, and, subsequent to 1971, he climbed without pitons or a hammer, with only one or two notable exceptions.

Erickson's free climbing criteria may seem overly rigorous to climbers steeped in earlier mountaineering traditions. It would not have been surprising had he climbed, using his style for a while during the early seventies, and then disappeared from the climbing scene forever, as many young climbers do. This was not to be the case. Erickson climbed regularly between 1967 and 1977, accomplished more than a hundred first free ascents, and with each passing year adhered more and more stringently to his free climbing principles.

Unsure of the value of his contribution, in 1977 Erickson ruefully commented, "I sometimes wonder if I've set an example which other climbers respect, or I'm just some kind of weird climbing anachronism." His concern was needless. His influence contributed in a major way to a quiet revolution in Colorado, to a point where, in 1977, a majority of climbers use free climbing techniques.

Diving Board

In 1964 a young school boy named Roger Briggs, who had been climbing for only a year or so, was picnicking with his family at Castle Rock in Boulder Canyon. He watched open-mouthed as Royal Robbins and Pat Ament struggled to free climb Athlete's Feat. Two years later in 1966, he watched Pat Ament leading Supremacy Crack. In 1966, he accompanied Ament on ascents of two difficult climbs: Vertigo and the Northwest Corner of the Bastille. He climbed regularly after that, and, as was the style, became an expert in direct aid climbing. His direct aid ascent in 1967 of a climb which he called Wide Country on the Bastille was a technically difficult route up an improbably blank section of the wall. Briggs recalls the first ascent:

> ...I'd always fantasized about a route up there in the middle of all that blank stuff....I was seventeen at the time, and I did it with Leo Foster who was just a kid of fifteen. It was pretty hard for us and we put in a bolt on

Roger Briggs.

the first pitch.

The third pitch was interesting when we nailed it. We had to get across a blank slab, and there was no free way to do it. I drilled a little hole and used a cliff hanger. It was terrifying. I remember the section distinctly. I stood in the cliff hanger and then reached over and grabbed an edge and did a 5.8 free move. I wasn't much of a free climber. I moved out of my stirrups, thinking I could get back in them, when the hanger fell out, taking my stirrup with it. I was committed to the move. I was right at my limit, 5.8, and at the time it felt very serious.

Following on from these early beginnings, Briggs developed into one of the leading free climbers of the 1970's. In 1971, two months before Erickson and Ferguson free climbed the Naked Edge, Briggs attempted to climb a route very close to it—the Diving Board, the same route which Layton Kor had led with the young and apprehensive Larry Dalke in 1962. His account of his ascent graphically demonstrates how conditions can change between first and subsequent ascents of a route.

I was thirteen and standing at the top of Redgarden Wall, mesmerized and trembling with my first view of the Diving Board. Kor and Dalke first climbed it in 1962. It was strenuous aid, requiring numerous bongs, and had a rotten A.4 section. In the mid-sixties it was quite an undertaking to tackle the Diving Board. In 1968 Tom Ruwitch and I did the fourth ascent—an all day affair requiring all the strength, stamina, and equipment we had. The appearance of the climb from the canyon floor probably kept more climbers off of it than anything else. It looms over its surroundings, beckoning or threatening, depending on one's frame of mind.

In 1967 Ament mentioned the idea of doing the Diving Board free. I considered it an outrageous dream—the whole climb overhung! In 1967 it seemed a major achievement to aid it; to free climb it— out of the question.

In July of 1971 I was planning a low key, fun sort of ascent of the Diving Board with two friends. I was not yet much of a free climber, but for some reason I decided to start out free climbing and go as far as possible without aid. It seemed safe enough—I would just use aid as soon as I could no longer free climb.

A short, rotten pitch took us to the top of pigeon flake. The difficulties began on the next pitch. The first 25 feet were rotten and overhanging—the A.4 section.... a ten-foot traverse left on portable blocks, then a place to rest next to a fixed pin driven into mud.... fifteen more feet up and out before a good crack and protection could be reached. What was I getting myself into? I didn't know but, what the hell, I'd give it a try....A mantle onto a crumbling, sloping shelf, using my fingernails to reach a standing position.

No protection!

Jesus, I've got to get out of here—but how?

It was dawning on me that I would not be able to

reverse the moves I had just made.... Ten feet out from poor protection, twenty feet out from my belayer, and aimed like a gun for a wild swing into pigeon flake—enough to dissect me, my rope, or both. Only three or four more feet to the crack and protection— I had to try. My strength was disappearing, but now it was a raw struggle for survival. This was no longer the fun game I had played in the past. I was in over my head.

Scratching, cursing, moaning and whimpering, I got a piton in. Someone must have wanted me to live. With renewed confidence I moved up, out of the rotten section and into the overhanging corner which extended 40 feet to the end of the pitch. Forty feet of climbing at my limit and beyond, but at least there was protection. Arms bloated and aching, I finally dragged myself into the belay cave. What a miserable excuse for a human! It was 100 degrees, my throat was like leather, and I wanted to throw up.

My partners jumared the pitch, not sure what to think about what they had just witnessed. I was still physically wasted, the heat was becoming intolerable, and I didn't even consider trying the last pitch free. We finished on aid, and I felt satisfied with having done as much as I had. I was sure that what I had done would be repeated by very few, and they would have to pay the same price in fear that I had paid.

Several weeks later, two climbers nailed the Diving Board. In the unprotected section they left two fixed pitons and a nut.

A month later I returned to try the last pitch free. We quickly nailed the lower section, and I was disappointed to find the protection left by the last party. This time I was fresh and ready for the last pitch. It was solid all the way, with tricky moves but always good protection. At the top, a lovely hand jam went off-width. Two difficult but very safe moves and moderate slabs to the end of the

Jamming the crux on the final lead of the Diving Board. 600 feet above the canyon floor, this is one of the most exposed positions in Eldorado.

Right. Looking down on the climber at the crux on the final lead of the Diving Board. (The climber is in the same position as in the opposite photograph). The haul line falls free for the full 150 feet.

climb. A hard pitch but nothing compared to the depths of psyche I had experienced climbing the lower pitch. Now all of the Diving Board had been done free, but not in a single ascent.

In 1976, the Diving Board still commands respect and has been done free perhaps 15 or 20 times. Few think the lower pitch is too hard—well enough protected, a little strenuous. To present day climbers, the crux is the last pitch. The soul left behind on the lower pitch by some terror-crazed glory seeker a few years earlier is invisible to all those who now do the climb.

It is always difficult to rate the difficulty of first ascents. In 1971, there were only a small number of new free climbs with which to make comparisons, and there was the ever present possibility of over-rating a new route as the result of too much ego involvement, only to have it down-graded on a subsequent ascent. Unwilling to risk having others downgrade his free ascent of Diving Board, Briggs rated the two difficult pitches 5.9+.

During the fall of that year, an incident took place which showed just how inaccurate Briggs' rating of the Diving Board had been. The first attempt at a second free ascent ended as an epic. Duncan Ferguson and Jim Erickson decided that the temptation of 5.9 climbing on an overhanging wall was too great, even if the rock was rather loose and rotten. They had free climbed the Naked Edge and X-M earlier that year, and they thought they shouldn't have too much trouble with the Diving Board.

Starting in the middle of the afternoon on a November day, Erickson took the first hard lead. From the top of Pigeon Flake he traversed left across the section which had given Roger Briggs such a difficult time on the first ascent. Then the line went straight up to a belay sixty feet above. Ferguson was out of range of the debris raining down, and he could only hear muffled curses and the sound of stones whirling by. One can well imagine the thoughts running through Ferguson's mind when he heard the sound of rock fragmenting, followed by, "There goes my best handhold," more rock breaking and, "There went my best foothold." One can imagine Erickson fiendishly scrambling upwards at a rate just slightly greater than the holds crumbling under his weight.

Finally, the dreaded signal came down from the other end of the rope. "Off belay. Your turn, Duncan." Ferguson does not describe his experience following the first pitch with much enthusiasm.

By the time Ferguson started out on the final lead, it was late in the afternoon. A crowd had gathered down below on the road to watch him working on the final section. He could not make the final moves and, after considerable effort, climbed back down to the belay and

gave the sharp end of the rope to Erickson. This sight alone, without the battle stories that were to come the following day, was enough to ward other climbers off the Diving Board for months to come. Ferguson was noted for his crack climbing ability, and his retreat was a good indication of the difficulty of the final lead. Erickson's efforts to lead the pitch ended in failure also, adding to the aura of difficulty. Both Erickson and Ferguson refused to use aid to surmount the final five-foot section. Instead they decided to rappel to the ground.

It was dark by this time, which made the rappels even less pleasurable. Rappelling from the cave at the start of the final lead put Erickson ten feet out away from the rock, hanging on the end of the rope. Erickson dangled in space, unsure of what to do, until Ferguson shouted down a suggestion for him to pull up the free end of the rope and to use it to lasso Pigeon Flake. Six more rappels in the dark landed them on the ground, each with a similar conclusion about the climb. Both agreed that one thing was certain. The Diving Board was 5.10 if it was 4th class. Ferguson never wanted to return.

The legends of the Diving Board began to grow. The first continuous free ascent was not made until a year later by Briggs and Erickson.

Death and Transfiguration

1972 was a transitional year for Roger Briggs. He had grown up in the traditional direct aid climbing school of the 1960's. His free ascent of the Diving Board was an important climb for him, but unlike Erickson, Wunsch and Ferguson, who were only interested in free climbing, Briggs maintained an interest in direct aid. He continued to search the Boulder region for new routes, and spotted an overhanging crack system on the north side of the Fourth Flatiron. He says:

At the time I wasn't much of a free climber. I just thought, "Wow, that looks like a great crack to nail up." I had just come back from Yosemite, where I had done the direct route on Half Dome, and was probably stronger than I had ever been before. I had been carrying nuts for quite some time, but was still using pitons. Erickson was the only person I knew of at that time who was climbing just on nuts. I had my hammer and rack of pitons, but I thought that I would do as much of it as I possibly could free before using aid. I pushed and pushed on the lower part, and kept thinking to myself that I'd go just a little further until I could find a resting place and then start aiding. There was a large roof about two thirds of the way up the crack, and I felt that if I could get over it free, that would be enough, and then I'd start aiding. I managed the overhang free and then realized how close I was to the top. It was only twenty-five feet away, but looked outrageous. I thought to myself, "Well, I've done

Duncan Ferguson.

and Erickson had attempted to free climb Wide Country, Roger Briggs' direct aid route up the blank section of rock between the Bastille Crack and X-M. Erickson had led the first pitch, which gave technically difficult climbing with poor protection. Ferguson returned in 1972, with Don Peterson, to complete the climb. Peterson, who had both flu and diarrhea that day, led the second 5.9 pitch, the easiest, leaving Ferguson to lead the first, third and fourth. Peterson attempted to lead the final pitch but retreated when, about thirty feet up, he pulled off a block which landed on the rope and cut it part way through. Ferguson decided to try to lead the pitch anyway. He was going great guns, and a "minor incident" like a damaged rope wasn't going to stop him. Peterson and he switched ends of the rope, and Ferguson led the final pitch, fortunately with no falls.

Ferguson showed little emotion after the first free ascent of Wide Country; he simply mentioned that, technically, the most difficult moves were on the first pitch.

Roger Briggs and Dave Ohlsen made the second

it all free up to here, might as well keep going." The closer I got to the top, the more determined I became that I was going to make it, and I did... by the skin of my teeth. I was climbing desperately for the last ten feet or so. As I was belaying my second up I was exhausted. I felt almost delirious. I was very happy to have done it and felt that it was a significant climb for me. I felt very inspired and was thinking about a name for it, and "Death and Transfiguration" floated into my head. It felt right immediately and matched my mood exactly. From that point on I was a free climber. It was a personal transfiguration for me, and I ceased to be an aid climber.

Death and Transfiguration was a significant climb for Briggs in 1972, and was later to become established as one of the finest one-pitch climbs in the Boulder region. It consolidated Briggs' feelings about free climbing versus direct aid, and also was the last climb in which he was to employ pitons for protection. Between 1972 and 1976, he put up a number of other difficult free climbs and repeated virtually all of Erickson, Wunsch, and Ferguson's routes, including the second free ascent of the Naked Edge.

Wide Country

A characteristic of many free climbs of the early seventies was moves of extreme technical difficulty, yet close to protection and made in relative safety. In 1971, shortly after the second free ascent of X-M, Ferguson

The Bastille. (1) Wide Country.

ft. Duncan
rguson leading the
al pitch of Werk
pp (5.9).

ght. The second
ch of Le Toit.

Spectacular climbing on good holds on the first lead of Le Toit. This was the first free climb to find its way through the long overhang which guards the lower section of Redgarden Wall.

Right. The steep wall leading up to the Guenese roof. Arm blowing moves, with only one resting spot, take the climber up to the roof, which is technically easier, but demanding for a tired climber.

ascent of Wide Country in 1973. Their ascent confirmed Ferguson's under-estimation of the difficulty. The final two leads turned out to be among the most difficult and serious in Eldorado at that time. On the third lead, the belayer is in a blind position and cannot see the leader. Briggs was leading and pulled on the rope to clip into a nut. There was a pause, followed by another strong pull on the rope, which Ohlsen assumed meant that Briggs was clipping into another piece of protection. (Actually, Briggs had fallen onto a tiny #1 stopper which broke.) Ohlsen, feeling the jerk, thought Briggs was pulling up slack to clip into protection, so he let more rope out and was surprised a moment later to see Briggs come falling into sight as the rope ran through his hands. After Ohlsen had seconded the final lead, he commented to Briggs that tying off a twig sticking out of the crack near the top of the lead was pretty funny. Briggs' reply was, "That twig was no joke. I hoped it would slow me down if I fell."

Wide Country represented a new level of a continuing trend in modern rock climbing—extreme technical difficulty in poorly protected situations. The crux moves were reasonably well protected, but the climb had extended, unprotected run-outs of 5.9 climbing in situations where a fall would have serious consequences. Layton Kor had done unprotected difficult moves above the lip of the Psycho roof in 1962. Larry Dalke had done unprotected hard free climbing on X-M in 1967. Wide Country continued this trend, but it was somewhat more difficult and more serious than anything done before.

In some ways, Duncan Ferguson in the 1970's was reminiscent of Larry Dalke in the 1960's. Extremely retiring, he climbed brilliantly, but assiduously avoided the public spotlight. Rumors trickled in that he soloed Werksupp (5.9) on the Bastille in a rainstorm, wearing socks over bare feet. He soloed the Wind Ridge in Eldorado Springs Canyon, at night by the light of a headtorch, in a blizzard. Frequently Ferguson took off by himself to solo other routes. Erickson says, "Duncan had more natural ability than any climber I have seen."

Guenese

It was a miserably cold day in 1972 in Eldorado Springs Canyon, and Steve Wunsch, Jim Erickson, and Scott Stewart were sitting at the base of Redgarden Wall trying to shake the effects of the morning-after-the-night-before's party. "How about Super Slab?" suggested Stewart. Wunsch had failed on that climb twice before and, noting the competitive gleam in Stewart's eye, diverted attention by airily waving his arm in the general direction of the large overhang

Left. Steve Wunsch moving out beneath the Guenese roof.

Right. Wunsch glued to the underside of the Guenese roof.

Left. "Hey you guys. There's a jug up here."
The climber is hanging from the flake on the
Guenese roof discovered by Scott Stewart on
the first free ascent.

Free Climbing - Seventies

capping the wall against which they were huddled and enquiring, "Jim, what goes up there?" "Oh, that's Guenese," responded Erickson. Erickson had privately entertained fantasies of free climbing the Guenese roof sometime in the dimly distant future, but he felt reasonably sure that the day hadn't yet arrived. The roof in question extended along the base of Redgarden Wall and was crossed in a number of places by direct aid routes put up in the sixties. At its western extremity, its narrowest point, a route called Le Toit (Kor and Culp, 1962) had been free climbed a year earlier in 1971, but at Le Toit the overhang merged into the wall and was not a roof in the same way as Guenese. The Guenese roof jutted out horizontally. In retrospect Erickson says, "The Guenese roof was the most ridiculous looking thing imaginable. When we looked up at it that day in 1972, I don't think any of us seriously considered that we would even be able to free climb the wall up to the roof, never mind the roof itself." Wunsch, eminently rational, pointed out that the wall up to the roof was one of the few relatively warm and sheltered spots in the canyon that day, and, since they were standing right next to it, they wouldn't aggravate their hangovers by further hiking. These brilliant insights readily convinced Erickson and Stewart and, in an atmosphere of light-hearted fun, they applied themselves to the problem at hand.

After a number of tries in which they took turns leading up the wall, exchanging wisecracks, fixing protection, groaning in mock anguish, and lowering off, Stewart found himself at the top of the wall directly under the roof. "Hey you guys," he shouted down,

"there's a jug up here!" Sure enough, right in the middle of the roof was a flake which they had not been able to see from the ground. Blown out from his efforts, Stewart lowered off, and it was Wunsch's turn to try next. With the security of an overhead belay through the highest protection, he was able to reclimb the moves up the wall and to reach the high point below the roof. The roof extended horizontally for four feet, but the flake gave promise of possibilities. Wunsch was in an awkward position under the roof and found it difficult to rest. The moves over the roof, if possible at all, were obviously going to be extremely tiring, and he could not hang on indefinitely. By strenuously laying out under the roof, holding on to the flake, Wunsch was able to gain a good handhold on the lip and to pull over. No one was more surprised than him, considering the way the day had begun. "I don't believe it," exclaimed Erickson down below, "that's just ridiculous." Both he and Stewart were unable to follow the pitch free, and in typical self-deprecating manner, Erickson later said, "I couldn't come near to doing the roof free. Wunsch just hauled me over it."

Wunsch had led most of the hard moves up the wall below the roof, and his first complete ascent was one of the most difficult, and surprising, ascents of 1972. Between 1972 and 1976, Guenese received a small number of repeat ascents, yet it maintained its reputation as a technically difficult and extremely strenuous lead.

Whittling Away The Myths

1973 was an important year for rock climbing in the Boulder region. Erickson, Wunsch, Briggs, and Ferguson had virtually monopolized the free climbing scene. Their ascents were shrouded in mystery and possessed an aura of great difficulty. During 1972, a small number of other climbers repeated the hardest new routes. As was the case with Wunsch and Ferguson, a number of young climbers appeared who had not grown up during the direct aid era of the sixties, and to whom free climbing was a natural, and in a sense the only, way to climb. Unfettered by the psychological need to "step out of their stirrups," repeat ascents of the existing hard free routes became commonplace, and pressure and competition increased to make free ascents of remaining direct aid lines. By the summer of 1973, many of the hardest free climbs such as the Northwest Corner of the Bastille, Rosy Crucifixion, Super Slab, Vertigo, Grandmother's Challenge, and Rincon, all had received a number of free ascents.

As the new free climbs were repeated, Jim Erickson's

Redgarden Wall. (1) Le Toit. (2) Guenese.

mythical anonymity was whittled away, but not his reputation for difficult free climbing. The climbing community slowly began to realize the tremendous advance he had made in sight-leading hard new free climbs between 1969 and 1972. Briggs has pointed out that "the difference between doing a climb for the first time and repeating it is very great, though only true pioneers like Kor and Erickson can fully appreciate this. Subsequent ascent parties have the considerable advantage of knowing that it is, in fact, reasonable for human beings to be where they are."

During the summer of 1973, Henry Barber arrived in Boulder on his way back to New York after a visit to Yosemite. "Hot" Henry had established a reputation for making difficult free ascents in very pure style, and for an approach to rock climbing which thrived on competition. His interest in the latest and hardest climbs, coupled with an extroverted eloquence on climbing, nurtured by both American and British beer, had made him well known, and he enjoyed his reputation as a "character" on the climbing scene.

Arriving in Boulder, Henry immediately wanted to know what the big remaining plums were. General opinion was that the direct finish to Vertigo was the climb to do. Barber led the pitch and John Stannard, not relishing the prospect of being lowered a full one hundred and fifty feet if he came off, seconded the pitch on aid. The climb became noted for a combination of technical difficulty and aesthetically fine positions. Barber also repeated a number of the established hard free climbs during this period.

Women Climbers of the 1970's

During the early years of Colorado rock climbing history, women played a secondary role. They were generally in the position of wife, or girlfriend, who occasionally came along to watch the men climb, and perhaps occasionally to second an easy route. Judy Rearick once remarked that, in almost a decade of being in the company of rock climbers, including her husband Dave, Pat Ament, and Royal Robbins, she never led climbs. During the 1960's there were very few women leading high standard technical rock climbs in Colorado. Jane Bendixen was an exception to the general rule in the 1960's and was a good climber in her own right. She had been known to lead 5.8 pitches.

In the 1970's, paralleling a re-definition of the role of women in contemporary society, a number of women in Colorado emerged as rock climbing leaders in their own right.

During Henry Barber's visit to Boulder in 1973, just

Connie Hilliard jamming the first difficult moves of the Bastille Crack.

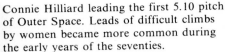

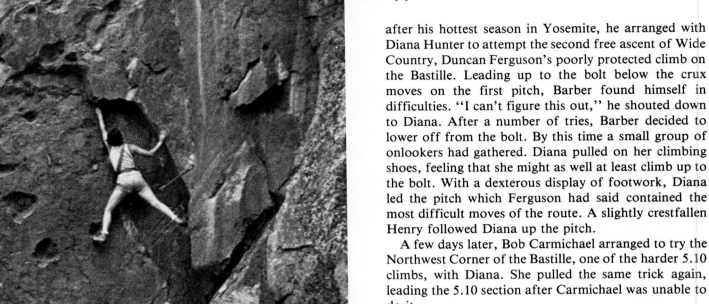

Connie Hilliard leading the first 5.10 pitch of Outer Space. Leads of difficult climbs by women became more common during the early years of the seventies.

after his hottest season in Yosemite, he arranged with Diana Hunter to attempt the second free ascent of Wide Country, Duncan Ferguson's poorly protected climb on the Bastille. Leading up to the bolt below the crux moves on the first pitch, Barber found himself in difficulties. "I can't figure this out," he shouted down to Diana. After a number of tries, Barber decided to lower off from the bolt. By this time a small group of onlookers had gathered. Diana pulled on her climbing shoes, feeling that she might as well at least climb up to the bolt. With a dexterous display of footwork, Diana led the pitch which Ferguson had said contained the most difficult moves of the route. A slightly crestfallen Henry followed Diana up the pitch.

A few days later, Bob Carmichael arranged to try the Northwest Corner of the Bastille, one of the harder 5.10 climbs, with Diana. She pulled the same trick again, leading the 5.10 section after Carmichael was unable to do it.

Diana Hunter worked hard at climbing. Her style was graceful, and the influence of her earlier training as a ballet dancer was evident. She was barely able to do a single pull-up, and compensated for her lack of brute strength by articulate footwork. Colorado climbing lost a remarkable person when Diana was killed in Rocky Mountain National Park in the summer of 1975, in an unroped fall on easy ground at the top of the Cathedral Spires.

A number of other women emerged in the 1970's who were able to lead technically difficult rock climbs. The following account was written by Molly Higgins shortly after she led her first 5.9 rock climb, the Green Spur:

My boyfriend's spending the week with another girl, my employer told me he'd rather hire men, I feel like I've been arguing for weeks and I'm sick of it!" I said, stomping over to the door of my cabin and looking out into Eldorado Canyon. The spring day was an interlude between storms, and Redgarden Wall beckoned warmly.

Charlotte said, "You've been wanting to lead Green Spur, let's go do it."

I'd never led 5.9 and Charlotte had never followed it. Our dubious glances met and we laughed nervously as I thought, "A climb like that should let me forget my troubles."

Hiking around the west side of Redgarden Wall, its massive buttresses and towers caught the afternoon sun. Stumbling up the scree, my eyes were at my feet until Charlotte exclaimed, "Look at the way the green and yellow lichens streak across the rock bands." I looked up, wondering at the color of the rock, at the pigeons soaring above, then at the pleasure of being out with a good friend.

When the climb came into view, we noticed another party using the fixed pitons to climb the second pitch. "If it's that hard will I be able to do it?" Charlotte smiled and patted my back.

Molly Higgins leading the Green Spur (5.9).

Right. Henry Barber beginning the sequence of moves across the Kloeberdanz roof. Hooking the left heel is the key to pulling into a dynamic move.

At the first belay stance we contemplated the pitch stretching above, the crux. A corner and a jam crack ran parallel for one hundred feet, where they merged in a thirty foot dihedral that was steep and smooth. As I tightened my shoes Charlotte said, "I feel like your sister at your piano recital."

The move off the ledge was tricky. "I'm gymnasting all around here and I can't seem to figure it out," I told Charlotte as a layback worked through to a jam. Climbing the parallel dihedral and jam crack grew progressively more difficult. With feet sometimes in the crack, sometimes on the face, balance was always changing; I worked back and forth between the two cracks like a dancer using the whole stage.

At the base of the steep dihedral, I found a face of minute holds. With no more secure jams, it required a change in dynamics like the Surprise Symphony. I moved up, thinking only of the small holds, of placing my feet precisely, of not shaking. The combination of control and anxiety enveloped me completely until I traversed right, deliberately, carefully, out onto larger holds. I flashed Charlotte, "OK," laughed joyously, and clambered to the belay ledge.

Charlotte followed. She looked like a spring nymph with her dark hair in braids, her rosy cheeks, and an ever-growing grin as she figured out the moves. "You're doing it, Charlotte!" I yelled.

When she pulled up on to the belay stance, we hugged one another, then prepared to rappel off. I said, "I loved the intensity of those hard moves, I loved the complete immersion of myself. Did I take too long, did you get bored?"

Charlotte smiled and answered, "It doesn't matter. I enjoy the sunshine, enjoy being up here; I love being as high as the birds!"

Women rock climbers are hampered by a lack of arm and shoulder strength on strenuous climbs. There were very few women able to lead 5.10 at the time of the publication of this book, and the hardest routes in Colorado had yet to receive female ascents. The cloak of male dominance is hard to shake and, to date, the best female climbers have generally restricted themselves to repeating established routes. In the future, it seems likely that more women will continue to do harder climbs, and there will undoubtedly come a time when women will develop important new routes.

Kloeberdanz

In 1973, Steve Wunsch spent an extended period of time climbing in the Shawangunks, and was strongly influenced by John Stannard. Stannard had an approach to rock climbing in which time was relatively unimportant, and major routes were approached as though they were boulder problems. Stannard would return time and time again to a particular move, and would eventually work out a solution. As he developed

Barber making a dynamic move for the lip of the roof on Kloeberdanz.   "Got it!" Barber pulling up on the lip.

his approach, he became an acknowledged master of arranging protection. He learned to organize complex systems of small nuts, none of which would probably hold a fall by itself, but which, in combination, provided adequate protection. His emphasis was exclusively on free climbing, and he had become well known for his prolonged attempts to free climb difficult routes. His classic "Foops" had been completed after many attempts extending over more than a year. A characteristic of Stannard's approach was his willing-

ness to take repeated leader falls onto protection.

After climbing with Stannard in the Gunks, Wunsch returned to Boulder. Prior to his trip east he had been very conservative about falling, and would also climb down difficult moves rather than lowering off from protection, feeling that in so doing he would become a better climber. After his climbing experiences in the Gunks, Wunsch says, "It was obvious that Stannard had become a pretty good climber by pushing himself to his limit and falling off. I decided to do the same."

"Whoops!" Barber retreating dynamically from the Kloeberdanz roof.

In 1973 Steve Wunsch began working on the Kloeberdanz roof, the next obvious break in the overhang at the base of Redgarden Wall. Sporadic attempts had been made to free climb the roof since 1971, but without success. Excellent protection existed, and the consequence of a fall was a spectacular, but safe, plunge through mid-air beneath the overhang. Wunsch made many attempts on the Kloeberdanz roof and took an approximate total of fifteen leader falls before finally working out a complicated series of moves out to the lip. The final solution involved an intricate sequence of two successive dynamic moves and heel hooks, followed by a strenuous pull onto the wall above the roof. Wunsch's account of the first free ascent of Kloeberdanz with Jim Erickson focuses more on the upper section of the climb after the roof pitch—on the notorious third pitch first free climbed by Larry Dalke in 1965:

> Kor named it. what's it mean? dance of the Kloebers? technical gymnastics for that horizontal leap on the first pitch?—the means by which i find myself here contemplating Dalke's third pitch lieback? he freed this pitch nine years ago and called it 5.9...i wonder was he innocent, ignorant or insecure? Dalke knew Kor, maybe he knows what Kloeberdanz means. Sunkloebers dancing on the water dripping twenty feet above. Erickson several bad nuts below grinning at my fear, babbling:
>
> "Can the young upstarts repeat the feats of their elders?" is there life after birth? can i reach that little hole, then maybe swing out to that foothold on the right and start lie-backing...over those nuts? Kloebers! try for the hole anyway...they'll probably hold bodyweight. wet as dogshit. don't fall here. how many falls did i take trying that leap before i?...count them. later. back to

Redgarden Wall. (1) Kloeberdanz. (2) Roof.

that foothold, quick. this ain't the first pitch.

"How was that?"

"Wet."

"Think it'll go?"

don't answer, look preoccupied...not hard when you're scared. up again to dig and clean, alternating between three longest first joints. down, rest, up, get the mud out, down rest up, more mud but deeper, down up and splash chalk to dry it. say something to Erickson before he mentions our strict canon of ethics. too late

"See them dip into their little bags of courage."

"Yeah, and Dalke was wearing a pack and mountainboots too, right?"

this up and down is calming, easy to the hole now. still, must declare it clean sometime and just use it. but be smart—don't lieback unless protection appears. where? well the foothold's only a few feet past what you've got. what have i got? jerk them a bit. bodyweight test imprudent just now. scared again. stall.

"Think you could throw up the no. 4 and no. 5 hexes?" am i superstitious? must be.

"Tie 'em to the rope in case I miss."

Technology. remember his three throws yesterday when i got over the first pitch roof unexpectedly and had no gear. his cackling when i had to clip my chalk bag into the fixed pin. then three perfect throws, the last about forty-five feet straight up. sell him to the Mets and buy Eldorado. first throw misses and the no. 5 drops off. how? technology versus human error in grand struggle for ubiquity. the no. 4 comes on the fourth throw. bad stance this time and harder throwing the rope with it. no excuses now. don't need nuts anyhow. solve by act of climbing. feet hurt. change stance. water drips—where from? Up there ice forms at night...sun melts, dries it Up. dripping Kloebers dancing in sun. Up? why not, can't dance. is there sex after death?

"Watch me."

"Got you good."

act of climbing...breathing...solve by...softly... unexpected hold...solution...water...dissolve...feels good...thanks, God. rock out right onto a foothold.

"Buckets."

wonder if Dalke saw these? probably not if he liebacked. looks easy and fun to belay. we've done it now. something old, something new, something bold, something true. no—borrowed, blue...right. who said i'm always thinking about marriage? climbing as sublimation. sublime pitch. sparkling, that water. thirsty. drink drips at belay. shady cave up here. comfort. loosen shoes. get good anchors. he won't have any trouble, though, unless the hole's out of reach for him. he'll figure something out.

"Your turn."

he always does. except the overhang on the first pitch. but he only tried it three times and how many did i? count them now...waste of time, but at least fifteen. his theory that once you fall you fail. seems to get him some very hard things on the first try. Insomnia. he dreamt last night that he found a fourth class chimney through the overhang. wonder if we could have finished it yesterday if it didn't get late? be a while before that lunge seems fourth class...took two tries today even after doing it before. how hard is it? 5.10a for the left hand, 5.10c for

the right hand, 5.10b for the right foot and 5.10d for the left foot. like any other problem in the Flagstaff gymnasium, but we must be exact or newcomers to the area might get in over their heads and have to be rescued. trying to shorten eternity with numbers. he's reaching for the hole now.

"Oh that's not fair!"

My turn to grin. he's not going down to rest. how can he hold on there for so long? he's moving his feet... reaching...got it. looked like he stood one foot on top of the other. magic. are we conquering nature or mastering ourselves? neither—all done with mirrors. raping or seducing the rock? polemics. is a free Kloeberdanz a happy Kloeberdanz? give me liberty or give me death. the Russians are coming.

"Comrade Erickson, how did you like that?"

"That'd be a really neat pitch if someone would rappel and put about twenty bolts in it."

"Yeah right. Say, does anybody know what Kloeberdanz means?"

"I don't. Maybe Kor does."[1]

With the successful free ascent of the Kloeberdanz roof, Steve Wunsch brought Shawangunks style climbing to Colorado. Wunsch was interested in climbs of ultimate technical difficulty and had formulated his own particular approach. He specialized in working out intricate series of chess-like moves in high places, treating long routes like extended boulder problems. His solution to free climbing the Kloeberdanz roof was the first major climb in Colorado where dynamic moves were intentionally employed and refined, though undoubtedly there had been earlier climbs where desperate, unanticipated lunges had been made. His ascent after fifteen falls, using dynamic moves to reach the lip, seemed an ultimate in terms of technical difficulty. Many top climbers would subsequently attempt the roof, by various methods, but would be unable to surmount it.

Sometime after Wunsch's successful ascent, Roger Briggs was attempting the Kloeberdanz roof. His tape-recorded account tells of the remarkable second ascent:

My brother and I were attempting the Kloeberdanz roof. I'd been trying it without much success when a young kid came wandering by. We were struggling, and I was finding it damned hard. He was kind of cocky and said, "That doesn't look too hard. It looks like a jug out there on the lip." I replied, "It's not a jug. Why don't you try it if you think it's that easy?" He climbed up and gave it one try, the way that Wunsch had done it, but couldn't do it. After a short rest, he climbed out and found a small handhold in the middle of the roof. He just hung on by one hand, found another hold, reached out to the lip of the roof, and pulled over. I couldn't believe it. He climbed it statically. I'd been trying the climb for years. John Stannard, Erickson, Henry Barber, all sorts of people had tried it. Wunsch had finally worked out his

Dave Breashears making the first ascent of Krystal Klyr. Perilous Journey takes the blank wall to the right.

exotic dynamic combination, and everyone thought it was the only way to do it. Not only did this kid do it, but he did it statically without even thinking. Just classic.

Perilous Journey

The "Kloeberdanz Kid", as he came to be known, was a high school youngster of seventeen named Dave Breashears. He had little experience of high standard extended rock climbs at the time, but he was a superb boulderer. His technical ability and strength developed on boulders had enabled him to sight lead the Kloeberdanz roof with only one fall, leaving the local experts shaking their heads in wonderment.

High up on Mickey Maus Wall, close to the Red Dihedral, was a steep, blank-looking wall on which Hurley had established his difficult and poorly protected "Offset" in 1970. In 1974, Duncan Ferguson led a more difficult and also poorly protected route straight up the steep wall to the left of the Offset, which became known as Duncan Donuts. To the left of Duncan Donuts the wall became even blanker. Steve Wunsch once commented, "It was the kind of buttress that I'd walk by and just thank God that no one would

Dave Breashears. *Pat Ament.*

ever try to climb it.'' Even in 1974, with the tremendous increase in technical standards that had taken place, it was hard to imagine anyone attempting to lead it. After his ascent of the Kloeberdanz roof, Breashears climbed with Erickson and his style matured. He learned Erickson's careful method of climbing up and down difficult, poorly protected pitches, systematically working out each move, and being sure that he could reverse each one. His bouldering experience had made him a master of climbing on tiny face holds. In 1975, he led two new routes up the blank wall to the left of Duncan Donuts, called Krystal Klyr and Perilous Journey. Of Perilous Journey the 1975 guidebook writes, ''protection imaginary.'' Both routes included sustained 5.9 climbing with 5.10 crux moves, and became recognized as the most serious leads in the area. They are important indications of the shape of things to come in future years of Colorado rock climbing as climbers seek out further challenges.

Dave Breashears recounted the first ascent of Perilous Journey in a tape recorded interview:

It was the most emotional climb I've ever done—it was really deep-rooted in the style of climbing that I believe in. First of all, it was not a good climb to fall off of at the crux—you'd certainly hit the ground. You probably wouldn't die. . . . but you might. Art and I had first seen the line of Perilous Journey in 1974. The sun had gone down behind the hill, and it was real quiet and peaceful. We started traversing back and forth across the wall. Art and I had been buildering a lot on the university walls, and I had learned a lot of tricks from him about this kind of climbing—on small quarter-inch or eighth-inch holds, and edging. So, we marvelled at this wall. . . .everywhere you went were little holds. I went up to Mickey Maus a number of times. . . .and just looked at the climb. It was exactly the kind of climbing I liked to do at that time—a relatively flat wall, with little holds on it, and real steep. Finally, I got it up to do it. I had been doing a lot of climbs in the Canyon, like the West Buttress and X-M a lot. And I was really wanting to do the first free ascent of Jules Verne. One day I got real obnoxious with Wunsch, and told him that I was gonna go up there before him—this was on the morning of his last attempt. And he got kind of pissed off, so I never went up. When he did it, I should have been really happy that he had done it, but I was real disappointed. All of my efforts, all of my training my fingers for that kind of climbing, and soloing for mind control, and really wanting to do that climb. . .I had to divert my efforts elsewhere. So, I decided, well, heck, let's go up there. I've always wanted to do this route. So I went up to Perilous Journey with Mammon. Looked at the wall. Got really ready for it. I just started up it and it all fell into place. About thirty-five feet off the ground, I got established at the crux. There's about an inch-and-a-half wide ledge in a remarkable spot. You can lean against the wall and let go with both hands, at a place where you'd never expect anyone to be able to drop their hands. I thought it was all over. I'd seen a number of

shadow pockets from down below, and thought they were gonna be buckets. I searched everyone of 'em. There wasn't a hold in any of 'em. So, finally, I ran my hand down the last set of pockets, and found a quarter-inch bump. I thought, well, I'm never gonna make this. So, I started thinking of ways to get down—and I couldn't think of any ways to get down. So, I just started working out the moves. I practiced one a couple of times, and I felt real secure on it. Finally, I had to do a real stretch move, real extended, to a bucket. And I had a hard time reversing that. I finally made the move, and the rock is real slick there. There were three or four more tricky moves, and that was it.

Discussing the unprotected difficulties of Perilous Journey and Krystal Klyr, in 1976 Wunsch commented, ''They seem like real jumps into the future to me.'' Erickson, never slow to respond, replied, ''They sure do; you'd jump right into eternity if you fell off either of 'em.''

Jules Verne

In 1967, Pat Ament and Larry Dalke climbed a complicated route on Redgarden Wall, between T.2 and the Naked Edge. The climb, which they called Jules Verne, included 5.9 free climbing and stretches of difficult direct aid. Jules Verne was the only climb in the guidebook to receive a Grade V overall rating, and was the longest route on Redgarden Wall.

During the spring of 1972, after the successful free ascent of the Naked Edge, climbers began to consider free climbing Jules Verne. A Boulder climber, Bill Putnam, was the first person to attempt a free ascent, and writes:

After the Naked Edge, I think it became obvious that free climbing possibilities were almost unlimited. It really broke a psychological barrier. I don't think I would ever have considered Jules Verne as possible if the Edge hadn't been done first.

On Jules Verne, the original direct aid line involved scary A.5 climbing close to the ground. On his first attempt with Duncan Ferguson, Putnam was able to traverse left under the lip of the overhang after starting on the first holds of T.2., and to then cross the lip at the same point as the original aid route. The technical difficulty and certainty of a ground fall made it an extremely serious lead. Ferguson was unable to follow, and Putnam descended on rappel.

A few days later, Putnam and Erickson were able to free climb the first three pitches of Jules Verne up to a large shelf half-way up the wall, called the Meadow; this left four more pitches on the upper wall unclimbed. Putnam writes:

After doing the lower part, I was climbed out and the upper pitch just scared the shit out of me, but I always wanted to climb it. I just didn't feel ready for the upper half. We never really pushed it very hard. I just came down with my tail between my legs. [2]

The fourth pitch of Jules Verne, above the Meadow, was to receive a number of attempts between 1972 and 1975. In 1974, Roger Briggs was inspired to write:

...the fourth pitch...has turned all climbers back. It will demand 25 feet of continuous, intricate 5.10 face climbing, with a 50 to 60 foot fall possible. The climbers who have attempted this pitch do not doubt that it will be free climbed some day. Such an undertaking lies in a realm which, seemingly, no man has yet entered, and epitomizes well the future of rock climbing.

Jim Erickson and Duncan Ferguson were two of the first to explore the fourth pitch. After their free ascent of the Naked Edge, they had decided to climb completely without pitons. Erickson gives the following account of their exploration of the fourth pitch of Jules Verne in 1973:

We climbed up above the roof, and it became obvious that a pin would be very nice in a crack out to the right. But, we had made a vow never to use pins again. We had none with us, and there wasn't anything fixed up there. We went up and gave it a little try, and I climbed up a couple of moves. It looked scary. I climbed back down again. Eventually, I climbed up about ten feet above the roof to a crack which looked as though it might take nuts. It was 5.10 to get across. I wanted to see if I could get a nut in the crack, and could only spend about one second standing there. I reversed the moves and got all the way back. Then I went up and did it again, and as I was coming back this time, my foot slipped off the hold and I fell about five feet. Duncan went up and also came down. Then he took an amazing fall. He was standing on a ledge trying to remove a nut when all of a sudden he just fell off and started spinning down through space, cartwheeling down the wall. We decided that the omens were just not with us that day for leading unprotected 5.10, and I gave up my attempts at trying to lead the pitch. After taking the fall, I didn't want to come back and try to lead it.

After this attempt, a number of other climbers tried the fourth pitch of Jules Verne. All of the attempts were unsuccessful. After Erickson and Ferguson's first attempt without pitons, all of the subsequent attempts were also made on nuts. There is no doubt that, had a protection piton been placed in 1973, one of the subsequent attempts would certainly have been successful, but the pitch was to remain unclimbed until 1975, despite the fact that it had been well publicized as a "last great problem." The commonly held agreement not to place a piton represented a remarkable commitment to a particular pure form of free climbing,

Steve Wunsch.

Bill Putnam leading the unprotected moves over the lip on the first free ascent of the first pitch of Jules Verne - with moral support from below.

a position which some climbers have difficulty appreciating, but one which characterizes developments which have occurred in top grade rock climbing in Colorado during the 1970's.

Steve Wunsch had made an unsuccessful attempt on the fourth pitch in 1973. In 1974, he returned to attempt Jules Verne with Briggs. They reached a point slightly higher than the previous high point, but, again, were unsuccessful.

In 1975, Wunsch returned to Colorado. With John Bragg belaying, he spent most of an afternoon working on the fourth pitch of Jules Verne, and eventually was able to find placements for two #1 stoppers (tiny nuts the size of a fingernail) in a small crack which previous parties had overlooked. Erickson comments:

> I'd been watching from down on the road through binoculars, and we all thought Wunsch was going to make it. He got up to within one move of the top of the difficult section.

Wunsch had succeeded in climbing the 5.10 section of rock which had turned back all previous attempts; he had reached a point very close to the end of the difficulties after a sustained series of 5.10 moves taking him high above his protection, to a point where the #1 stoppers most likely would not have withstood a fall. In a display of climbing which was even more impressive than his lead, he painstakingly reversed each move of the pitch and successfully regained the belay without falling.

The following day, Bragg did not feel like a repeated extended belaying session, and declined to return with Wunsch. Jim Erickson was not willing to attempt to lead the pitch after his earlier fall, because of his tainting philosophy, but he agreed to accompany Wunsch and belay for him. Wunsch carefully climbed up to his high point, clipped into the protection which he had left in place the day before, reclimbed the 5.10 section, made the final difficult move, and completed the pitch. They climbed the remaining four pitches to the top of the wall, Erickson leading a difficult 5.10 finger crack, and all of the pitches of Jules Verne had been climbed free. Roger Briggs had previously written, "The climb waits for someone with stainless steel testicles." After the successful ascent, Erickson commented, "I remember when we got to the top I was gonna ask Steve to pull down his pants to see if he really did have stainless steel testicles."

With Wunsch and Erickson's ascent, all the pitches of Jules Verne had been free climbed, but not in a continuous ascent. In January 1976, Bob Candelaria and Roger Briggs made the first continuous ascent from the ground to the top of the wall in one day. Candelaria

Briggs attempting the
fourth pitch of Jules Verne
in 1974.

An unsuccessful attempt to repeat the Psycho roof.

did not place the #1 stoppers, and he took a hairy thirty foot fall on the crux section of the fourth pitch onto a lower protection nut, but he was unhurt and climbed back to successfully lead the pitch.

Psycho

During 1974, Steve Wunsch and Jim Erickson were hiking around Eldorado Springs Canyon, talking about which of the other roof routes might go free. They speculated on the possibilities of Psycho, the route which Layton Kor and Huntley Ingalls had first climbed in 1962. The roof extended for approximately eight feet, and there were three expansion bolts in place from the earlier direct aid ascent. Wunsch recalls:

> We were wandering around under the roof routes after Guenese had gone free, and thinking about which other ones might go. We were speculating about Psycho, and noticed a big pointy flake about ten feet down the lip. I was thinking that if there was a foothold on the wall, it might be possible to get an undercling under the roof and to just leap straight out and get the flake; just jump straight out backwards.

Erickson and Wunsch made an attempt to free climb the wall directly below the roof, following the line of the original direct aid ascent, and immediately ran into difficulties. Erickson recollects:

> Steve had been up once to try the first pitch. He got up about a third of the way, saw that it was going to be really cruddy protection on one move, and didn't want to try it. I went up with him on another day, got up a little ways, and also came down. About thirty feet above the ground was an old bashie for protection, and an obvious hard move across to the next crack system. I came back

Redgarden Wall. (1) Psycho. (2) Roof.

Left and right.
Working on the
Psycho roof.

later with Art Higbee and decided that I was a chicken-shit for not going for it, because I could see the moves. I clipped into the bashie and led across. I think it was one of the scariest leads I've done in Eldorado.

Erickson and Higbee established themselves on a small stance at the top of the first pitch and were inspecting the problem of the roof, when Wunsch and Chris Reveley came hiking by down below, after an unsuccessful attempt on the Wisdom. Wunsch shouted up, "Waddya think Art? Think it's gonna go?" Higbee bent down, whispered something to Erickson, and then tucked himself into a crouch, as though to leap for the lip, just as Wunsch had speculated earlier. The incredulous Wunsch watched amazed, visions of someone else beating him to his dream flashing past his eyes. Suddenly accompanied by a great scream, "Whaaa...," Higbee jumped out backwards into mid-air and wrenched Erickson up off the stance tight against his belay anchor, leaving the two of them suspended from the direct aid bolts in the roof!

Reassembling themselves on the belay, feeling content at the surprise they had given the astonished Wunsch and Reveley, they examined the roof. To Erickson, it seemed unclimbable using his free climbing criteria of no falls. For the fun of it, they climbed up on direct aid, and Erickson lost interest in trying to lead the roof.

In 1974, Steve Wunsch hiked up to Psycho with John Bragg, trying to figure out how to avoid leading the first poorly protected horror pitch. Reaching the wall, inspiration struck, and with a straight face he said, "Well, John, you can have the first pitch, I'll try the roof." Fortunately, Bragg was tall enough to reach across and to clip into a fixed pin before making the hard move.

Their attempts on the roof were unsuccessful, and they made no further tries during 1974. In 1975 they returned to try again. With Bragg established in the stance, Wunsch was able to clip into the first two old expansion bolts for protection. Underneath the roof he found small, friable flakes. During the remainder of the day, Wunsch and Bragg took turns trying the roof and took a total of fifteen short falls onto the bolts as they experimented, trying to work out a sequence of free moves across the flakes. They were able to reach a point three feet from the lip, but the final moves evaded them, and they eventually rappelled off.

Two or three days later, Wunsch and Bragg were again in Eldorado Springs Canyon. It had become an Eldorado phenomenon to watch them attempting, and occasionally succeeding, on the itinerary of climbs in which they were interested. To warm up, they would try to free climb Genesis. They would then try Cinch Crack, and fail on that. Then they would move over to try

Psycho. The next day they would repeat the same thing, or a variant of it, all over again, usually trying one or two climbs each day.

On this particular day, they had decided to make an attempt to free climb the Wisdom roof. Wunsch recollects:

> We decided to go up and try the Wisdom. For some reason I'd been having dreams about Psycho. It kept running through my head a lot. I was just not feeling right. I didn't exactly know why at the time. It was a turmoil period in my brain, having to do with why I climb, or something. I realized I was pushing myself to do climbs because there was a gamut to be run. We got up underneath the Wisdom, and I was just sitting kicking my feet in the dirt, thinking, "I don't wanna go climbing. I don't feel like doing this," and generally mumbling to myself. We started talking about philosophies of climbing, and about why people do all this stuff. I suddenly thought to myself, "I don't care about the Wisdom. What I really want to do is Psycho." John said, "Why don't we go and do Psycho?"

Established at the belay underneath the Psycho roof, Wunsch resumed his attempt. Again, fall followed fall. The falls were short, since the moves were close in to the two bolts. Then, unexpectedly, after a series of dynamic moves on small flakes, Wunsch found himself out with one hand almost at the lip of the roof. Again he came off, and this time the consequence was a stomach-wrenching fall of some fifteen feet through mid-air, until the rope came tight. The bolts held, and Wunsch repositioned himself on the small stance. He had come awfully close, and he felt a surge of excitement that perhaps the roof might go. Finally, after a sequence of approximately ten very short, dynamic moves and heel hooks, he was able to reach a good hold on the lip, pull over, and establish himself on the wall above. The Psycho roof had been free climbed.

Despite his calculated employment of leader falls on Kloeberdanz and the Psycho roof, Steve Wunsch was a conservative climber by standards of 1976, and was very calculating about when he was willing to take repeat leader falls. The move had to be close to protection, and in a situation where he would not hit anything when he came off. On Jules Verne, he took no leader falls and demonstrated a remarkable ability to downclimb unprotected 5.10 moves. Some contemporary rock climbers are willing to take falls of twenty feet onto protection, and have the ability to remain in control. Wunsch, twenty nine years old in 1976, sounding a little bit like the old man of the mountains and demonstrating how rapidly modern rock climbing evolves, ruminated, "I think it's fantastic that some of the young climbers can take twenty to thirty foot falls and stay in control."

Inaptly christened the "Prophet of Purism" in a

Mountain magazine article in 1973, Wunsch's leads of the Kloeberdanz roof, the fourth pitch of Jules Verne, and the Psycho roof demonstrated his range of approaches and his determination to free climb last great problems. Kloeberdanz subsequently received other ascents, its well protected security and ease of access inviting regular attempts. The fourth pitch of Jules Verne on nuts is likely to remain a serious and rarely attempted lead. On a later attempt to repeat Psycho, a key flake broke off, and it is questionable if it is now possible to free climb the roof; but rock climbing history has repeatedly indicated that premature answers to such questions only invite contradiction.

Third Classing

Throughout the history of Colorado rock climbing, there have been individuals who have delighted in the unencumbered exhilaration of solo climbing. Elkanah Lamb and Enos Mills made unroped solo descents of the East Face of Longs Peak, and members of the Rocky Mountain Climbers Club had considered the use of a rope to be "cheating" in ascents of the Third Flatiron. In the early 1960's, Layton Kor and Bob Culp had responded to Buhl's maxim that a climber must solo if he was to realize his potential. These historic threads came together in the 1970's, resulting in the unroped soloing of climbs of maximum technical difficulty.

Modern climbers term unroped solo climbing "third classing," in a take-off on the grading which normally refers to unroped scrambling on very easy rocks. It is also known as "free soloing." When Larry Dalke soloed X-M and the Nord Wand in the 1960's, he used a self protection system of ropes and pitons. The contemporary climber who chooses to third class has no such insurance and faces the prospect of serious injury, or death, as the consequence of a fall.

The underlying motivation for third classing can range between two extremes. Some climbers solo for the sensation of unrestricted climbing and for the aesthetically pleasing flow of continuous upward movement, without the interruption of belays. Climbers in this group tend to solo easy routes. The other extreme involves third classing routes of maximum technical difficulty, and can be approached on two different levels. A climber can free solo hard climbs to discover his own personal limits and to satisfy his own inner needs, or he can free solo to impress other climbers with his boldness in a competitive vein.

In 1972, Jim and Dave Erickson met Steve Wunsch in Britain, and the three climbed together in the Llanberis Pass in North Wales. Wunsch had rented a caravan in the village of Llanraig, and one day Jim said he wasn't feeling too well and didn't want to climb that day. Wunsch took off with Dave and returned in the afternoon to hear that Jim was feeling much better after having taken a little bike ride. It was a number of months later that Wunsch found out the full story of the little bike ride. A few days before, Erickson had made a roped ascent of a short, viciously overhanging 5.10 jam crack called Grond. He says, "I'd always told myself that if I found an overhanging 5.10 handcrack, that I would solo it." He rode the bicycle eight miles back to the cliff, not telling anyone of his intentions, and third classed Grond!

Returning to Boulder that fall, Erickson found that leading new 5.10 climbs was less satisfying than before. He decided to attempt to third class some new routes. He pointed out, "I'd never go up and solo just any line. I picked climbs very carefully." He chose climbs which he felt were secure, usually involving jam cracks.

An overhanging crack on the Bastille attracted his attention. It became harder and harder as he moved up, but the jams were good, and Erickson felt that he could reverse down to the ground at any time. The crux was the final section of the crack, which Erickson gave a 5.9+ grading. He called the climb Blind Faith.

The ascent of Blind Faith by Erickson in 1972 represented climbing of a kind not previously seen in Colorado. His free solo of this previously unclimbed line required superb confidence in his own ability.

High up on the West Ridge of Eldorado Springs Canyon was a climb called Sooberb, involving A.2 nailing over an exposed overhang on the third pitch, first climbed by Pat Ament and Larry Dalke in 1965. In 1972, Erickson wanted to see if the route could be free climbed and decided to find out solo. Using the style which he employed during roped free climbing, he carefully climbed up and down the pitch, making sure he could reverse every move. Finally, he reached a point at the lip of the overhang. It was the crux move, but he could see a bucket within reach. Committing himself, he reached the bucket. Sooberb proved to be 5.10 at the crux overhang. Erickson's ascent was the first time a route of this difficulty had received a free solo first ascent.

Erickson free soloed a number of other new routes during 1972 and 1973, and commented, "I'd just get on my bike, take a pair of shoes, pick out a climb, and do it. Or not do it. I probably backed off as many climbs as I did."

Free soloing hard climbs became addictive for Erickson. The aesthetics of being alone on rock were important to him, but he says:

At the time I was doing them, I don't think anyone in

Colorado had previously soloed such hard new climbs. I don't think anyone had even soloed new 5.9 routes. I wanted to do something that no one had done before. I wanted to do something that epitomized the thing I was into—complete control climbing—which is what solo climbing is all about. I guess I was, in a sense, trying to emulate the myths that I had heard about John Gill.

By the mid-1970's, a few people had soloed established hard climbs on sight, but to solo a new hard climb on sight is an undertaking of a different nature. The grade is unknown, and no one has previously tested the solidarity of the holds.

As with Grond, Erickson rarely discussed his solo climbs, even with close friends, feeling that he was soloing for personal satisfaction, and not wanting to spoil that sense with competitive overtones.

Erickson soloed regularly during 1972 on difficult climbs, and visited Yosemite in the spring of 1973 on one of his annual pilgrimages to attempt to free climb Half Dome:

> When I got back that summer, I got back into it. Probably half the things I did were solo. It got to the point where I was doing it too much, and this is what caused my accident. I had a ho-hum attitude about soloing. I just wasn't psyching up for it. I couldn't maintain the fine-tuned edge which you need. I went up on a climb of the Fourth Flatiron that I'd seen, down to the left of Death and Transfiguration. It was only about 40-50 feet long. I climbed up a chimney that led up over a roof. It was a very hot day. Monday, August thirteenth, I jammed out. There was a thin hand crack leading up for about five feet. I chimneyed out and had my hands in two cracks. I swung out of the chimney position and stuck my foot on a tiny little edge, and was liebacking up on handjams, and apparently, due to the heat, and not chalking, it just torqued out. The next thing I knew I was falling through space and landed on the ground. Luckily, I was only 30 feet up when I fell. For several months it put an end to my climbing. They had to rescue me. I came to, and I was delirious and had two broken legs and a broken wrist. I was in shock and my head was bleeding badly. I was able to crawl a ways. A lady came hiking up the trail, and I was able to yell to her. She fetched help. I could have crawled out under my own power, I think, but at the rate I was going it would have taken about six hours. By which time it would have been dark.

The ever-present possibility of a mistake while free soloing had caught up with Erickson. He fell only thirty feet, but the landing was on broken ground, and he was lucky to crawl away with only two broken legs and a broken wrist.

After his accident, Erickson commented, "I don't have the push these days that I used to have. I used to be able to say to myself, 'Well, if you get killed doing this, it doesn't matter very much.' But these days I seem to value my life more. I still solo occasionally. But I would never solo things at the level I did before."

Henry Barber.

Gorilla's Delight - Solo

In a letter written to *Mountain* magazine in 1974, Royal Robbins called Henry Barber's free solo of the Steck Salathé route (on the North Face of Sentinel Rock in Yosemite) in two and a half hours, "a work of climbing genius. . .an act of vision."[3] During the 1970's Barber became noted for his ability to third class difficult climbs.

In 1973, on one of his many visits to Colorado, Barber overheard Duncan Ferguson say, "All of the routes on the Dome (a cliff in Boulder Canyon) have been soloed, except Super Squeeze and Gorilla's

The Dome. (1) Gorilla's Delight. (2) 5.9 slab.

Delight.'' Henry's ears pricked up. Super Squeeze was a 5.10, and he wasn't up for that, but Gorilla's Delight was only 5.9. ''Hm...'' Barber decided to attempt to third class the climb.

The guidebook description of Gorilla's Delight states, ''a vertical dihedral leading to some high angle walls....jam to the top of the dihedral, (5.8). Traverse right and layback a flake to the 5.7 or 5.8 slabs above.'' Barber remembers, ''I was feeling good at the time. The first crack went real smoothly. I was feeling flowing and really hyped up, kind of in a music mood.'' At the top of the first crack, he traversed right and laybacked up a flake, which, as the guidebook had stated, was 5.7. From good holds at the top of the flake, he was able to reach around a corner and could see a smooth, steep slab of granite leading upwards. The guidebook had called the slab ''5.7 or 5.8.'' ''There should be some nice fat holds up here, thought Henry to himself. At this point he was some 150 feet above the ground. Holding on to the layback crack with his left hand, his right hand explored the surface of the slab for holds, but there were none to be found.

Henry began to sweat. Reversing the layback crack, he moved back down to a resting place and took stock of the situation.

''5.7 or 5.8 slabs? I must be missing something.''

Climbing back up again, his searching right hand still could not find good holds. He considered reversing the route down to the ground, but something inside him kept pushing to go on. With a ''shit or bust'' prayer, he decided to go for it, hoping that good holds would appear as soon as he moved up.

They didn't. Henry found himself poised on minute ripples in the smooth granite, contemplating a one hundred and fifty foot fall to the ground. ''It's the nearest I've ever come to buying it,'' he recalls. The slab proved to be 5.9 friction, and was notorious among local climbers. Henry hadn't checked with anyone before his solo attempt, preferring to climb without prior knowledge. He was able to make the moves, but at the limit of control, with panic threatening to sweep over him.

Barber could hardly have picked a worse route to third class. Moving from a good crack onto irreversible 5.9 friction, with the hardest moves at the top of the climb, high above the ground, was probably the most dangerous combination he could have chosen.

Barber is noted in the climbing community for his superb gamesmanship, and in 1974 he was interviewed by *Mountain* magazine. On being asked about his soloing experiences, he casually mentioned that Gorilla's Delight was particularly scary, and said, ''The trouble was that the ground was sloping and I couldn't predict where I would land if I fell off. I don't mind falling from some height, as long as I've got some

control over my landing, to miss boulders''*...inferring that he normally doesn't mind falling off when a hundred and fifty feet up, as long as he can see his landing!

Erickson and Barber were not the only climbers active in free soloing during the seventies. Ferguson was noted for quietly disappearing on sunny afternoons and soloing difficult routes. People knew he had third classed the Umph Slot on the Dome (5.8 for midgets and up to 5.10 for those of normal girth). Rumors about his activities were passed around, but no one knew for sure what else he had done. Many of Colorado's hard climbs were third classed by other good climbers who appeared on the scene between 1973 and 1977. Blackwalk (Jim Erickson's intimidating 5.10 climb on Redgarden Wall) received a free solo ascent by Dave Breashears. After making a roped ascent, Pat Adams third classed the Kloeberdanz roof — yet another commentary on the possible fate of yesterday's ''ultimate'' climbs.

During the mid-1970's, one hears of more and more free solo ascents of difficult routes. Free soloing has become vogue, the ultimate way of notching one's way up the rock climbing social ladder. Robbins' statement that extreme free soloing is ''an act of vision,'' though true on one level, is clearly not the main motivation for many contemporary climbers; forces of competition all too often outweigh the aesthetic and spiritual rewards of being alone on the rock.

The Diamond - Free

During the early 1970's, free climbing was pushed to extreme limits on low elevation cliffs close to Boulder and Colorado Springs. As had happened during earlier periods, it was not long before attention began to turn towards free climbing long routes in the high mountains. Free climbing had always played an important part on extended mountain routes but, because of the importance of speed, direct aid was generally employed to overcome difficult sections. During 1973, after such routes as the Naked Edge and Guenese had been climbed free, a small number of climbers began attempting to apply modern free climbing techniques to difficult routes in the high mountains.

During 1973 and 1974, a number of difficult free routes were done in the high mountains. Ferguson and Hesse climbed a bold new free route on Hallett Peak in 1973. In 1974, Briggs and Reveley made the first all free ascent of a climb called Directissima (5.8-A.2, originally climbed by Kor and LaGrange in 1960), which involved 5.10 moves, on the lower East Face of Longs Peak. Briggs and Hamilton free climbed a long new route on Notchtop Mountain in 1974, which included 5.10 climbing, and which they called White Room. Dan

Mclure and his partner made the first free ascent of the Barb on Spearhead in Rocky Mountain National Park, eliminating A.2 nailing by means of hard 5.10 free climbing. In the context of these developments, climbers began to speculate on the possibility of free climbing the Diamond.

The Diamond routes were well known, and many Colorado climbers had previously made direct aid ascents. As the topic bounced back and forth in conversation, it was thought that it might be feasible to free climb the Diamond, but that it would be very hard, and that luck, in terms of having good weather, would play an important part in the outcome of any attempt.

During the summer of 1972, Duncan Ferguson and Bill Putnam made an attempt to free climb D.7, the easiest and shortest of the Diamond routes on the left side of the face. They were able to free climb the first five pitches, but wet, difficult cracks on the sixth pitch necessitated rappelling off. A week later, Roger Briggs and Scott Stewart followed in their tracks and reached a slightly higher point. The cracks were still wet, and they searched unsuccessfully for an alternative to the left, where the wall seemed to present other free climbing possibilities.

The summer of 1973 was wet, and no attempts were made. In 1974 Briggs made another attempt, this time accompanied by Chris Revely. They again explored crack systems to the left of the wet section, and again were unsuccessful in finding a free climbing line that would go. That same summer, Duncan Ferguson returned with Kevin Donald and Jim Logan and they, too, were repulsed by the wet cracks. By this time, virtually all of the route had been climbed free. The remaining section was only about fifty feet long.

During the winter of 1975, the Diamond became a big talking point among Colorado climbers, and it became obvious that a number of free climbing attempts would be made when the summer months arrived. The race was on, and a number of different parties were quietly preparing and weighing their chances.

Wayne Goss and Jim Logan were two "old timers" who had both started climbing during the mid-1960's. They were known as experienced climbers, but they had not figured in the free climbing developments of the 1970's. Young climbers who knew of Goss vaguely remembered that he had done the winter ascent of the Diamond with Kor, and Logan tended to be remembered as a climber who had "once climbed with Dalke."

Logan had been drafted from 1969 to 1971, and on his return to Colorado found that his head was no longer into hard climbing. "I just found myself getting too scared," he says. Goss had remained active, but was

Wayne Goss.

Jim Logan.

The Diamond. (1) Goss-Logan free ascent.
(2) Dunn-Wood free ascent.

not climbing the newer 5.10 and 5.11 routes.

In 1972, Goss and Logan got together "for old times' sake," to attempt a climb which had been long talked about during the 1960's—the Nose of Chasm View in the Black Canyon of the Gunnison. They completed the climb, but, in Goss's words, "Did it in terrible style and used too much aid and too many expansion bolts."

During 1974, Logan had accompanied Ferguson and Donald on their free attempt on D.7, but had not expected to play a leading part on the harder sections of the route, feeling that Ferguson was the more accomplished free climber. The experience whetted his appetite, however, and during the fall and winter, he and Goss began to talk of making a free attempt on the Diamond the following summer. Considering their reputation as "climbers of the sixties," anyone running

a book would probably have given odds of a hundred-to-one against their chances of success.

Goss and Logan climbed regularly during the spring of 1975, and after a number of easier climbs to get into shape, were able to free climb Country Club Crack. In early July, they embarked on some of the newer free climbs in Eldorado Springs Canyon. Goss led the Guenese roof with no falls (one of the few pure ascents of this difficult route). After a day of rest, they free climbed the Naked Edge, also in good style. Feeling that they were in as good a shape as they would ever be, they took one full rest day, and then headed up to Longs Peak.

Goss and Logan both were familiar with the Diamond from their earlier climbs, and knew that speed would be essential if they were to have any chance of success. The sun leaves the wall before noon, making free climbing more difficult, and thunderstorms are common in the afternoon. They banked all of their hopes on making a fast ascent, and travelled as lightly as possible. Taking minimum bivouac gear, they carried just down jackets and cagoules, only a small amount of food, and, to avoid having the weight of heavy mountain boots on the face, Goss plodded up the snow to the base of the North Chimney wearing Adidas running shoes. Logan wore Robbins' boots and carried a pair of P.A.'s for the hard sections.

Their hope was to make a free ascent in the best modern style. To this end, they left pitons and hammers behind and were determined to make a clean ascent, using only nuts. Logan knew that there was a good number of fixed pitons in the route and was optimistic that these, coupled with nuts, would provide adequate protection. Also, they did not carry jumars, and both planned to climb every pitch.

Reaching Broadway, they found three women bivouacked. Molly Higgins, Stephanie Atwood, and Laurie Manson were intent on making the first all female ascent of the Diamond. It was obvious that a conflict of interests existed. Climbing etiquette gave the women the right to be first on the wall the next morning.

Goss and Logan fretted over the situation for a while. They knew that a party of three using direct aid would be slow, and that their chance of free climbing the route would be eliminated if they were behind. Goss tactfully approached the situation, and inquired if they might be allowed to go first. For a while it was touchy. The women, rightfully, were somewhat reluctant to move into second place, one practical reason being that they would be targets for any stones knocked down by Goss and Logan. Diplomacy won the day, and after more discussion, it was decided that Goss and Logan could start first. Not satisfied with talking themselves into first place, Goss and Logan somehow presented themselves in such a good light that the women took pity on their foodless state and fed them hamburgers for dinner—a royal feast for the Broadway bivouac.

The next morning, Goss and Logan were away at first light, swinging leads up the first five known pitches. The pitches increased in difficulty as they moved up the wall, with 5.10 moves on pitches four and five. At the foot of the sixth pitch, which had turned back previous attempts, it was Goss's lead. Again the pitch was wet, and he began to explore alternatives. They knew that previous attempts to the left, even though it looked like the easiest alternative, had proven unsuccessful. A downward traverse thirty feet to the right, via a narrow ledge, took Goss across the wall past the Black Dagger

crack to a belay high in the crack system which Bill Forrest had soloed in 1970. Logan led the next 5.10 pitch up the Forrest Finish. Clouds had moved in and it had begun to rain and hail. From the belay ledge, Goss was faced with a choice of five different cracks leading to Table Ledge.

By this time, both were feeling the effects of the first seven pitches. They had climbed fast, and the effects of altitude contributed to their feeling of fatigue. Rain mixed with hail continued, and they sat dismally on the ledge for almost an hour, wondering if they were going to be robbed of success so near the top.

It was Goss's lead, and eventually he felt sufficiently rested to examine the crack which was the continuation of the Black Dagger. It was an inside corner, reminiscent of the first pitch of the Naked Edge, but containing many fixed pitons. A brief exploration made it clear that it would not go free in their tired condition. Examination of two other cracks to the right produced similar conclusions. The crack directly above the belay also looked hard. By elimination, this left only a four-inch crack splitting an eighty degree wall above the Black Dagger chimney. Forty feet of reasonable climbing took Goss to a bolt, five feet below a dirt-filled section of the crack.

The rain, which had been falling steadily for the past hour, stopped. The dirt-filled crack looked infeasible to Goss in his tired state, but he thought that small, wet holds on the right wall might be climbable. His account conveys the narrow margin by which he made this crucial section:

"Logan! Watch my ass! I'm right on the limit." The climbing is no worse than before, but I am. Up into a layback. Ever wonder why there's not a book called the *Joy of Laybacking*? Water running down the wall makes a wake around a swimming R.D. Concentrate Motha. Right toe to nubbin. Peek-a-boo round the corner reveals a misplaced chess problem. Possibilities are chalked... three...four times, to absorb the water. Left hand turns white on its own. Exit out on little holds. This is where it's at! Eye balls wide. Two inches away a tenuous hold...still out of reach. Some hero, squinting because it's too wet to wear glasses, reaching across a gulf of fear to deliberately finger an eighth-inch indentation just two fingers wide. Which ones to put there? Decisions, decisions. Left foot lifts off the pucky in the crack, and with pluck defying better judgment, belaying a mind of its own, replaces the right. Right is relegated to a newer, but not better, bump. This is art? Climbing on zits. Switch fingers one at a time. Contrapuntal elegance. Left foot slides—up, now or never, and place it under the same side's fingers....in slow motion cartwheel upwards thinly...a vertical hold slips by..."Got it!" Ape-like up on buckets.

From the buckets, Goss was able to move back left into

the main crack and to continue more easily to a belay. Logan, seconding, could not make the moves on the wall, but with the security of an overhead belay, was able to climb straight up the dirt-filled crack. A nut jammed as he was seconding the pitch, and Logan, nearing the end of his reserves, left it and a carabiner hanging from the crack.

Above them, a short fifteen foot pitch led to Table Ledge. Tired, exhausted, but exuberant, they grinned at each other. The Diamond had received its first free ascent. They had made good time and were able to hike over the summit of Longs and down to the Boulder field before dark. The next day, they learned that Higgins, Atwood, and Manson had been successful in making the first female ascent of the Diamond.

Goss and Logan's ascent was particularly notable for the style which they employed. To embark on the face traveling light, without hammers, pitons, or jumars, was an act of calculated boldness, in keeping with the finest free climbing developments of the 1970's.

If two "old timers" can accomplish such an incredible climb in such good style in 1975, who can possibly predict what may lie ahead in years to come?

One week later, Jimmy Dunn and Chris Wood made the second free ascent of the Diamond. Their climb extended over three days in between snowstorms, and they left fixed lines and jumared back up the first few pitches. They carried more food and bivouac gear than Goss and Logan, hauled a relatively heavy sack up the face, used pitons for protection, and belay anchors. The route they followed was more direct, however, and followed a straight line up the first three pitches of the Yellow Wall to connect with the line followed by Goss and Logan at the Forrest Finish. Seeing a nut and carabiner in the crack just below Table Ledge, they speculated on whether Goss and Logan had possibly rappelled or lowered off from it. Dunn, after cleaning dirt from the crack, was able to lead the pitch, and the Diamond received its second free ascent.

Shortly after returning from the first free ascent of the Diamond, Goss commented, "If freed routes had new names, we'd call it the 'Komito Freeway,' and if

they had dedications, this one would be dedicated to all the young hot shots who made it conceivable for us old farts to come steppin' out of the old rocking chair."

Both of these ascents were outstanding achievements, with an effect on free climbing in the high mountains comparable to the effect which the first free ascent of the Naked Edge had had on free climbing on lower cliffs.

REFERENCES

1. Steve Wunsch, "Kloeberdanz," *Climbing Magazine*, May/June, 1974, pp. 6-10.
2. Bill Putnam, *personal communication*, 1976.
3. Royal Robbins, "Letter to the Editor," *Mountain Magazine*, No. 35, 1974, p. 42.
4. Henry Barber, "Interview," *Mountain Magazine*, No. 35, May 1974, p. 36.

An Interview with
JIM ERICKSON and
STEVE WUNSCH

Jim Erickson and Steve Wunsch were two of the most active free climbers in the Boulder region during ithe 1970's. Both climbed extensively in other areas: Yosemite, the Shawangunks, Devil's Lake, and Great Britain. They have much in common; a dedication to free climbing, the use of nuts for protection, and the ability to consistently pioneer difficult new routes. The main difference between them is expressed in Erickson's "tainting" philosophy, contrasted to Wunsch's willingness to take repeated leader falls. For a number of years these two, firm friends and climbing companions, have sparred as intellectual adversaries on points of philosophy and style. In the following interview, they discuss their approaches, and rock climbing in general.

Godfrey: *Steve, how did you begin free climbing?*

Wunsch: I didn't evolve from being an aid climber. I just started doing things free. Free climbing was an extension of soloing for me, which is the way I started to climb.

Godfrey: *So free climbing wasn't a conscious decision for you?*

Wunsch: My style of climbing hasn't been developed by thinking about how I climb. . . .

Erickson: Cogito ergo klettere?

Wunsch: Yes, but it's the other way round. It's klettere, ergo. You figure out why you climb afterwards. When I first started, for the first two or three years, my climbing didn't have anything to do with what people normally think of as climbing. I was just a little kid, and we'd play follow the leader on rocks and try to punch each other out. I was in seventh and eighth grades at the time, living near a grungy little heap of rocks in Missouri. We didn't know that climbers used ropes, and we didn't know anything about climbing. Then I spent summers at a camp near Colorado Springs, and I'd sneak away from the counselors, because we weren't allowed to climb, and go off and solo a lot. I spent two years like that, and an automatic free climbing response developed. It just wasn't something I thought about.

Godfrey: *But that's a very different situation from, say, trying the Kloeberdanz Roof, in the center of a popular rock climbing gymnasium, knowing that other people had been trying to climb it for two years. Are you saying that your approach is still instinctive, and that even on Kloeberdanz you didn't have to think about not grabbing protection?*

Wunsch: Well, everybody knew that you could grab a sling and do it. When I first started trying the Kloeberdanz roof, I had ten years of free climbing behind me, and my original response to soloing had become a reflex. Even on Kloeberdanz I just didn't have to think about whether to use a sling or not. The slings were just not there. They were there for protection, but that's all.

Godfrey: *Have you ever been involved in direct aid climbing?*

Wunsch: Aid climbing has just never seemed interesting to me. When I started climbing, back in the Tetons, it sounded just as hard to pull up on slings as it was to climb on the rock. Though I once figured out how to do a tension traverse on the Jensen Ridge, and thought that was pretty brilliant at the time. But I've just never really been interested in the challenge of aid climbing.

Erickson: You figured out how to do a tension traverse. . .and after that it was all down hill.

Wunsch: Very funny.

Godfrey: *Jim, how did you start climbing?*

Erickson: It was in 1962 at Devil's Lake. I had three pitons, two carabiners, and a rope. I tried to climb up a crack, and couldn't do it free. I had read in books that you were supposed to use pitons, so I hammered one in, clipped into it, but couldn't figure out how to pull myself past it. My brother was holding me tight on tension, and I just couldn't figure out how to get loose and move up above it. When he slacked off the rope, I went down rather than up. It baffled me. I eventually managed to get a second piton in, and by a desperate effort pulled up to it. But by this time I was exhausted

Left. The C'est la Vie dihedral (5.11). The crux is a few feet below the climber where chalk marks can be seen on the right wall. A tiny crystal for the right foot supports full body weight. Handholds are non-existent.

Above. The awkward unprotected moves above the overhang on C'est la Vie (5.9+).

Right. The direct finish to C'est la Vie. Note that the climber's left foot is level with his head.

Interview

Right and far right. A free ascent of the first pitch of Temporary Like Achilles.

and had to back off. I think it was a 5.4 climb.

Godfrey: *Do you think that the majority of climbers today think consciously about using free climbing techniques?*

Erickson: I think it's the herd instinct. Most climbers do things free because they think they're supposed to. You see, if you reach a spot where you can't climb free, and you have to pull up on a sling, that doesn't appreciably depreciate the enjoyment of that particular move unless you have a free climbing orientation. Most people have a free climbing orientation because they think they should have it, and because it's the best way to compete these days. It's a syndrome that the climbing media has generated.

Godfrey: *Do you feel that modern distinctions between free climbing and direct aid are meaningful?*

Erickson: I think the distinction is a meaningful one, even though it's somewhat artificial. Pulling on one sling on a two thousand foot climb makes very little difference. But the difference between aiding up the Dawn Wall on El Cap, and soloing the Wind Ridge (5.6) in Eldorado in barefeet, is a big difference. So the line is drawn somewhat artificially in-between. Climbing shoes are O.K., chalk is O.K., and it's still thought of as free climbing. The trend is towards less and less equipment. People are giving up this, and giving up that, and trying to get back to their roots. It takes you back to what I see as the ultimate in free climbing: the unroped, nude, solo climber. The closer you can come to approximating this, without killing yourself, of course, the more you'll get out of climbing.

Godfrey: *What do you see as the main differences between free climbing in the sixties and in the seventies?*

Erickson: I think that most of the climbers during the sixties were good free climbers. Kor certainly was. He just never had the kind of direction and desire that Robbins had. Robbins had climbed at Taquitz, where free climbing was pursued as an end in itself. Kor never seemed to think about really pushing free climbing, not in the sense of working and working on a problem until finally a free climbing solution was found. His approach was very different from the thing I'm into, namely, going out and specifically trying to free climb a pitch.

Godfrey: *You mean being prepared to spend long periods of time working on a problem?*

Erickson: Yes. Though my style of trying to free climb something just for the sake of it can at times get in the way of the climbing experience. Like the fellow who wrote the letter to *Climbing* magazine, saying that he was never going to let a move of aid get in the way of his enjoyment of a route. I think a lot of people are like that. People like myself, unfortunately, who are intent

only on doing things free, and coming down if they can't do things free, are missing some of the pure animal joy of the experience.

Wunsch: I don't think that's true. People tend to enjoy what they know how to do. If you get used to free climbing, you just don't think in terms of aid. For someone who's totally into free climbing, there's just no way you could enjoy aid. In fact, quite the opposite. Once you start pulling on things, you're not going to enjoy it anymore.

Erickson: I agree, but I did some aid climbing back in the sixties, and I know how enjoyable it can be. But I suppose it's true for people who started out climbing in the last few years, and who know only free climbing.

Godfrey: *Steve, how do you feel about the traditional idea that the climber is an artist, that climbs are creations, and that the climber who makes the first ascent has the right to determine such things as fixed protection?*

Wunsch: I think it's complete bullshit. It's a classic tenet of climbing in certain areas, but not one that I subscribe to. It really spoils a climb if it's obvious how it has been done on previous ascents.

Erickson: The question is, who has the right to do first ascents? Is it legitimate for some nurd to go up on a last great problem, such as Jules Verne, and do it with pins, or use bolts?

Godfrey: *It seems as though the myth of "climber as artist" has encouraged those kinds of approaches.*

Wunsch: Right, and that's where Robbins has really blown it. He's encouraged that as much as anyone I can think of. I think it's completely ridiculous to think of climbers as artists.

Erickson: Oh, I think that there are some climbers who possess some degree of artistic sense in their more lucid moments.

Wunsch: Well, I'm not meaning artistry in that sense, I'm meaning in the sense of sculpting routes, like Robbins, Bridwell, and Harding have done in Yosemite. They are artists in the sense that the rock is a piece of canvas, and they paint their ego on it. Everyone can come and view it afterwards, and they have to view it the way it was painted, which is unfortunate. It's a characteristic of the Yosemite scene, and Robbins has been a chief perpetrator. The idea that it makes rational sense to morally draw the line at one hundred bolts per three thousand feet of rock just doesn't hold water. This application from big wall climbing has carried over into the Yosemite free climbing world today and manifests itself in fiascos like some of Bridwell's routes, which go to the ultimate artistic extreme of chopping holds. They were once going to present Bridwell with a hammer and chisel for his birthday, but I guess they didn't. These

things probably wouldn't be occurring today in Yosemite free climbing if the concept of the climber as artist hadn't developed under Robbins and the big wall boys. That's the real sadness of the artist philosophy. It worked well in Britain and held back the excesses of pitons, but in Yosemite, it's just a terribly confused situation, with first ascenters claiming that they have all kinds of rights to their routes. People have even got into fights about it. Henry Barber arrived in the spring of 1975, fresh back from Australia, in great shape, and blitzed up a bunch of new routes. The Valley regulars were up in arms. They wanted to gang up on him and beat him up. It was ridiculous. He gave the Valley the first rejuvenation shot-in-the-arm it had had in ages...and they wanted to beat him up! All of this is just an unfortunate extension of the climber as artist philosophy.

Godfrey: *Talking of Henry, what do you think the main effects of the wandering minstrels of the climbing world, including yourselves, and Henry, and Robbins, have been?*

Wunsch: Well, styles have been brought from one area to another, and stories have been brought from one area to another.

Erickson: Inter-area competition has really increased. People want to know if the climbs in the Gunks are harder than the climbs in Boulder.

Wunsch: It contributes to the homogenization of opinion.

Erickson: It's a lot of fun for the climbers who do it. They see new places, meet new people...

Wunsch: Drink different beer...meet new women... and it helps to shake up the climber-as-artist syndrome a bit. Locals usually revere first ascenters, and feel they have to repeat climbs in the same manner. When somebody comes drifting in from another area, they are less concerned about this and just go up and do them in their own way. A lot of the British climbers, for example, were really pissed off when Henry came breezing in and did things like Vector all on nuts, ignoring the fixed belay pins. I love doing things like that. I do things the way I've always done 'em, and it doesn't matter if it accords with some local tradition or other.

Godfrey: *Siege climbing is a game that is played frequently these days. What is your definition of siege tactics, Steve?*

Wunsch: My definition of sieging stops at the point where one person leads a pitch, and never falls. Anything else is sieging.

Godfrey: *Historically speaking, doesn't sieging carry connotations of massed hordes camped for extended periods of time around medieval cities? Aren't many*

people and long time periods necessary conditions?

Wunsch: That's so, but I think that in climbers' colloquial it covers a wider range of situations. It includes people who fall a lot, or lower to the ground many times.

Godfrey: *You wouldn't call that just bad style, rather than sieging?*

Wunsch: You could, I suppose. No one has really attempted to define sieging before, so I guess you can draw the line wherever you choose and see how many people argue with you. Perhaps you can construct the first definitive work of scholarship on the finer points of siege tactics.

Godfrey: *I think I'll probably leave that for somebody else.*

Erickson: I think that any time you put an over-abundant amount of effort into a climb it constitutes a siege, and this can apply to a short route on a small cliff or a long route on a high mountain. The principle remains the same. For me, once I've fallen and lowered off, it becomes a siege to return and try it again. Most people I know would consider Psycho a siege. But was Jules Verne sieged, because you went back up on it a number of times even though you didn't fall? And in the same way, was Dead Bird Crack sieged because I returned four or five days without falling?

Wunsch: It's a very useful word, but deciding its connotation is real hard. You see, what Erickson calls a taint, I call a siege. If just one person goes up on a climb, falls, and tries again, it's a siege by my standards.

Erickson: Wunsch, you get more like me every day. I can't believe that you've lumped everything other than "no falls" into a siege category. Glad to see you're starting to shape up.

Wunsch: I've always seen clearly the difference between falling and not falling. I just think that ropes are too damned expensive these days not to use them. If you're gonna pay that much, you might as well use them by taking falls occasionally.

Godfrey: *Didn't climbers like Robbins and Ament swap places and take turns trying to lead hard moves during the sixties?*

Wunsch: Sure they did. People have done that forever. If one or two people go climbing and come up to something that's real hard, I imagine the next guy's going to go up and give it a try. Siege tactics are just the natural social consequence of this line of development.

Erickson: Sieging is probably due to the fact that, these days, people who go out climbing together have more equal abilities. Kor took other people up climbs a lot of the time. There was hardly anyone around to match his abilities. I suspect that Northcutt and Carter swung leads on their climbs, but I imagine that on most earlier

climbs there wasn't all that much swinging of leads. In recent years, with more people climbing, swinging leads has become more usual, and hence the development of what we now call sieging.

Godfrey: *Steve, do you think that the intuitive free climbing approach you have is shared by a majority of climbers today?*

Wunsch: Yes, I do. Among the people I climb with, I don't know anyone who climbs on the small cliffs who thinks about going out and doing little aid routes. But some of those people are prepared to go to the Valley and climb a big wall using aid.

Godfrey: *So it depends on the particular game they are playing?*

Wunsch: Yes.

Godfrey: *How do you feel at that very moment when you're up on the climb, within grabbing distance of protection. Then, is it intuition, or do you have to make a decision not to grab? Is it a conscious discipline, or is it so well internalized that thought isn't necessary?*

Wunsch: It's not conscious. It's on a completely different level.

Erickson: I don't think that's true. I think free climbing is conscious and contrived.

Wunsch: Look at it this way. The goals that are generally formulated in the imaginations of myself and those I climb with are free climbing goals. Therefore, when we get to the crags, the goals have been set. There is no question of grabbing for protection. Grabbing is simply an expression of failure, of extrication from fiasco.

Godfrey: *Steve, I'm hearing a difference between your approach and Jim's when you talk about what you experience when you are actually up on the climb. Jim says that his decision not to grab protection is conscious. You seem to be saying that, by the time you get up there, the decision has been made and you operate on a more intuitive, reflex level.*

Erickson: The behavior is the same, though. If you can't do the climb free, you have to grab something, or aid up, just to get off.

Godfrey: *Yes, but I'm talking about before you actually reach that point.*

Erickson: When I first started climbing at Devil's Lake, I pounded in a piton. I didn't try to move delicately upwards around it, trying to avoid using it. I just pulled up on it. It seems to me, based on that experience, that the decision to climb free is a cerebral decision. It's made in your conscious mind.

Godfrey: *Is this how you feel, Steve?*

Wunsch: Yes, but in my case, the decision is made before I get on the climb. Once there, I don't think about it any more. For me, the decision was made during my early years as a kid when I was soloing easy little rocks. Later, when I thought about climbs in bars and other places . . . .

Erickson: Steve's motivation seems to come to him mainly in bars.

Godfrey: *You must have been really inspired climbing in England, with all that good beer.*

Wunsch: In the pubs . . . yes . . . as a matter of fact . . . I did a lot of thinking and talking in pubs. But they talk about ethics in England more than any other place I've been. It used to annoy me to death. But a lot of my desires were born in the pubs.

Godfrey: *You seem to be implying that, for you, there is a difference between climbing ethically and climbing according to your personal values.*

Wunsch: Yes. Ethics are a code, a set of rules, by which to climb. When a leader's mind is cluttered by having to make ethical judgments, he cannot think clearly nor creatively enough to perform greatly.

Godfrey: *So, you climb according to your own personally-internalized values, and they are separate from ethical proscriptions, the rules that govern climbing in general.*

Wunsch: Yes. Ethics are the rules of the masses. My climbing mode is that which feels right for me, and which works for me. It's habit almost. It's just my natural way of doing things. That's the distinction I make. A mode involves no conscious decision on a climb. Ethics do. Ethics involve a restraint where probably there should be none, and they are counter-productive to doing the best of which you are capable.

Godfrey: *Do climbers today really have the opportunity to develop their own individual approach to climbing, their mode, as you call it? Don't they get swamped by contemporary ethics and go along with the crowd?*

Erickson: That's the herd instinct. Unless you have the luck to be in a situation where you have a lot of options to be individualistic, or have the personal courage and integrity to be an individual amid the sweaty masses, you are very likely to be caught up in ethical approaches without thinking too much about them. So, it's very difficult for someone who is just getting into climbing to do his own thing. There are very few climbers these days who are in any way individualistic. One of the problems is that everything has already been done, pretty much. I suppose if you really wanted to climb creatively, you could go out and nail routes sideways, just using bat hooks, or descend routes with a rope from below, or something equally esoteric. These days it's just harder than ever to make a mark.

Godfrey: *How many climbers do you see these days who are performing creatively?*

Wunsch: Probably about the same proportion as before. I think the percentages remain constant. These days, there are a lot more options for those who are just entering climbing. In the very early days, the only option was to get to the top of peaks. Now there are many different ways to be active, both mentally and physically. There are far more choices. If someone chooses to go and aid climb because he has been reading about Warren Harding or Charlie Porter, that's a good thing for him. If he stays in climbing for ten years and only does that, then he has probably isolated himself too much from some of the other possible choices. If he comes in and has been reading Buhl and Erickson and wants to solo. . . .

Erickson: Watch those comparisons.

Godfrey: *But are the choices really realistic choices? Isn't there a strong tendency for the majority to drift into a pattern of free climbing, with a little bouldering occasionally to keep in shape?*

Wunsch: I think the choices are realistic. There are free climbing, aid, bouldering, soloing, mountaineering, and ice climbing. And they're all becoming well-defined little pockets. Unfortunately, these decisions are capable of being manipulated—by media, and by ethics. This is what I would like to see climbing move away from if possible. Climbing is moving toward a complete homogenization of opinion at an alarming rate, and that's lamentable. There exists a moral pool which the pundits who write magazine articles use to try and push the herd in one way or another. Any individual who has the strength to resist this is probably going to get a lot out of climbing and be distinctive. In this sense, a lack of morals is sometimes a prerequisite for genius in climbing.

Godfrey: *So you don't see climbing as a moral activity?*

Wunsch: No. The introduction of morality into what is basically a soulless, evolutionary phenomenon is a common mistake of historians, and of some curly-haired local experts.

Erickson: How dare you.

Godfrey: *You'll have to explain that one a bit.*

Wunsch: I think what I'm getting at is that when people talk about morality, they generally talk about it after the fact. When they are actually climbing, morality seems a long way away. One does not need to strive for an ideal when striving to do the damn routes is hard enough. It's a mistake to look at climbers when they're actually climbing as though they are thinking in moral terms. It happens almost never with me. Once you've developed your own personal mode, it automatically dictates how you are going to climb, and modes change very gradually, if at all, over a climber's lifetime.

Godfrey: *Are you able to divorce yourself completely from contemporary ethical constraints and climb just in your own personal style?*

Wunsch: There's nothing wrong with those aspects of current ethics which make sense becoming part of a particular climber's mode. When you make what is originally possibly an ethical decision, such as deciding not to use pitons, which may have come to you from a whole lot of sources, it becomes a mode just like any other, once you have internalized it.

Godfrey: *You have said that ultimate difficulty is not pursuable while considering means. Can you explain that?*

Wunsch: It is related to the distinctions I make between ethical considerations and a climber's mode. It's very easy to get bogged down in external criteria and waste a lot of energy on questions such as, "Does this climb's difficulty justify two points of aid, or three?" as used to be the case in Britain. Whillans, for example, aided the 5.8 move on Erosion Groove by means of a pin on the first pitch, and did some incredible 5.10 face climbing a long way above protection on the second pitch, where it was impossible to get a pin in. The first pitch generated an ethical response, the second allowed a primal mode to operate. In terms of what I said about it not being possible to pursue ultimate difficulty while considering means, it's quite likely that Whillans wouldn't have done such brilliant 5.10 climbing if a pin placement had been available. The ethics of that time said that a pin for aid was fine in that situation, and he would probably have used one. Today, the trick seems to be to develop a personal mode which ensures that one constantly gives of one's best. Jim's and my so-called "strict canon of ethics" are in reality finely evolved modes which automatically draw from us our best.

Godfrey: *Jim, you've said something that is an apparent converse of Steve's position.*

Erickson: I have?

Godfrey: *Yes.*

Erickson: Hm. . . . I feel as though I'm being set up for something.

Wunsch: I knew we should have done this interview before he had a chance to prepare tricky questions.

Godfrey: *You've said, Jim, that historically, ultimate climbs have usually been achieved by dubious means.*

Erickson: That's a pretty categoric statement, I guess. What I should say is that most ultimate rock climbs that I've had experience with, or knowledge of, seem to have been done by means which were slightly outside the accepted set of ethics at that particular point in time. Cenotaph Corner was first climbed, for example, by Joe Brown using more pitons than apparently Peter Harding thought was ethical. Great Wall on Cloggy was first climbed by Pete Crew using more aid than Joe

The long stretch for the mantleshelf move on the headwall of the fourth lead of Bishop Jaggers (5.9). Protection is sparse and the ground three hundred feet below on this exquisitely delicate slab climb.

Brown thought was justifiable. Supremacy Crack was climbed using more time and lowering off than was generally considered acceptable in the Boulder region in the mid-1960's. Whenever people are trying to do something that is billed as a last great problem, whether it's Cenotaph Corner, Great Wall, Supremacy Crack, or putting a bolt ladder up Cerro Torre, the means adopted seem to be outside the generally accepted style of the times. The thing that I wonder about is that people see Steve falling on Psycho and assume that that's the way they should be climbing, and that it's the way everybody is climbing.

Godfrey: *Is that any worse than people seeing you do your climbs by not falling, and thinking that your way is the way they should be climbing?*

Erickson: Is that worse? Well, I think people should make decisions for themselves. If people want to go up and fall off climbs, or use aid, it's their right. I guess I'm talking mainly from the point of view of competitive ethics.

Wunsch: Well, of course, people always have examples that they follow. The two styles that we are talking about have come into existence only very recently as separate categories of ways to try climbs. Once the two approachs exist, I look upon them as just different options for people.

Erickson: Yes, but people should recognize that there are differences between a well-protected climb that was done with falls, like Psycho, and a poorly-protected climb that was done without falls, like Wide Country. If you make a competitive comparison between those two climbs in terms of technical difficulty, you're missing the boat. In fact, you're drowning five hundred yards away from the boat. The two were conceived of, and climbed, under completely different sets of premises.

Wunsch: I feel that those distinctions are made by the rock rather than by people. The rock tells you that you'd better not fall on certain parts of Wide Country, and it tells you that you can fall just as much as you want to on the crux of Psycho. People don't need to make the distinctions, and in fact it involves a whole lot of mental bureaucracy to try to make those distinctions. The rock makes them perfectly naturally.

Godfrey: *Jim, Robbins has said that your style, of not taking leader falls, is a higher level. Do you feel that's true?*

Erickson: A higher level? Well, is free climbing a higher level than aid climbing? Is soloing a higher level than free climbing? I just think they're all kind of different things.

Godfrey: *Isn't that just fudging the issue?*

Erickson: No. How can you add six apples and six oranges? You get eighteen tangerines, or something equally meaningless.

Godfrey: *But people never get moralistic about apples and oranges, only about climbs.*

Erickson: O.K. Look at it this way. Is Charlie Porter's A.6 route at King Tutt's Tomb harder than Athlete's Feat? Or harder than Perilous Journey? Is the North America Wall harder than ice climbing on Bridal Veil Falls?

Wunsch: That's getting right at it.

Godfrey: *Is doing the first ascent of the Naked Edge with one or two falls better or worse than doing a later free ascent with no falls?*

Erickson: The question of doing the first ascent with one or two falls, compared to a later ascent with no falls—that's a difficult question to answer. Is doing the second ascent of Kloeberdanz with only one fall better than doing the first ascent with fifteen falls? Many people would think it is, but maybe it isn't. If Wunsch had never existed and the Kid had come up to it first, perhaps he would have taken a lot of falls trying to work it out for the first time. It does make a big difference doing a climb for the first time.

Godfrey: *Hence your conclusion that the majority of first ascents of ultimately difficult climbs in any given period are achieved by somewhat dubious means?*

Erickson: Yes.

Wunsch: But that's not the most important issue. What's important is what happens to you after you take a fall. My feeling is that it's unnatural to say, "I'm not interested in this climb any more." If I've gone right to my limit, and fallen, then I'm intrigued all the more. I just want to get right back up and try it again.

Godfrey: *Steve, in your approach, do you ever go up a climb thinking, "Well, I'll just go up and fall off a few times," as Henry Barber says he does?*

Wunsch: Oh, I sometimes talk like that. Especially if it's a climb I've fallen off before.

Godfrey: *Is it a regular approach for you?*

Wunsch: I have a million approaches.

Erickson: "I got a million of 'em." You sound like Jimmy Durante.

Godfrey: *Let's say it's a climb that's going to be maximum difficulty for you, that it has never been free climbed, and that you really want to do it.*

Wunsch: I usually go up with the mind of not getting hurt. That's foremost. Whether I'll fall off, that I decide later on the basis of the protection and how hard it gets. Do you ever wonder why people consider a climb which is inescapable to be more aesthetic than one you can get off easily part way up?

Godfrey: *Tell me.*

Wunsch: Because it's natural. You have to keep going up. I find a similarity between that and my mode, which

David Breashears demonstrating his mastery of thin cracks on the direct start to Wunsch's Dihedral (5.11). He made the first ascent of this finger-wrecking problem.

Right. Wunsch's Dihedral

says that you do whatever seems natural. If there is good protection, it is natural to push yourself to the ultimate limit, and to search into all the realms of creativity that you have, to seek solutions for the problem. Even to the extent of attempting things that you're not sure you can do, but which you are going to try anyway. Sometimes you find yourself in the middle of a finger-tip pull up, harder than you've ever done before, and you try something real quick. Maybe it doesn't work and you fall off. If you have protection and it's safe, to me it's usually very instructive. And it's usually very instructive to immediately think about what you did right and wrong, and then go and try it again. You may learn something really worthwhile from trying it again. It's very important to me that I learn more and more about climbing. When I do certain climbs by falling off, I'm learning something every time, and I'm searching as far as I can into myself in doing them that way.

Godfrey: *And you are saying that if even a small part of you is thinking about retreating before you reach the point of falling off, or thinking about grabbing for protection, that both of these are inhibiting factors in terms of creativity and learning.*

Wunsch: Yes. That's just what I feel.

Godfrey: *But for you, Jim, there is a different benefit in that situation?*

Erickson: No, I think I get the same benefit but in a different way.

Godfrey: *But you generally try to keep enough in reserve to be able to climb back down without falling or holding on to protection?*

Wunsch: But I do that too, whenever I'm scared and there isn't good protection. It's natural to keep something in reserve in those situations.

Godfrey: *Sure. You demonstrated that on Jules Verne. But Jim does it all the time.*

Erickson: I figure that if you are going to do a climb, it should be within your ability, something your body is physically capable of doing at that point in time.

Wunsch: Your mind is more important than your body in that instance.

Godfrey: *You mean in a safe, well protected situation?*

Wunsch: Yes. I can't think of anything that involved my mind more than Psycho—even including Jules Verne. I can think back to the ridiculous gyrations I had to push my mind through to make myself cool enough on the inside to perform just perfectly to do the moves. I was right at my total limit all the way. It involved a digging into resources that I know I couldn't have come to by just trying it once.

Godfrey: *When you say, "cool enough on the inside," you are implying that there was a lot more to doing*

those moves than just hurling yourself at the lip?

Wunsch: You never do anything hard if you just hurl yourself at it.

Erickson: When Steve makes a dynamic move, he climbs it very meticulously, and carefully, and cerebrally.

Wunsch: But there does come that moment when you just have to launch yourself.

Godfrey: *Steve, you once objected to my pejorative way of describing dynamic moves and appended, virtually in capital letters, the description—"magnificent lunge." Can you talk about that a little more?*

Wunsch: Well, it's easy for people to talk pejoratively about dynamic moves. Stannard's real good at that, though he does it tongue-in-cheek. He occasionally says, "Well, I finally gave up trying to climb it and lunged." And an even better one: I once introduced Diana Hunter to that dynamic boulderer Bob Williams, who was taking us on our first tour of the Fort Collins boulders. Diana asked shyly, as always, toes in the sand, "Aren't you the lunger?" To which Williams coolly replied, "I prefer to be called a swinger." Maybe describing a climb will give you a sense of how I feel about lunging. Have you heard of a climb called Crash and Burn in the Gunks?

Godfrey: *No, I haven't.*

Wunsch: Well, it involves climbing up a detached pinnacle. From the top of the pinnacle, you have to jump for a ledge on the lip of an overhang about six feet away. The protection consists of a sling around the top of the pinnacle. So, if you miss, you're going to come crashing back down into the pinnacle. In order to understand why a lunge move is magnificent, put yourself into that position, on top of that pinnacle. Imagine yourself there, imagine where your protection is, and the kind of fall you're going to take if you blow it. Try and muster resources inside yourself until you can see yourself jump and grab the lip. It's a matter of foreseeing exactly what's going to happen. There is real spine-chilling magnificence when you get the feeling that it can go. The only situation I can think of that comes close to it, is in old fashioned dueling where the participants have to stay calm, knowing they're gonna die if they blow it, and keep their hand completely still as they fire. The first time I had a sense of lunging as being magnificent was watching Stannard trying a variation on Matinee in the Gunks. He did some 5.9 moves and clipped into a fixed pin, then made a number of tries to reach a hold that was way out of his reach, and couldn't get it. Suddenly, he said in a very calm and level voice to Bragg, who was belaying him, "Two feet of slack please, John." And.....Wooooosh! He made an amazing lunge for the hold and fell straight off! I

thought that was just great! I just couldn't imagine anyone asking for slack like that when it was likely he was going to fall off. That's as neat as marching into battle and not looking to the right or the left, just keeping straight on going toward the enemy. Not even trying to duck bullets. I think it's magnificent. It's a mustering of resources that enables you to perform, knowing, without a shadow of a doubt, that you're going to be able to do it. At the moment of taking off, every single part of you has to feel completely confident that it's going to work out. When you see slow motion films of gymnasts, you realize all that goes into doing one of those incredible moves. One of the real secrets is the preparation that gets you into a mental state that will allow you to do the moves as a reflex, without thinking, and that gives you just the right combination that's going to work. Climbing gives you a much better opportunity than gymnastics to do these kinds of things.

Godfrey: *Why so much better than gymnastics?*

Wunsch: Because the moves aren't determined beforehand. They are determined by the rock in a natural way, and the body and mind work together in a natural combination. It is very important to do whatever the rock dictates at any given time.

Godfrey: *Is this what you mean when you talk about listening to the rock?*

Wunsch: Yes, but it also has another associated meaning. Climbers usually relate to rock by means of two main senses, seeing and touching. Zen masters tell us that in looking, you only see a part of the picture. Likewise, touching is restricted. Listening calms you down, makes you very still inside. It allows aspects of sight, touch, and other more mysterious bodily senses to operate. You just can't do anything perfectly if you are mentally concentrating on doing it perfectly. Listening calms everything down and helps prevent you from getting cornered into a constricted pattern; it also brings into play a lot of non-climbing-oriented resources. Putting all this together in the context of a particular move, responding as openly as possible to that situation, gives the greatest likelihood of being able to come up with a creative solution to the problem. You need to accept whatever the climb gives in terms of handholds and footholds and protection, accept whatever gear you have with you, including shoes, and sink right into that mode as it exists in the present. If you are somewhere other than the present moment, fighting with an unnatural stricture such as not falling, or not clipping into a fixed pin or bolt, you are not going to be as capable of figuring out the moves. You are going to end up muddled and not be able to give of your best.

Erickson: Well, obviously, in that sense, my approach is muddled, and I can't climb quite as hard routes in my

The undercling at Split Rocks (5.9).

style as can people who are prepared to fall off.

Wunsch: Obviously you could do harder climbs if you fell off them a lot. If there were two Jim Ericksons, the one who was prepared to go ahead and fall would be able to do a harder climb, even close to protection, on his first try, than the one who says he won't fall.

Erickson: Wait a minute. I don't say I won't fall. Do you think I don't go for it ever?

Wunsch: No, obviously you do go for it. But what is in your mind at the moment you're gonna have to go for it is an ethical decision, based on competitive ethics—that you don't think you should fall, that you don't think falling is a good way to climb—and having to make that decision detracts a little from your ability.

Godfrey: *Jim, how does that relate to your need to maintain a sense of adventure on a particular climb?*

Erickson: If I get to know too much about a climb, it ceases to have any adventure for me, and falling is a very good way to learn about a climb.

Wunch: I decline to believe that you didn't get a sense of adventure out of going back up to the Naked Edge after you had fallen off.

Erickson: I had most of my adventure on the Naked Edge on the last pitch, where I didn't fall at all, and slightly less adventure on the fourth pitch, which is harder, where I did fall. The only adventure on the fourth pitch after I'd fallen off, was whether or not I could get up the moves.

Wunsch: I think that was plenty. I don't think I'd want any more.

Erickson: Well, at the time it was plenty.

Wunsch: But these days I think you probably miss a lot of adventurous possibilities by not coming back to climbs that you have fallen off. What do you think you would experience if you came back to a route after you had fallen off?

Erickson: I'm not saying I wouldn't get any adventure. I could enjoy it, but it would be in a completely different framework. It would be in a bouldering framework. But then, I might as well go back and use a top rope.

Wunsch: Oh, no. There's a big difference between going back and trying to lead it again, and going back and top roping it. Once you get your feet up above that last protection, you're going to start worrying a lot more than you would if you had a top rope above you.

Erickson: To me, there isn't much difference between going back and top roping, or aiding back up, or hanging on the protection again. All of those ways teach me something about the climb, in the same way that falling does, that I'd rather not know, and they end up feeling like boulder problems.

Godfrey: *But don't you also learn about a climb by climbing up and down a lot?*

Crack climbing at Split Rocks (5.8).

Erickson: Well, obviously, there are many adventures that I could be having that I'm missing. I could even go out race car driving.

Godfrey: *Jim, can you talk a little about the feelings you have and the values you see in not falling? Is it just a gimmick?*

Erickson: No. For me it's an operational definition of not failing on a climb, and secondly, it involves less encumbrances and reliance on equipment than other approaches. I'm not saying that other people can't get adventure out of climbs that involve technology. Charlie Porter's aid routes, and Steve's solutions that involve falling are obviously highly adventurous endeavors for them. The South Face of Everest was also, obviously, a highly adventurous undertaking, despite the massive amount of technology employed. All other things being equal, the closer I approximate nude solo climbing, the better. I am more likely to depend on my own resources in a crux situation, and therefore the experience is more meaningful.

Wunsch: I think you ought to be clear that you are not eliminating technology just by the fact that you don't fall on your equipment. I'd say that once you've got the rope on, and the protection in, you are being no more natural to climb the pitch without falling than you would be to climb it with falling. In fact, you are being quite unnatural by not accepting falling as a possibility within the environment you have defined for yourself. It is just very unnatural to impose such an artificial limitation on your brain in such a tricky environment. Saying, "I'm not gonna fall on my gear, I'm gonna pretend that it's not here, I'm gonna pretend that I'm soloing," is unnatural. It takes a little segment of your brain to convince the rest of your brain that the equipment is not there, and that energy could be better employed doing the moves.

Godfrey: *Steve, are you saying that it would be better for Jim if he took falls?*

Wunsch: Yes. It would be better for Jim. Though...no, ...wait a minute. Any change in his mode probably wouldn't help. He's obviously very interested in climbs that he hasn't fallen on. That interest is probably intensified by the fact that he doesn't go back to climbs he has fallen on. Losing this intensified feeling, if he changed his mode, probably wouldn't be worth it for him. He ought to stick with what he's doing, unless he gets some intuition that convinces him that a change would be beneficial.

Erickson: I do see the other point of view, and I do enjoy going out once in a while and engaging in uproarious bouldering-type climbing. Guenese was an example. That was a boulder problem-type of adventure for me. I viewed Guenese much as I view the boulder

Left. The J-Crack on Lumpy Ridge above Estes Park (5.9). (500mm. telephoto).

Above. The J-Crack.

Right. Delicate slab climbing at the top of the J-Crack. This variation traverses right to avoid the 5.11 headwall.

The first pitch of T.2.

problems on Flagstaff.

Wunsch: Guenese is a whole lot safer than the boulder problems on Flagstaff, and one problem in particular, King Conquerer Crack, scared me a lot more than Psycho. But you do have a certain amount of disdain, and don't seem to feel that bouldering-type climbs on the high cliffs are as valuable as the climbs you do.

Erickson: Well, I probably do project that, but I don't really think it's right. When I make distinctions, I'm not really trying to say that bouldering-type climbs are done in bad style. Do you derive more adventure from trying to solo a boulder problem like King Conquerer Crack than you do from trying to work out the moves on Psycho?

Wunsch: No. They're different.

Erickson: Do you experience the same kinds of feelings? Are they the same kinds of challenges?

Wunsch: You can talk about intensity of challenge, but you can't say that they are the same kind. On Psycho I was not scared, except of failure, which is a huge fear. It was not fear of falling. It was fear of non-control. I became intensely afraid trying to work out the moves on Psycho. I was afraid that I wasn't going to be able to control myself well enough to do moves that I knew I could do if I controlled myself. Do you follow that?

Erickson: Yes.

Wunsch: My climbing approach is not a moral thing. In fact, I might even applaud people who pull up on slings and lie about it later, because it's not a damn moral situation. I just don't think it's all that important.

Erickson: Oh, now wait a minute. . . . You don't think it's important if people lie?

Wunsch: Well, I've got as much good as bad out of lies.

Godfrey: *How about the effect of lies on the climbing community as a whole?*

Wunsch: I think the climbing community is better off because of lies about Oliver Moon, and better off for watching Pitman Orr cavort in the bars, impressing four girls with his stories of climbing Country Club Crack. Once when Henry and I were trying Super Crack, we were going to come back and tell everyone we had done it, and we waxed philosophical about the effect it would have on the climbing world and the effect it would have on us. I don't think the effects would have been particularly detrimental to anyone.

Godfrey: *I can see you having more hesitation in that situation, which involved generating a myth about yourself, than in the Oliver Moon situation, which involved a completely imaginary figure.*

Wunsch: That's true, but we were still gonna do it. We

Lichen to Like (5.10).

thought it would be real fun, and we thought it would shake up the information sections of the magazines. Between Henry and I, we probably would have been able to pull it off in a really good way.

Godfrey: *But, historically, when certain individuals misrepresent what they have done, it hasn't usually been done with the idea of building a myth that will benefit the climbing community.*

Wunsch: You mean they do it for an ego trip?

Godfrey: *Yes. And usually it bounces back on the individual in question in a way that has adverse effects for him.*

Erickson: As long as it's well intended, and isn't maliciously done, it's fine. I think that it was cute that someone told Northcutt that Kor had previously free climbed the direct start to the Bastille, just to get him going. But if someone does it just to move himself up the climbing hierarchy, it's not so good because the reasons are poor.

Godfrey: *Jim, does it bother you that you have missed a number of important first free ascents because of your unwillingness to return to a climb on which you have taken a leader fall?*

Erickson: No. I feel very happy with the climbs I've done. I don't feel that I cheated myself out of anything by not doing the first free ascent of Kloeberdanz, for example. Let's assume that I might have been able to do Kloeberdanz after twenty-five falls. It just would not have been that rewarding an experience for me. But it's very easy for me to say that, because I was fortunate enough to be in a place in time where there were a lot of climbs within my ability that I was able to do. I had countless plums to pluck off. Consequently, if anyone today was to adopt my climbing style, they probably wouldn't make much of a name for themselves unless they were extraordinarily talented, because there just aren't that many plums remaining.

Wunsch: I don't think that's true. The Kid is following your mode today pretty closely, and he's doing some amazing things.

Erickson: But he's extraordinarily talented.

Godfrey: *But you could change your style, push harder, take falls, and probably pull off more climbs than you do.*

Erickson: If I wanted to stay on top of the climbing scene, in the public eye so to speak, that would be the way to do it. But I feel that, in my own way, I'm improving every day, becoming a better climber. Each time I go climbing I'm evolving. I've been steadily improving ever since I started climbing, but technical

The strenuous crux on the airy second lead of the Rosy Crucifixion (5.9+), one of the most aesthetic leads in Eldorado Canyon.

Right. Strenuous hand jams across the roof on the final lead of Art's Spar (5.10).

standards have also been rising in recent years. For a brief instant in time on October 3, 1971, when I did the Edge, those two planes intersected.

Godfrey: *So you feel that the personal value you get out of climbing is more important than creating a public reputation?*

Wunsch: There are all kinds of values to be gotten out of climbing. Sometimes you can take a girlfriend up a climb and get laid for it.

Erickson: In terms of my being in the right place at the right time, it seems clear that history makes men, rather than men making history. With the exception of unique individuals like Napoleon and Hitler, everything that has ever been done would have been done by someone eventually. This applies to the climbs I did between 1968 and 1977. If I hadn't done them, someone else certainly would. This is partly what I base my approach on these days. It just seems to me that people are eventually going to come along who are going to be able to put up new routes without falling and without using other means that I feel are dubious, and I think that maybe it's best to leave good lines for them, rather than trying just anything to get up them right now. This is why I said that ultimate climbs tended to be done by dubious means. Because the people who are doing them are just a step ahead of everybody else, the vision of the climb seems so much more important than the means adopted for doing it. That's how it was for me on the Edge. I wanted to free climb it, and that's all I cared about. Taking falls in the context of that climb, at the time, seemed all right.

Godfrey: *And that's true for you today in your approach to trying to free climb Half Dome?*

Erickson: Well, I'm not sure how I'm approaching Half Dome. I used to hike up the backside, but now the Muir Lake trail seems to be a slightly easier way.

Godfrey: *Seriously though?*

Erickson: I tend to view Half Dome the same way I viewed the Naked Edge. I'm not so concerned about being pure, because it seems such an outrageous thing.

Godfrey: *So you are saying that because it seems like an ultimate climb for this point in time, you don't mind employing slightly dubious means, according to your own criteria?*

An early attempt to free climb Genesis, Turner and Culp's original A.5. route on Redgarden Wall.

Right: At the top of the expanding flake during a free attempt on Genesis.

Erickson: I guess that's true. There seems to be plenty of adventure because the climb is so long. I guess I'm not interested in doing just hard climbs. I'm mainly interested in impossible climbs. Anybody who's good can do hard climbs. But I don't think people will be standing in line to try to free climb Half Dome, for a while yet, anyway. Last year I got up fifteen feet higher than I'd managed the previous year. At that rate of progress, it's gonna take me about a hundred and fifty years to get to the top. So far, the pitches I've led I've managed to do without falling. I just don't know if I'm going to be able to maintain this for the rest of the route. If I get up to the last slab pitch and slip and end up hanging on protection, I wouldn't rappel the whole face.

Wunsch: That would be pretty dense. We used to do things like that, but we've developed a bit more sense in our old age. I used to retreat from routes rather than aid past the one move that would get me to the summit. Jim and Duncan rappelling all the way back down the Diving Board when they couldn't make the final move or two is a good example of that kind of approach.

Erickson: Don't you mean retreat?

Wunsch: The time I quit doing that was when I realized that it was an ethic rather than a mode, and how really unnatural it felt to me. It became obvious that it was just a pain in the ass and busy work. A mode always operates along the line of least resistance once you've had some kind of fiasco. A moral decision throws monkey wrenches into the process. Sometimes rappelling might be the easiest way to get off, but in the cases of Half Dome and Diving Board, it would sure be a lot easier and sensible to aid over the last few moves and get up to the top. There is just no difference between using gear to rappell down, or to aid up. You just get off the climb as easily as you can once you fail.

Godfrey: *Jim, does the uniqueness of your style of not returning to climbs you have fallen off encourage you to maintain your approach? Would you feel as committed to it, if other climbers started using it?*

Erickson: Well, I suppose that's part of it, but I'm sure I'd maintain it even if everyone else adopted it.

Wunsch: I find the opposite. I think I enjoyed free climbing more when hardly anyone else was into it. Everyone thought I was a real weirdo. I think I enjoyed being a weirdo. Now that everyone is free climbing, it's not quite as satisfying as it was in the old days. Particularly in the Valley, people thought I was really screwy for not just using short climbs as a way to get in shape for the big walls. It was hard to find people who even wanted to go up and do the established 5.9's. They had to find time between their big wall routes and equipment-racking exercises. I'd tried for a long time to find somebody to go up with me to try the Salathé-Steck

Above. Art Higbee making the crux moves over the lip on the first free ascent of the Wisdom roof.

Left. Jim Erickson leading the poorly protected first pitch of the Wisdom.

Right: Higbee making the first free ascent of the Wisdom roof.

on Sentinel free, and it wasn't until Jim came out for a visit to Yosemite that we were able to get together and do it. Though I must say that back then I was really miffed when that *Mountain* magazine article called me the Prophet of Purism. I'm really glad that it's becoming recognized that some of my climbing has controversial aspects.

Godfrey: *Jim, can you describe how it feels right at that moment when you really go for it on a particular move, not sure if you are going to be able to do it, and that you might end up falling?*

Erickson: In situations like that, I have a very warped sense of perception. When I finally commit myself, I don't have any fear. I'm not sure of the outcome, but just go for it. Mentally, I seem to be extremely aware of what is going on. My mind moves at an extremely fast pace. I find myself concentrating fully on what I'm doing, and I divorce myself completely from thoughts of falling, from thoughts of protection, from thoughts of fear, or anything like that. The only thing that is important is concentrating totally on what needs to be done to get myself to where I want to be. Time is completely altered. Thinking back to the Naked Edge, many of the details of the lower pitches of that climb are blurred in my memory now, but the details of the final pitch, especially the jam crack, are still crystal-clear. I knew I had only enough strength for one try. It was happening just like the baby floating through space in the movie *2001*. Just eons of time drifted by. I could see my hand slowly drifting up for that last jam.

Postscript to the Seventies:

The English writer, Harold Drasdo, has commented that the more effort expended on a particular climb over the years, the more its character (in a historical sense) is enhanced. Climbs.... "are enlarged by their dramatic histories,"[1] he writes. In this sense, the climbs considered in this book have become part of Colorado climbing lore. There are many, many others, of course, and their will be many more in the future. Even as we go to press, reports of new ascents come in......Cinch Crack received its long-awaited free ascent...and so it goes. As one observes the "kids of Kloeberdanz" sniffing around the base of climbs that make the hair of old-timers like Wunsch and Erickson stand on end—who would be silly enough to predict the future?

1. Harold Drasdo, *Education and the Mountain Centers,* (N. Wales: Welsh Universal Press, 1973), p. 18.

BOB GODFREY

DUDLEY CHELTON

INDEX

Able, John F., 76
Adams, Pat, 233
Alexander, Chuck, 87, 97
Alexander, Professor J.W., 27, 28, 31
Ament, Pat, 58, 91-92, 113-116, 138-139, 143, 151, 152, 153, 156, 159, 160, 164, 167, 174, 178, 181, 186, 193, 194, 210, 219, 230
Armstrong, Baker, 18, 19, 41
Auld, John, 76
Baillie, Rusty, 120, 132-133
Baldwin, Ivy, 78, 152
Barber, Henry, 210-211, 217, 231-233
Beckey, Fred, 54
Bedayn, Raffi, 59
Bendixen, Jane, 210
Bird, Dick, 78, 81, 86
Bird, Isabella, 8
Black Canyon of the Gunnison: 3, 41, 43, 45-48, 117, 120, 130, 133, 135, 152; Chasm View, 117, 235; Death Valley, 136; Painted Wall, the, 3, 120, 133, 135
Blanchard, Paul, 18
Blaurock, Carl, 27, 30, 40-41
Bonatti, Walter, 132
Borghoff, Mike, 76
Bossier, Tex, 117, 124-126, 153, 167
Boucher, Bob, 112, 152
Boucher, Stanley, 70, 72, 73, 75
Boulder Canyon: 3, 86, 129; Athlete's Feat, 143, 193; Castle Rock, 58, 143, 151, 193; Cosmosis, 186; Country Club Crack, 143, 153, 186, 235; Final Exam, 143, 148; Gorilla's Delight, 155, 231-233; Super Squeeze, 231, 233
Bouldering, 159-163
Braddock, Brad, 58
Bragg, John, 222, 227
Breashears, Dave, 218, 219, 233
Briggs, Bill, 159
Briggs, Don, 133
Briggs, Roger, 156, 193-195, 197, 199, 202, 208, 210, 217-218, 220, 222, 233, 234
Brinker, Dexter, 64
Buhl, Herman, 27, 30, 99, 116, 132
Byers, William, 6
Candelaria, Bob, 222, 225
Carmichael, Bob, 211
Carter, Harvey, 66, 68, 72-73, 75-76, 81-82, 84
Chapin, Frederick, 6, 7, 97-98
Cheyney, Steve, 76
Chidlaw, Ben, 87
Chief's Head: 102-105, 116, 121, 138, 172,
Chouinard, Yvon, 82, 84, 93, 97, 114, 116, 174
Cole, Gary, 97
Colorado Mountain Club, 20, 21, 40
Covington, Mike, 120, 126
Crack of Fear: 148, 149, 151

Cranmer, Chappel, 50
Crestone Needle: 31, 62
Crestones: 2
Croff, Pete, 76
Culp, Bob, 86, 92-93, 98-99, 101-107, 112, 116-117, 120-121, 124, 126-127, 129-130, 133, 138-139, 153, 160
Dalke, Larry, 24, 52, 91-92, 108, 113-117, 120, 133, 138, 152, 160, 164, 166-169, 172, 181, 194, 202, 216, 219, 230
Davies, Eleanor, 31
Davis, Dan, 148
Diagonal, the: 90-93, 105, 112, 121, 124-126, 152, 172
Diamond, the: 2, 61-63, 68, 90, 93, 97-98, 121, 123-129, 132-133, 138-139, 152, 172, 234-237
Disney, Jim, 120
Diving Board, the: 116, 153, 194-195, 197
Dolomites, the: 105-106
Donald, Kevin, 181, 186, 234
Dornan, Dave, 139, 164
Doucette, Don, 76
Dunn, Jimmy, 117
Eldorado Springs Canyon: 3, 78, 86-87, 98, 108, 115, 129, 152, 175, 186, 225, 227, 235; Bastille, 78, 90-91, 98, 108-109, 115, 155, 177, 178, 186, 193, 199, 211, 230; Black Jack, 178; Blackwalk, 181, 233; Blind Faith, 230; Bulge, the, 87, 98, 101, 138; Dirty Deed, 113; Diving Board, the, 116, 153, 194-195, 197; Duncan Donuts, 218; Genesis, 116-117, 227; Grand Giraffe, 98, 138; Grandmother's Challenge, 179, 181, 208; Green Spur, 164, 211-213; Gueneses, 208, 233, 235; Jules Verne, 219-221, 227, 230; Kloeberdanz, 116, 164, 216-217, 219, 230, 233; Krystal Klyr, 219; Micky Maus Wall, 117, 218-219; Naked Edge, the, 112, 117, 139, 153, 164, 172, 186-195, 199, 219, 220, 233, 235-237; Offset, 218; Outer Space, 109, 115, 153; Perilous Journey, 219; Psycho, 138, 167, 178, 225, 227, 230; Red Dihedral, 117, 172, 218; Redgarden Wall, 78, 81, 98, 112-113, 116, 152, 155, 181, 203, 208, 219; Redguard Route, 81, 84, 87, 116, 177; Rincon, 113, 181, 208; Rosy Crucifixion, 113, 208; Ruper, 102, 152; Sooberb, 230; Supremacy Crack, 152-153, 193; T2, 90, 98, 138, 139, 181, 219; "Toit, le," 116, 208; Wide Country, 178, 193, 199-203, 211; Wind Tower, 178-179; X-M, 115, 164, 166-172, 195, 199, 203, 219, 230; Yellow Spur, 113, 139, 151, 164, 178
Ellingwood, Albert, 21, 22, 24, 26, 31,

38, 43, 61, 62, 70, 73, 75, 177
Ellingwood Arete: 31, 40
Erb, Dick, 149
Erickson, Dave, 181, 186, 230
Erickson, Jim, 169, 173, 174, 177, 178-179, 181, 186, 189, 191, 193-195, 197, 199, 202, 208, 210, 216, 217, 219-220, 222, 225, 227, 230-231, 233; **Interview**, 240-271
Ervin, Bill, 40
Eubank, Bill, 57, 61-62, 64
Ferguson, Duncan, 169, 181, 186, 189, 191, 194, 195, 197, 199, 202, 208, 211, 218, 219, 220, 231, 233-235
Field, Ernie, 50
Fitschen, Joe, 90
Flatirons, the: Death and Transfiguration, 197-199, 231; Northwest Passage, 57, 59, 61-62, 63, 78, 81, 101; Third Flatiron, 10-11, 15, 18, 19, 22, 27, 45-49, 56, 230
Forrest, Bill, 132-133, 135-136
Foster, Leo, 193
Fralick, Jack, 50-52
Fredericks, Chris, 149, 151
Frost, Tom, 90, 116
Garden of the Gods: 2, 22, 33, 62, 70-76; "Borghoff's Blunder", 76; Ellingwood Ledge, 22; Greyrock, 22; Kissing Camels, 33, 71; North Gateway Rock, 71, 76; "Pete and Bob's", 76; Pipe Route, 76; "Psychic Grandma", 76; South Gateway Rock, 76; "Tidrick's", 76
Garbert, Gary, 132
Giesecke, Lewis, 41
Gill, John, 159, 160-164, 231
Glenwood Canyon: 3, 106-108, 152
Gorrell, Warren, 49, 50, 62
Goss, Wayne, 120, 126-129, 133, 164, 234-237
Greenman, Ernest, 11, 15, 18, 19, 45
Gregory Canyon: 101
Griffiths, Melvin, 41, 44-46, 48
Hallett Peak: 2, 233; North Face, 82, 84
Hardin, Charles, 49-50
Harding, Earl, 8
Harlin, John, 126, 130
Harrel, Lee, 138
Hart, Stephen, 31, 40
Hempel, Mort, 90
Hendricks, Herby, 76
Herbert, T.M., 116
Higbee, Art, 227
Higgins, Molly, 211, 213, 236
Higgins, Tom, 159
Hoag, Barton, 24, 26, 38
Holubar, Roy, 59, 112
Horn, Rick, 117
Hornbein, Tom, 54-55, 57-58, 61-66, 68, 78, 86
Hornsby, Dave, 62
Howells, Art, 76
Hunter, Diana, 211

Hurley, George, 98-100, 156
Huston, Cary, 59, 61, 65-66, 78, 86
Ingalls, Huntley, 105, 108, 116, 138, 225
Jackson, Dallas, 78, 86, 164
Johnson, Dale, 19, 58-59, 61, 68, 78, 81, 86, 90, 93, 97
Johnson, Rudolph, 10
Jules Verne: 219-221, 227, 230
Kamps, Bob, 91-93, 97-98, 121, 123-124, 138
Kane, Charles, 46
Kiener, Walter, 30-31
Kloeberdanz: 116, 164, 216-217, 219, 230, 233
Komito, Steve, 108-109, 112, 117, 159
Kor, Layton, 84, 86, 87, 90-93, 98-99, 100, 102-109, 112-117, 120-121, 123-130, 133, 138-139, 143, 148, 151-152, 164, 166, 167, 172, 177-178, 181, 194, 202, 210, 216, 225, 233
LaGrange, Bob, 108, 117, 233
Lamb, Reverend Elkanah, 7-8, 27, 30, 230
Lamb, George, 90
Laughlin, Jack, 97
Lavender, Dwight, G., 40-41, 43-44
Lizard Head: 24, 26, 31, 38, 40, 62, 68
Logan, Jim, 148-149, 151, 234-237
Lone Eagle: 40, 52, 68
Long, Carleton, 41
Long, Everett, 41, 48
Longs Peak: Alexander's Chimney, 28, 30-31, 37, 48, 125; Broadway, 7, 28, 30, 37, 50, 63-64, 90-91, 93, 97, 121, 123-127, 129, 236; Chasm Cutoff, 64; Chasm View, 62, 64, 97-98, 132; Diagonal, the, 90-93, 105, 112, 121, 124-126, 152, 172; Diamond, the, 2, 61-63, 68, 90, 93, 97-98, 121, 123-129, 132-133, 138-139, 152, 172, 234-237; East Face, 2, 6, 7, 8, 22, 27, 28, 30-33, 37, 49, 50, 52, 61, 63, 68, 78, 82, 92, 98, 121, 124, 127, 152, 233; Grand Traverse, the, 152; Keiners, 91, 123; Homestretch, the, 7, 27; Jack of Diamonds, 121, 123; Keyhole, the, 7, 8, 27, 30; Lamb's Slide, 7, 8, 30, 37, 123, 127; Mills Glacier, 63, 123, 125; North Chimney, 30, 97, 124, 127, 236; Notch Couloir, 7, 37, 50, 62, 126; Stettners Ledges, 38, 40, 50, 52, 61, 63, 90; Table Ledge, 68, 133, 236, 237; Window, the, 62-63; Zumies Thumb, 63-64
Macomber, William, 46
McCarthy, Jim, 117, 121
McCarty, Cleve, 57-58, 143, 174, 178
McClintock, Henry L., 41
McClure, Dan, 105, 234
McCracken, Jim, 117
Maiden, the: 56, 57, 58, 186; Northwest Overhang, 59, 61, 68, 78, 81; Crow's

Nest, 58, 59, 61
Matron, the: 57, 166; Nord Wand, 166, 172
Mayrose, Paul, 117, 148
Millard, Earl and Floyd, 10
Mills, Enos, 8, 27, 30, 48, 230
Monitor Peak: 51-52, 68
Moomaw, Jack, 27-28, 48
Moore, Dean, 97
Mount Sneffels: 43-44
Murchison, Roy, 40
Murley, Chuck, 78, 81
Naked Edge, the: 112, 117, 139, 153, 164, 172, 186-195, 199, 219, 220, 233, 235-237
Needles-Grenadiers: 40, 43
Nelson, Ax, 54-55
Northcutt, Ray, 78, 81-82, 84, 86, 90-93, 105-106, 112, 121, 124-126, 152, 160
Ohlsen, Dave, 199, 202
Ormes, Bob, 40, 50, 65, 70, 73
Orr Pitman, 181
Oxford Mountaineering Club, 21
Painted Wall, the: 3, 120, 133, 135
Peak, Roy, 57
Peterson, Don, 199
Peterson, James, 58
Pike, Zebulon, 6
Pike's Peak: 2, 6
"Powder Puff Kids", 175
Powell, John Wesley, 6
Powers, Margaret, 57
Pownall, Dick, 93
Pratt, Chuck, 90, 138, 139, 174
Proboscis: 117
Putnam, Bill, 219, 220, 234
Radigan, Paul, 76
Raley, Francis, 116
Raubauch, Roger, 108, 152, 153
Rearick, Dave, 91-93, 97-98, 121, 123-124, 138-140, 143, 148, 151-152, 159, 172, 181, 210
Rebuffatt, Gaston, 58
Redgarden Wall: 78, 81, 98, 112-113, 116, 152, 155, 181, 203, 208, 219
Redguard Route: 81, 84, 87, 116, 177
Reveley, Chris, 227, 233, 234
Riley, Bob, 55, 57, 65
Rinsberger, Jack, 97
Roach, Gerry, 87, 90, 138
Robbins, Royal, 93, 116-117, 121, 123-124, 132-133, 138-139, 143, 148, 151-152, 153, 156, 160, 164, 174, 181, 186, 193, 210, 231, 233
Robertson, Dave, 59, 61
Robertson, Phil, 58
Robinson, Pete, 178
Rocky Mountain Climbers Club, 10-11, 18, 20, 230
Rocky Mountain Rescue Group, 97, 113, 127
Rogers, James Grafton, 20
Roskosz, Charlie, 97, 121

Rouillard, Ted, 143
Ruwitch, Tom, 194
Salathe, John, 54
San Juan Mountains: 2, 22, 51; Lizard Head, 24, 26, 31, 38, 40, 62, 68; Needles, the, 24
San Juan Mountaineers, 40, 43-46
Sangre de Cristo Mountains: 2, 22, 31, 68
Shawangunks, the: 71, 73, 178, 179, 186, 213, 215, 217
Shepherd, Stanley, 86, 112, 117
Sherman, Dick, 55, 57
Shiprock: 59, 71, 132
Simmons, Corwin, 160
Smith, Dudley, 27, 30
Speck, John, 51-52
Spielman, Andy, 76
Squires, Ralph, 11
Stannard, John, 193, 210, 212, 215, 217
Stauch, Bob, 76
Steck, Allen, 54-55
Stettner, Paul and Joe, 33, 37, 38, 40, 43, 50, 51, 52, 72
Stettner, Paul, Jr., 52
Stewart, Scott, 202, 208, 234
Stocker, Gordon, 97
Sundance Buttress: 87, 143, 148
Sutton, Bob, 58, 68
Taggart, Mark, 57
Tahquitz Rock: 90, 139
Tangen, Ed, 18
Tidrick, Rick, 76
Turner, Jack, 112-113, 116-117, 143
Turnkorner: 143, 148, 151
Twombly, Vernon, 72
Van Diver, Brad, 57-59, 61-62, 64
Vertigo: 208, 210
Von Alman, Otto, 64-65
Waldrop, Harry, 64
Walker, Chris, 133, 135-136
Walsh, Jim, 179
Walton, Harold, 62-63
Warner, Marion, 31
Watson, Eddie, 50
Weeks, Ken, 82, 84, 93
Westbay, Billy, 105, 126
Wexler, Arnold, 54-55, 61
Whillans, Don, 152, 153
Wiessner, Fritz, 50
Williams, Bob, 160, 162
Williams, Gordon, 41, 44, 46, 48
Wilson, Tink, 108
Wright, Ed., 181, 186
Wunsch, Steve, 159, 181, 186, 189, 193, 197, 199, 202, 208, 212, 215, 216, 217, 218, 219, 222, 225, 227, 230; **Interview,** 240-271
Yosemite Valley: 71, 73, 82, 84, 93, 99, 116, 123, 124, 130, 139, 151, 186,
Young, Geoffrey Winthrop, 43, 54
Ziegler, Gary, 70, 76
Zumwalt, Clerin, 63